Creating the Ethical Academy

For those who believe in the promise of *higher* education to shape a better future, this may be a time of unprecedented despair. Stories of students regularly cheating in their classes, admissions officers bending the rules for VIPs, faculty fudging research data, and presidents plagiarizing seem more rampant than ever before. If those associated with our institutions of higher learning cannot resist ethical corruption, what hope do we have for an ethical society?

In this edited volume, higher education experts and scholars tackle the challenge of understanding why ethical misconduct occurs in the academy and how we can address it. The volume editor and contributing authors use a systems framework to analyze ethical challenges in common functional areas (e.g., testing and admissions, teaching and learning, research, fundraising, spectator sports, and governance), highlighting that misconduct is shaped by both individuals and the contexts in which they work, study, and live. The volume argues compellingly for colleges and universities to make ethics a strategic, institutional priority. Higher education researchers, students, and practitioners will find this volume and its application of empirical research, real-life examples, and illustrative case studies to be an inspiring and applicable read.

Dr. Tricia Bertram Gallant is the academic integrity coordinator for the University of California, San Diego.

D0303229

* 000286145 *

Creating the Ethical Academy

A Systems Approach to Understanding Misconduct and
Empowering Change in Higher Education

Edited by Tricia Bertram Gallant

Routledge
Taylor & Francis Group

NEW YORK AND LONDON

First published 2011
by Routledge
270 Madison Avenue, New York, NY 10016

Simultaneously published in the UK
by Routledge
2 Park Square, Milton Park, Abingdon, Oxon OX14 4RN

Routledge is an imprint of the Taylor & Francis Group, an informa business

© 2011 Taylor & Francis

The right of Tricia Bertram Gallant to be identified as author of this work
has been asserted by her in accordance with sections 77 and 78 of the
Copyright, Designs and Patents Act 1988.

Typeset in Minion Pro and Futura BT by Prepress Projects Ltd, Perth, UK
Printed and bound in the United States of America on acid-free paper by
Walsworth Publishing Company, Marceline, MO

Library of Congress Cataloging-in-Publication Data
Creating the ethical academy : a systems approach to understanding
misconduct and empowering change / edited by Tricia Bertram Gallant.
p. cm.
Includes bibliographical references and index.
1. Education, Higher—Moral and ethical aspects. 2. College
administrators—Professional ethics. 3. Cheating (Education)—United
States. 4. Plagiarism. 5. Downloading of data—Ethics. I. Bertram Gallant,
Tricia, 1970–
LB3609.C74 2011
378'.014—dc22
2010017985

ISBN13: 978-0-415-87468-7 (hbk)
ISBN13: 978-0-415-87469-4 (pbk)
ISBN13: 978-0-203-84048-1 (ebk)

Dedication

This book is dedicated to my brother, Scott Trevor Bertram (1967–2009). Scott modeled some basic principles of integrous living—being true to one's calling, giving up luxuries to afford luxuries for others, and prioritizing fundamental values before profits. Scott also taught me that it if it isn't enjoyable or doesn't help others, it's not worth doing.

Contents

Figures

Tables

Acknowledgments

I would first like to thank all of the contributors to this volume. They were gracious with their time and knowledge, lending me their wise words for my first edited book attempt. John and Melissa were especially gracious during the initial proposal brainstorming phase, and, as always, Adrianna, Mike, and Pat gave of their time to mentor me and provide a friendly ear when needed.

I also would like to acknowledge all of the folks at the University of California, San Diego and the International Center for Academic Integrity (Clemson University) who support my work and also influence my thinking about the topic. This book is the result of years of accumulated thoughts as we struggled to connect student ethics and misconduct with the ethics of the broader academy and education system.

This book would not have been possible without the guidance of Sarah Burrows, Alexandra Sharp, Catherine Bernard and Alex Masulis (in order of appearance) at Routledge/Taylor Francis who helped successfully guide this project through the publishing process despite minor setbacks and personnel changes.

Finally, I must acknowledge the support of my family and friends, from those who simply inquire about the book's progress to those who actively helped and supported me. My parents deserve special mention because during the last few months of this book project, they modeled for me the importance of acting ethically despite immense stress, pressure, and personal pain. And, as always, thanks to my husband Jamie who loves and supports me unconditionally.

I

Opening the Door

The State of Corruption and the Hope of Academic Ethics

1
Introduction

TRICIA BERTRAM GALLANT AND LESTER F. GOODCHILD

It should not be a surprise that many are concerned about the ethicality of the academy and the integrity of higher education in America and around the world. A quick review of two of the most prominent higher education press publications in the United States, *Inside Higher Education* and *The Chronicle of Higher Education*, reveal numerous stories of unethical conduct on the part of professors, administrators, researchers, and students (e.g., Brainard 2008; Brazao 2008; Jaschik 2008; Lederman 2008; Mills 2008; Monastersky 2006; Neelakantan 2008; Overland 2008; Wong 2010; Young 2007). Headlines such as "Science Journals Must Develop Stronger Safeguards against Fraud" or "Cheating Incident Involving 34 Students at Duke Is Business School's Biggest Ever" should cause us to pause. Are there many people behaving badly in the academy? And, if there are, are we heading down a road of inevitable corruption? Or is there an alternative way forward?

In *The Cheating Culture: Why More Americans are Doing Wrong to Get Ahead*, David Callahan (2004) argues that indeed many people are behaving badly. According to Callahan (2004: 13), "the prominence of cheating in every sector of society, including higher education, represents a profound moral crisis that reflects deep economic and social problems in American society." Callahan cites such problems as (1) a worldwide competitive economy that has little concern for individual success, security or well-being, which entices people to do whatever it takes to ensure their own survival; (2) a growing gap between the richest and the poorest, which encourages people to take risks they might not normally; (3) weakened (or non-existent) regulations and limited infrastructures that have abdicated ethical oversight to individual actors; and (4) corruption within the larger system of government entities, businesses, and organizations that has created a situation in which individual actors believe they have to cheat to "level the playing field." These four problems in particular, Callahan argues, are encouraging Americans to behave badly rather than ethically or morally.

And, in fact, higher education research suggests that these four problems are encouraging misconduct in the academy as well, not just in America but around the world. For example, the worldwide competitive economy may exacerbate institutional corruption and the increasing dependency on a higher education degree for economic survival may invite individual misconduct (Decoo 2002; Eckstein 2003; Hallak & Poisson 2007). The research by Eckstein, as well as Hallak and Poisson, also argues that the growing gap between the "haves" and the "have-nots" contributes to educational corruption around the world. And, as with other industries, higher education seems to have abdicated ethical oversight to individual actors and systemically ignored ethical misconduct and misbehavior, leaving people without guidelines or normative understandings for making ethical choices (Bertram Gallant, Beesemyer, & Kezar 2009; Kelley, Agle, & DeMott 2005). Likewise, system-wide efforts to conduct ethical audits, enhance public transparency, and ensure accountability to public funds have not been successfully widely implemented in higher education, inviting opportunities for corruption (Hallak & Poisson 2007). Finally, something not specifically noted by Callahan but particularly relevant to the academy is the effect of the internet and other sophisticated technologies; technology is enabling misconduct particularly because the academy has yet to adequately address the way it influences teaching, learning, research, and assessment (Duderstadt, Atkins, & Van Houweling 2002, Gumport & Chun 1999).

Certainly, higher education has not reached a level of untenable corruption in most countries, and it may not be as systemically corrupt as other sectors of society. However, this does not mean that we should ignore possible systemic causes of the ethical failings that are occurring in the academy. Given the complexity and challenges of a global economy, supporting an ethical college and university may be one of the most important tasks of our time. Higher education need not be perfect, but because its graduates, activities, and research affect every sector of society, it should be a model of the constant quest for the ethical high ground.

The quest for the ethical high ground has been a subject of research and literature for almost fifty years now. We can point to the beginning of the field of academic ethics in 1965. University of Michigan higher education historian and philosopher, John S. Brubacher, in his *Bases for Policy in Higher Education* (1965: 78) broached the initial quest for confronting the ethical dilemmas within higher education administration this way:

> It has already been mentioned that two principal functions of the university are to transmit and to advance knowledge. We are so accustomed to accepting this statement of fact, however, that we fail to be sensitive to some of its subtle implications. The question arises, for instance, does the performance of these functions entail any ethical responsibilities or obligations?

Brubacher's work represented one of the first comprehensive attempts to address ethical issues in the academy. Two years later John D. Millett (1967) suggested in his article, "The Ethics of Higher Education," how the freedom of inquiry, self-direction of academic activity, and the free use of knowledge may lead to certain vices within academe, if they are pursued to excess.

His concerns foreshadowed the realities of higher education during the late 1960s boom period. The Carnegie Council on Policy Studies then began a sustained effort to address certain ethical issues in higher education in its series, namely student rights in *Dissent and Disruption* (1971); the role of women in the academy with *Opportunities for Women in Higher Education* (1973); promoting diversity in hiring in *Making Affirmative Action Work in Higher Education* (1975); teaching moral values in the classroom in *Missions of the College Curriculum* (1977); problems with the admissions process in *Selective Admissions in Higher Education* (1977); and, finally, a declaration of ethical decay in higher education with its *Fair Practices in Higher Education: Rights and Responsibilities of Students and Their Colleges in a Period of Intensified Competition for Enrollments* (1979).

In the early 1980s, scholars and professionals gave new attention to ethical problems in the academy. Articles, monographs, and edited books appeared describing the ethical dilemmas of the presidency to sexual harassment of students. The best critical work of the decade came from Harvard President Derek Bok, whose *Beyond the Ivory Tower: Social Responsibilities of the Modern University* (1982) provided the richest systematic work yet produced about the ethical problems in colleges and universities. Other works focused on administrative or campus-wide issues: Ronald H. Stein and M. Carlota Baca's *Professional Ethics in University Administration* (1981); M. Carlota Baca and Ronald H. Stein's *Ethical Principles, Practices, and Problems in Higher Education* (1983); John B. Bennett and J.W. Peltason's *Contemporary Issues in Higher Education: Self-Regulation and the Ethical Roles of the Academy* (1985); or George M. Robinson and Janice Moulton's *Ethical Problems in Higher Education* (1985).

Other works centered more on the faculty and ethical roles and responsibilities: David Dill's article, "Ethics and the Academic Profession," in the *Journal of Higher Education* (1982); John Martin Rich's *Professional Ethics in Education* (1984); and Stephen L. Payne and Bruce H. Charnov's *Ethical Dilemmas for Academic Professionals* (1987). Out of this faculty focus came a small monograph, which would galvanize the academy because of the importance of its author and the university press that published it. Edward Shils, Distinguished Service Professor in the Department of Sociology and the Committee on Social Thought at the University of Chicago, offered his thoughts on the ethical dilemmas and responsibilities of faculty in *The Academic Ethic* from the University of Chicago Press (1983). Gradually the force of his work and title became the new banner for this emerging applied field of study in higher education. The drumbeat to deal with ethical problems on campus was greatly heightened by the publication of Steven M. Cahn's *Saints and Scamps: Ethics in Academia* (1986) and Charles

J. Sykes's *ProfScam: Professors and the Demise of Higher Education* (1988). As the decade came to a close, President Bok again made a more direct appeal for ethics within higher education administration in his *Universities and the Future of America* (1990).

The plethora of these calls for academic ethics resulted in the new decade being launched with the most systematic treatments to date. The most promising effort to achieve greater philosophical sophistication occurred with Steven M. Cahn's edited work, *Morality, Responsibility, and the University* (1990), in which such renowned philosophers as Alan Gewirth, Judith Wagner DeCrew, Norman E. Bowie, David A. Hoekema, Robert Audi, Theodore M. Benditt, and Alan H. Goldman explored the ethical dimensions of campus issues. Written primarily to faculty, this work remained more for the enlightened than for those struggling with ethical challenges in college and university trenches.

The need for an ethics book for the trenches was filled by the most practitioner-oriented comprehensive work on academic ethics to date, the then-definitive work *Ethics and Higher Education* (1990), by Associate Professor of Religious Studies and Director of the Business Ethics Program William W. May from the University of Southern California. His hefty tome attempted to bring professional decision making to a wide range of administrative issues in academic planning, admissions, advancement, and athletics, to racism, sexual harassment, graduate education, and the presidency. May's edited volume was the first to propose a framework for enabling administrators to resolve the ethical issues that had been the subject of commentary in previous books. This applied ethics task, then rather commonplace in medical and business ethics, began with Charles H. Reynolds and David C. Smith's chapter, "Academic Principles of Responsibility" (1990: 45–47), in which they proposed a five-step framework for making a moral decision on campus (see Goodchild's later chapter in this volume for more information on decision-making frameworks). Together, the writings in May's volume demonstrated a necessary next step in the development of the field of academic ethics.

The next two decades would see the emerging field of academic ethics reach a major developmental stage as full book-length treatments of major ethical issues and problems were released. Substantive credit for this development must go to Professor of Philosophy Steven M. Cahn at the City University of New York Graduate Center and his work with Rowman & Littlefield publishers. They supported his effort to create an "Issues in Academic Ethics" series. Their collaborative work led to seven volumes during the 1990s, five of which were published in 1994: Peter J. Markie's *A Professor's Duties: Ethical Issues in College Teaching*; David A. Hoekema's *Campus Rules and Moral Community: In Place of In Loco Parentis*; Normie E. Bowie's *University–Business Partnerships: An Assessment*; Robert L. Simon's *Neutrality and the Academic Ethic*; and Kristin Shrader-Frechette's *Ethics of Scientific Research*. Two others followed that addressed faculty and administrative issues: Richard T. De George's *Academic*

Freedom and Tenure: Ethical Issues (1997) and Rudolph H. Weingartner's *The Moral Dimensions of Academic Administration* (1999). Cahn sought "to do justice to the complexities of academic ethics" in his series; his work along with the editors at Rowman & Littlefield greatly fostered the emergence of the field of academic ethics.

During these decades, specializations began to develop within the field. Scholars produced in-depth treatments of particular areas of academic ethics. Academic integrity and faculty teaching received significant path-breaking scholarship. Ralph D. Mawdsley's *Academic Misconduct: Cheating and Plagiarism* (1994) offered a comprehensive legal and ethical overview of the issues for administrators, faculty, and students. Thirteen years later, Bill Marsh took on the difficult task of exploring the ethical and practical issues of plagiarism in *Plagiarism: Alchemy and Remedy in Higher Education* (2007). A major contribution to this area next came with Tricia Bertram Gallant's *Academic Integrity in the Twenty-First Century: A Teaching and Learning Imperative* (2008), which took a more comprehensive and cultural approach to address academic misconduct through teaching and learning strategies.

The ethics of teaching and learning is a growing area of study within academic ethics. One of the groundbreaking academic ethics works in this period was John M. Braxton and Alan E. Bayer's *Faculty Misconduct in Collegiate Teaching* (1999), in which they explored teaching problems in the disciplines of biology, history, mathematics, and psychology (for more on this, see Braxton's chapter in this volume). Other works pushed academic ethics research further into areas of campus values (Thompson 1991), institutional research (Schiltz 1992), campus environmental responsibilities (Eagan & Orr 1992), affirmative action (Cahn 1993), sexual harassment (Dziech & Hawkins 1998), college student moral reasoning (Davey & Davey 2001), governance (Hamilton 2002), and the university presidency (Keohane 2006).

Few comprehensive treatments of academic ethics have occurred since May's 1990 volume. Only two stand out as attempting to explore systematically ethical problems across the campus. M. N. S. Sellers at the University of Baltimore's School of Law edited *An Ethical Education: Community and Morality in the Multicultural University* (1994), which took up issues of the aims of the university, undergraduate curriculum, campus speech, and affirmative action. Similarly, Stephanie L. Moore's *Practical Approaches to Ethics for Colleges and Universities* (2008) included four chapters on undergraduate curricular issues, strategic planning, codes of professional ethics, and athletics. Our volume addresses this need for a major comprehensive contemporary assessment of the emerging field of academic ethics as we enter the second decade of the new century.

This brings us to the first purpose of this edited volume, which is to raise awareness about *academic ethics as a systemic issue that is broader than (but inclusive of) individual ethical failures* and create a sense of urgency to attend to academic ethics as a way to stem off possible corruption. The breadth of awareness we hope to stimulate is more expansive than that of many of the earlier volumes on academic ethics which tend to focus readers on *individual* ethical failings (such as students cheating, administrators stealing, researchers deceiving, and admissions officers lying). Of course, individuals do make ethical mistakes and we should continue to address those in both proactive ways (by developing individual capacity for ethical decision making—see chapter 9) and reactive ways (by removing unethical members from the academy).

Our thesis, however, is that ethical corruption will occur if the academy continues to treat misconduct as only an individual dysfunction rather than as being also shaped by underlying systemic factors and the environment in which individuals live, study, and work (Bertram Gallant 2008). Individual dysfunctions can be handled within the context of a "healthy ethical environment" (Haydon 2004: 121), but in an unhealthy ethical climate, individual acts of misconduct can spread, become institutionalized, and corrupt the integrity of the academy. After Stephen Heyneman overviews the state of educational corruption today in chapter 2, Bertram Gallant and Kalichman describe the characteristics of the "ethical academy" and introduce a systems framework for understanding misconduct and empowering change. This framework is used throughout the book by many of the contributors, but most specifically in Part II as various functional areas of misconduct are examined—standardized testing and admissions (chapter 4), teaching and learning (chapter 5), research (chapter 6), fund-raising and spectator sports (chapter 7), and governance (chapter 8).

To the second purpose of our book, we thus now turn—*to encourage college and university campuses to make ethics a strategic priority*. This second purpose is focused on empowering higher education faculty, students, and administrators to change organizational structures, processes, and cultures to diminish opportunities and temptations for misconduct and encourage ethical behaviors. Traditionally, academic ethics has been a silent partner in the academy; everyone wants and expects ethics to be a part of the organizational culture and operations, yet it is seldom openly addressed at an institution-wide level. We have left student ethics largely to student affairs professionals or to the philosophy department, research ethics to the institutional review boards, and other ethical conversations or issues unexplored. There is evidence that this is changing, and we believe that college and university actors are more than capable of doing what it is that we suggest in this volume. Thus, in Part III, contributors offer suggestions for empowering ethical change at all levels of the system: among individuals and groups through ethical decision-making frameworks (chapter 9); within higher education organizations through leadership (chapter 10); within the education system through teaching and curriculum (chapter 11) and connection with external stakeholders (chapter 12); and in the larger society through a global academic ethics movement (chapter 13). Part III provides a valuable resource to individuals looking to forward the creation of the ethical academy.

As May (1990: 1) has argued, although scholars within higher education have done "a great deal to address ethical issues in the professions and business ... very little of this attention has been focused on higher education itself." Bringing together in one volume some of the leading scholars and researchers on academic ethics and misconduct, this volume seeks to remedy this campus myopia by offering a comprehensive and thorough treatise on ethical problems and misconduct in the academy, based on a unifying framework. These chapters present not just treatments of individual campus problems, but rather solutions and ideas for future, proactive efforts by the academy writ large to address its continuing academic ethics crisis.

References

Baca, M.C. and Stein, R.H. (1983) *Ethical Principles, Practices, and Problems in Higher Education*, Springfield, IL: Thomas.

Bennett, J.B. and Peltason, J.W. (eds) (1985) *Contemporary Issues in Higher Education: Self-Regulation and the Ethical Roles of the Academy*, New York: American Council on Education/Macmillan.

Bertram Gallant, T. (2008) *Academic Integrity in the Twenty-First Century: A Teaching and Learning Imperative*, San Francisco: Jossey-Bass.

Bertram Gallant, T., Beesemyer, L.A., and Kezar, A. (2009) 'Creating a culture of ethics in higher education', in J.C. Knapp and D.J. Siegel (eds) *The Business of Higher Education Volume 1: Leadership and Culture*, Santa Barbara, CA: Praeger Publishers.

Bok, D. (1982) *Beyond the Ivory Tower: Social Responsibilities of the Modern University*, Cambridge, MA: Harvard University Press.

Bok, D. (1990) *Universities and the Future of America*, Durham: Duke University Press.

Bowie, N.E. (1994) *University–Business Partnerships: An Assessment, Issues in Academic Ethics*, Lanham, MD: Rowman & Littlefield.

Brainard, J. (2008) 'Science fraud at universities is common – and all commonly ignored', *The Chronicle of Higher Education*, 19 June. Available at http://chronicle.com/article/Science-Fraud-at-Universities/914 (accessed 19 June 2008).

Braxton, J.M. and Bayer, A.E. (1999) *Faculty Misconduct in Collegiate Teaching*, Baltimore: Johns Hopkins University Press.

Brazao, D. (2008) 'Phone degrees catch up to buyers', *The Toronto Star*, 13 December. Available at http://www.thestar.com/printarticle/553330 (accessed 13 December 2008).

Brubacher, J.S. (1965) *Bases for Policy in Higher Education*, New York: McGraw-Hill.

Cahn, S.M. (1986) *Saints and Scamps: Ethics in Academia*, Lanham, MD: Rowman & Littlefield.

—— (ed.) (1990) *Morality, Responsibility, and the University: Studies in Academic Ethics*, Philadelphia: Temple University Press.

—— (ed.) (1993) *Affirmative Action and the University: A Philosophical Inquiry*, Philadelphia: Temple University Press.

Callahan, D. (2004) *The Cheating Culture: Why More Americans Are Doing Wrong to Get Ahead*, Orlando: Harcourt.

Carnegie Commission on Higher Education. (1971) *Dissent and Disruption: Proposals for Consideration by the Campus*, New York: McGraw-Hill.

—— (1973) *Opportunities for Women in Higher Education: Their Current Participation, Prospects for the Future, and Recommendations for Action*, New York: McGraw-Hill.

Carnegie Council on Policy Studies in Higher Education. (1975) *Making Affirmative Action Work in Higher Education: An Analysis of Institutional and Federal Policies with Recommendations*, Carnegie Council Series, San Francisco: Jossey-Bass.

—— (1977) *Selective Admissions in Higher Education*, Carnegie Council Series, San Francisco: Jossey-Bass.

—— (1979) *Fair Practices in Higher Education: Rights and Responsibilities of Students and Their Colleges in a Period of Intensified Competition for Enrollments*, Carnegie Council Series, San Francisco: Jossey-Bass.

Carnegie Foundation for the Advancement of Teaching. (1977) *Missions of the College Curriculum: A Contemporary Review with Suggestions*, Carnegie Council Series, San Francisco: Jossey-Bass.

Davey, J.D. and Davey, L.D. (2001) *The Conscience of the Campus: Case Studies in Moral Reasoning Among Today's College Students*, Westport, CT: Praeger.

Decoo, W. (2002) *Crisis on Campus: Confronting Academic Misconduct*, Cambridge, MA: MIT Press.

De George, R.T. (1997) *Academic Freedom and Tenure: Ethical Issues*, Lanham, MD: Rowman & Littlefield.

Dill, D. (1982) 'Ethics and the Academic Profession', *Journal of Higher Education*, 53: 243–381.

Duderstadt, J.J., Atkins, D.E., and Van Houweling, D. (2002) *Higher Education in the Digital Age: Technology Issues and Strategies for American Colleges and Universities*, Westport, CT: Praeger.

Dziech, B.W. and Hawkins, M.W. (1998) *Sexual Harassment in Higher Education: Reflections and New Perspectives*, New York: Garland.

Eagan, D.J. and Orr, D.W. (eds) (1992) *The Campus and Environmental Responsibility*, San Francisco: Jossey-Bass.

Eckstein, M. A. (2003) *Combating Academic Fraud: Towards a Culture of Integrity*, Paris: International Institute for Educational Planning.

Gumport, P.J. and Chun, M. (1999) 'Technology and higher education: Opportunities and challenges for the new era', in P.G. Altbach, R.O. Berdahl and P.J. Gumport (eds) *American Higher Education in the Twenty-First Century: Social, Political and Economic Challenges*, Baltimore: Johns Hopkins University Press.

Hallak, J. and Poisson, M. (2007) *Corrupt Schools, Corrupt Universities: What Can Be Done?* Paris: International Institute for Educational Planning.

Hamilton, N.W. (2002) *Academic Ethics: Problems and Materials on Professional Conduct and Shared Governance*, Westport, CT: Praeger.

Haydon, G. (2004) 'Values education: Sustaining the ethical environment', *Journal of Moral Education*, 33: 115–29.

Hoekema, D.A. (1994) *Campus Rules and Moral Community: In Place of In Loco Parentis*, Lanham, MD: Rowman & Littlefield.

Jaschik, S. (2008) 'Another inappropriately awarded degree', *Inside Higher Ed*, 19 August. Available at http://www.insidehighered.com/news/2008/08/19/degree (accessed 19 August 2008).

Kelley, P.C., Agle, B.R., and DeMott, J. (2005) 'Mapping our progress: Identifying, categorizing and comparing universities' ethics infrastructure', *Journal of Academic Ethics*, 3: 205–29.

Keohane, N.O. (2006) *Higher Ground: Ethics and Leadership in the Modern University*, Durham, NC: Duke University Press.

Lederman, D. (2008) 'Another case of academic fraud involving athletes', *Inside Higher Ed*, 21 August. Available at http://www.insidehighered.com/news/2008/08/21/newmexico (accessed 21 August 2008).

Markie, P.J. (1994) *A Professor's Duties: Ethical Issues in College Teaching*, Lanham, MD: Rowman & Littlefield.

Marsh, B. (2007) *Plagiarism: Alchemy and Remedy in Higher Education*, Albany, NY: State University of New York Press.

Mawdsley, R.D. (1994) *Academic Misconduct: Cheating and Plagiarism*, Topeka, KS: National Organization on Legal Problems of Education.

May, W.W. (1990) *Ethics and Higher Education*, New York: American Council on Education/ Macmillan.

Millett, J.D. (1967) 'The ethics of higher education', *Educational Record*, 48: 11–21.

Mills, A. (2008) 'Egypt's high-stakes university entrance exam is tainted by corruption charges', *The Chronicle of Higher Education*, 8 July. Available at http://chronicle.com/article/Egypts-High-Stakes-Univers/41277/ (accessed 8 July 2008).

Monastersky, R. (2006) 'Science journals must develop stronger safeguards against fraud, panel says', *The Chronicle of Higher Education*, 8 December. Available at http://chronicle.com/article/Science-Journals-Must-Develop/17231 (accessed 8 December 2006).

Moore, S.L. (ed.) (2008) *Practical Approaches to Ethics for Colleges and Universities*, San Francisco: Jossey-Bass.

Neelakantan, S. (2008) 'In crackdown on corruption, Bangladesh removes 4 university presidents', *The Chronicle of Higher Education*, 21 May. Available at http://chronicle.com/article/In-Crackdown-on-Corruption/40999/ (accessed 21 May 2008).

Overland, M.A. (2008) 'Your education in hock', *The Chronicle of Higher Education*, 12 December. Available at http://chronicle.com/article/Your-Education-in-Hock/32335/ (accessed 12 December 2008).

Payne, S.L. and Charnov, B.H. (eds) (1987) *Ethical Dilemmas for Academic Professionals*, Springfield, IL: Thomas.

Reynolds, C.H. and Smith, D.C. (1990) 'Academic Principles of Responsibility', in W.W. May (ed.) *Ethics and Higher Education*, Phoenix, AZ: American Council on Education/Macmillan.

Rich, J.M. (1984). *Professional Ethics in Education*, Springfield, IL: Thomas.

Robinson, G.M. and Moulton, J. (1985) *Ethical Problems in Higher Education*, Englewood Cliffs, NJ: Prentice-Hall.

Schiltz, M.E. (ed.) (1992) *Ethics and Standards in Institutional Research*, San Francisco: Jossey-Bass.

Sellers, M.N.S. (ed.) (1994) *An Ethical Education: Community and Morality in the Multicultural University*, Oxford: Berg.

Shils, E. (1983) *The Academic Ethic: The Report of a Study Group of the International Council on the Future of the University*, Chicago: University of Chicago Press.

Shrader-Frechette, K. (1994) *Ethics of Scientific Research*, Lanham, MD: Rowman & Littlefield.

Simon, R.L. (1994) *Neutrality and the Academic Ethic*, Lanham, MD: Rowan & Littlefield.

Stein, R.H. and Baca, M.C. (1981) *Professional Ethics in University Administration*, San Francisco: Jossey-Bass.

Sykes, C.J. (1988) *ProfScam: Professors and the Demise of Higher Education*, New York: St. Martin's Press.

Thompson, D.L. (ed.) (1991) *Moral Values and Higher Education: A Notion at Risk*, Albany, NY: State University of New York Press and Brigham Young University.

Weingartner, R.H. (1999) *The Moral Dimensions of Academic Administration*, Lanham, MD: Rowman & Littlefield.

Wong, G. (2010) 'Rampant cheating hurts China's research ambitions', *Associated Press*, 11 April. Available at http://news.yahoo.com/s/ap/20100411/ap_on_re_as/as_china_academic_cheating_2;_ylt=AmTwLPT7ale9jnJazfdJ5AflWMcF (accessed 11 April 2010).

Young, J. (2007) 'Cheating incident involving 34 students at Duke is business school's biggest ever', *The Chronicle of Higher Education*, 11 May. Available at http://chronicle.com/article/Cheating-Incident-Involving-34/25714 (accessed 11 May 2008).

2

The Concern with Corruption in Higher Education

STEPHEN P. HEYNEMAN

As stated in the introduction of this volume, this book has two purposes: to illustrate that ethical misconduct in the academy should be viewed as a systemic (rather than an individual) issue and to encourage higher education stakeholders to make ethics a strategic institutional priority. This chapter, which surveys the state of ethical corruption in higher education around the world, should help to meet both purposes. While an individual can be corrupt, that is, abusing authority for personal as well as material gain (Anechiarico & Jacobs 1996; Blizek 2000; Kalnins 2001; Victor & Cullen 1988),[1] an ethical academy could handle such individual misconduct without significant damage to institutional integrity (Bertram Gallant, Beesemyer, & Kezar 2009).

However, from the perspective of social development, systemic education corruption (that which is beyond a few individuals "behaving badly") must be of concern because, more so than corruption in the police, customs service, or other areas, it contains both immoral and illegal elements, involves minors or young people, and damages the ability of education to serve a public good, most notably the selection of future leaders on a fair and impartial basis (Anderson & Heyneman 2005; Heyneman 2005; Noah & Eckstein 2001). Much of education corruption might be classified under the term "professional misconduct" (Braxton & Bayer 1999), but corruption may contain implications beyond other professional misbehavior. It may include corruption on the part of universities who bribe officials to become accredited, whose quality of public service may then be compromised and may produce graduates whose skills and professional levels could be a danger to the public (Heyneman 2003, 2004). Corrupt education officials and institutions collect an illegal "rent."[2]

To help readers recognize education corruption and feel a sense of urgency to address it, in this chapter I define educational (i.e., organizational, institutional and systemic) corruption, survey the state of it around the world, examine the consequences of unfettered corruption, and review possible strategies for reducing misconduct.

What Is Education Corruption?

Corruption, the abuse of authority for personal as well as material gain, can be understood in terms of the stakeholders involved and their actions. In terms of *corruption for personal gain* the categories of victims and perpetrators are generally students and faculty (Table 2.1). When personal favoritism is shown by a faculty member for a particular type of student, the victims are other students. Favoritism may be based on family or friends. The mother of a young faculty member in Georgia might telephone her daughter to observe that her best friend has a son in her class and would she be kind enough to give the boy a high grade. This category is most common in societies that have not yet established the priority of universalistic (based on one's achievements) over particularistic (characteristics set at birth—nationality, class, race, etc.) values.

A faculty member may use his or her position as teacher to exploit a student for sexual or other favors. In this case the victim is the student directly affected. But the opposite may be the case in which a student uses sexual favors to gain an educational advantage (Bakari & Leach 2009; Collins 2009). In the instance of cheating on an examination and plagiarism on term papers both the perpetrator and the victim are students. Likewise, with respect to the falsification of research findings and research plagiarism among faculty, both the perpetrator and the victim are the faculty themselves. Moreover, faculty who plagiarize or who falsify research may adversely affect the reputation of their university, their profession, and, in some cases, their nation, and they may cause irreparable harm to the uses of research (see chapter 6 for details on research misconduct).

In terms of *corruption for monetary gain*, Table 2.2 provides just eight examples of the kinds of misconduct that can occur in education.[3] For example, in the case of procurement and accreditation, the buyer is the educational institution, and the seller of the bribe is the government, usually the minister of education.[4] In the case of obtaining illegal entrance to specialized programs, raising a grade on the basis of an illegal payment, or illegally paying for what should be a normal education service (student housing, borrowing a book from the library, and

Table 2.1 Types of Professional (Non-Monetary) Corruption

Perpetrator	Type of Corruption
Faculty	Research falsification
	Plagiarism
	Sexual favors
	Personal favoritism
Students	Sexual exploitation
	Exchange cheating
	Plagiarism

Table 2.2 Types of Monetary Corruption

Sellers	Buyers		
	Rector	Students	Suppliers
Ministry of education	Accreditation		Procurement
Rector		Entrance exams	
Administrators		Bribes needed for: Transcripts Housing Library use	
Faculty		Grades	

administrative procedures such as the transfer of transcripts),[5] the buyer is the student and the seller is either a faculty member or a member of the university administration. The agents vary but can be broadly classified as teachers, rectors, and other university administrators, and the ministry of education.

What Is the Current State of Education Corruption?

As a problem, education corruption is universal. Transparency International monitors the perception of corruption in general and in education specifically. Of the eight regions being monitored, the region perceived as having the most corrupt education systems was the Middle East and North Africa. Seventy percent of the respondents described education systems in the Middle East and North Africa as being either "corrupt" or "extremely corrupt." This was followed by Latin America and the Caribbean where 60 percent of the respondents described the education system as "corrupt" or "extremely corrupt." In the case of sub-Saharan Africa, 55 percent of the respondents described the education systems in this manner; in the low-income countries of Asia and Europe and the Central Asia Region (including the fifteen republics of the former Soviet Union) it was 50 percent; in North America it was 40 percent; and in the high-income countries of Asia it was 35 percent. The region where the perception of education corruption was least was Western Europe, but even there 20 percent of the respondents described the system as "corrupt" or "extremely corrupt" (Heyneman, Anderson, & Nuraliyeva 2009: 14).

The type of corruption differs from one region to another. A major problem in North America appears to be student and faculty plagiarism and cheating on examinations (Cizek 1999; McCabe 1999, 2005). There are also illustrations of breaches in institutional ethics (Kelly, Agle, & DeMott 2005; Louis, Anderson, & Rosenberg 1995). This may include mistrust, misconduct, and misbehavior in conducting research (see chapter 6), the ethical questions with regard to raising funds and sports supporters (see chapter 7), misconduct in admissions and testing (see chapter 4), and ethical dilemmas in academic governance (see chapter 8), as well as classroom improprieties—showing up late for class, unfairly assessing homework assignments, showing preference to specific genders, nationalities, or opinions (see chapter 5).

Outside of Organisation for Economic Co-operation and Development (OECD) countries, the prevalence of education corruption is more frequent, but more importantly, it occurs in different ways. In Vietnam, Cambodia, South Asia, Eastern Europe, and the former Soviet Union, the main problem appears to be corruption for monetary gain and on the part of both individuals and institutions. This includes the propensity to seek bribes in exchange for higher grades, accreditation, and entrance to selective programs of study (Dawson 2009; Heyneman 2009a; McCornac 2009). On the other hand, in sub-Saharan Africa, corruption includes frequent instances of professional misconduct and sexual exploitation in the classroom (Bakari & Leach 2009; Collins 2009).

Some might argue that corruption and cheating is cultural, that it is imbedded within the moral standards of the community. This might suggest that students are in favor of it and have no shame when participating in it. It is common, however, for some students to express shame and remorse with respect to cheating (Heyneman, et al. 2009). Is the degree of remorse common from one country to the next? In Croatia 89 percent of the students asked said that it was "wrong" to cheat on an examination, approximately the same proportion (90 percent) as in the United States (Table 2.3). On the other hand, the Josephson Institute reports that American students who cheat also say that they are satisfied with their personal ethics (Josephson Institute 2009). This suggests that, in certain circumstances, cheating can become a cultural norm, "disconnected" in an individual's mind from personal ethics.

But however common it might be for a student to feel remorse, it is also common for students to participate. In Croatia, 76 percent of the students said that they would cheat on a test if they would not get caught. In the United States, 97 percent of the students claim to have seen another student cheat and 75 percent admit to having copied from the paper of another student (Table 2.4). Some evidence would suggest, moreover, that the propensity to cheat has increased in the United States. According to one estimate, 20 percent of the students admitted to having cheated in high school in 1969, but this increased to 27 percent in 1979 and to 30 percent in 1989 (Cizek 1999: 18). The fact that

Table 2.3 Is It Wrong to Cheat on an Examination?

Country	% Answering "Yes"
Bulgaria	79
United States	90
Croatia	89
Moldova	77
Serbia	87

Sources: Heyneman, et al. (2008: 5); Cizek (1999: 15).

Table 2.4 Incidence of Cheating on Examinations

Country	% Answering "Yes"
If you could cheat without getting caught, would you?	
Bulgaria	60
Croatia	76
Moldova	68
Serbia	69
Have you seen another student cheat?	
United States	97
Have you ever copied from another student?	
United States	75

Sources: Heyneman, et al. (2008: 5); Cizek (1999: 15).

almost all students feel remorse but almost all would cheat if they would not be caught suggests that the resistance to cheating is not autonomous or embedded as a moral principle, but rather based on the fear of sanction.

What Are the Systemic Causes of Education Corruption?

Because illegal or unprofessional actions are often regretted by those who participate in them, in one sense, every illegal or unprofessional action has a single cause—the absence of sufficient self-control (Stein & Baca 1981; Waite & Allen 2003). But there are ancillary characteristics that help explain frequency. The break-up of the Soviet Union and the subsequent privatization without precedent or regulation caused distortions in many parts of economic and social life. There was an upsurge of general corruption in the public sector. This was exacerbated by an absence of tradition concerning legitimate areas for private enterprise and what are essential public goods. Agricultural and industrial property was suddenly privatized, the lines between public and private having been drawn from scratch, creating confusion and misunderstanding in addition to outright corruption behavior (Hallak & Poisson 2007; Heyneman 2000; Heyneman & Todoric-Bebic 2000; Heyneman, et al. 2009). In Asia the penchant for individual achievement at any cost is one explanatory cause of education corruption (Dawson 2009). In North America, and many other parts of the world, cheating and plagiarism are motivated by a demand to acquire qualifications over the knowledge on which the qualifications are based. In chapter 3, Bertram Gallant and Kalichman describe in detail a systems framework for understanding the causes and solutions to corruption caused by misconduct. The chapters in Part III will then apply that framework to elaborate on the causes of corruption in various functional areas of the academy.

What Are the Consequences of Education Corruption and Why Should We Care?

Since the time of Plato it has been understood that a key ingredient in the making of a nation/state is how it chooses its technical, commercial, and political leaders. In general it is agreed that no modern nation can long survive if leaders are chosen on the basis of the ascriptive characteristics, that is, the characteristics with which they are born (race, gender, social status). On the other hand it is common for families to try to protect and otherwise advantage their own children and relatives. Every parent wishes success for their own child; every group wishes to see the success of children from their particular group. This is normal.

Schooling provides the mechanism through which these opposing influences can be carefully managed. It is the common instrument used by nations to "refresh" the sources of leadership. Economists have tried to estimate the sacrifice in economic growth if there is a serious bias in the selection of leaders (Klitgaard 1986). It has been estimated that developing countries could improve their gross national product (GNP) per capita by five percentage points if they were to base their leadership upon merit as opposed to gender or social status (Pinera & Selowsky 1981). In fact, by some estimates, the economic benefit to developing countries of choosing leaders on the basis of merit would be three times more than the benefit accruing from a reduction in OECD trade restriction on imports (Kirmani 1986).

Success in one's schooling is one of the few background characteristics seen as necessary for modern leadership. Although it is possible for leaders to emerge through experience or just good fortune, getting ahead in schooling itself is seen as essential.

But what if schooling itself is not fair? What if the public comes to believe that the provision of schooling favors one social group? What if the public doesn't trust in the judgment of teachers on student performance? What would happen if the process of schooling had been corrupted (Heyneman 2007a)?

The fact is that, in a democracy, the public takes a very active interest in the fairness of its education system. If the public does not trust the education system to be fair or effective, more may be sacrificed than economic growth. It might be said that current leaders, whether in commerce, science, or politics, had acquired their positions through privilege rather than through achievement. If the school system cannot be trusted, it may detract from a nation's sense of social cohesion, the principal ingredient of all successful modern societies (Heyneman 2000).

Education potentially serves two labor market functions. It is an investment in human capital and it develops the productivity of labor. One expects each additional year of education to increase earnings because a student will acquire new knowledge, skills, and attitudes that are transferable to employment. Both individual students and society gain from higher education in this way. Second, completion of education can signal to employers that the student is of high ability and integrity and has great potential to be a productive employee (Heyneman

2002/2003) or a status group selectivity market (Collins 1979). Only the most able students may complete higher education because the costs of completion (in time, resources, and effort) are lower for the more able than for other students. Higher education may not increase the productivity of labor directly, but it may help employers sort out the most productive and reliable from other more costly candidates (Heyneman, et al. 2009: 9).

Corruption affects the private and social returns to education investment through two avenues. If students obtain grades through corrupt means, they have less incentive to learn. Because economic growth is associated with the quality of education and the acquisition of skills (Behrman & Birdsall 1983; Dale & Krueger 2002; Griliches & Mason 1972; Hanushek & Wobmann 2007; Solmon & Wachtel 1975; Wales 1973), if students buy grades and exam scores, the economic rates of return for higher education investments will be degraded (Heyneman, et al. 2009). The signaling function of education is also reduced if there is significant corruption among faculty or administrators.

If entry into select programs and high grades are for sale, then the completion of education cannot be linked to student ability. The employer will not know whether a student completed the program and did well because she was a high-ability, low-cost student or because she acquired grades illegally or unfairly. The variance in ability for students completing a corrupt program is higher. Even if an individual student from a relatively corrupt institution is honest and of high ability, the signaling value of the degree is reduced. An employer with a choice of candidates reduces the risk of hiring an unproductive employee by avoiding graduates of corrupt institutions and programs and hiring only students from institutions, departments, or programs with a reputation for honesty. For this employer to hire a student from a corrupt program, the student would have to accept a significantly lower salary and prove his or her economic value through on-the-job experience.

Corruption as part of the undergraduate experience may affect the probability that a student can obtain a graduate degree. Graduate schools, particularly the selective ones, discount applicants from institutions in which corruption is perceived as common. Admission committees look carefully at statements of purpose and letters of reference that may be plagiarized or forged; and they constantly note students with a wide divergence in grades and Graduate Record Examination (GRE) scores on the grounds that the former may have been subject to artificial manipulation.

There are some who have argued that corruption and bribery serve a purpose; that bribes may help make weak institutions more efficient. In instances in which prices (tuition, fees, or wages) are distorted by regulation or lag in application, corruption has been known to improve efficiency (Ahlin & Bose 2007). On the other hand, because the purpose of education is to provide a way for society to model good behavior for children or young adults, allowing an education system to be corrupt may be more costly than allowing corruption in the police or the customs service. By design, one function of education is to purposefully teach the young how to behave in the future. If the education system is corrupt, one can expect future citizens to be corrupt as well (Bruhn, Zajac, Al-Kazemi, & Prescott 2002).

Efficiency also fails within an educational institution if corrupt officials are affected by non-monetary factors such as favoritism towards one's own ethnic, regional, or religious group or by pressure to show favoritism for relatives. In this case, university officials may admit unqualified students or faculty, and education becomes a high-priced, low-quality good. Instead of increasing competition within the university, bribery limits competition and reduces quality (Bardhan 1997).

If a college or university acquires a reputation for having faculty or administrators who accept bribes for entry, grades, or graduation, the power of the university in the labor market may be adversely affected. In the public sector and in domestic labor markets, particularly those with state-run enterprises, the risk is less because the job choices of graduates are fewer. But in the private sector and particularly with companies that draw from international labor markets, the effect of a reputation for corruption of a university may be more serious.

Thus, economic consequences occur to the individual, the employer, and the community or nation. Higher education becomes a less effective means to obtain a higher income and it lowers the effect of higher education on poverty. Corruption in education changes the ability of education to increase income, by as much as 50 percent in one estimate, and lowers the returns to the wider community or nation from public investments in higher education (Heyneman, et al. 2009: 20). Corruption also adversely affects employers. Not being able to trust the signaling mechanism of higher education, many employers construct their own selection mechanisms. They extend offers of employment but new employees then enter "as interns," which requires proving effectiveness over time. Moreover, employers may be reluctant to place employees with suspect abilities in sensitive positions or to promote them (Heyneman, et al. 2009: 21).

Education corruption also has a social and a political cost (Maricik 2009). If rampant, corruption may reduce the prestige of a nation's higher education system, reduce the ability to negotiate joint degrees and credit transfers, and limit the ability to attract new employers. If corruption were to reach a "tipping point" (when over 50 percent of the students have participated), the system itself is at risk of implosion, which raises the specter of social unrest and national insecurity (Heyneman 2010; Silova, Johnson, & Heyneman 2007).

What Can Be Done about Education Corruption?

However common it is to cheat or to take bribes, there remains a portion that refuse to participate. In the former Soviet Union, faculty leaders exist, even in the most austere and debilitating environments. There are some who lead by virtue of moral principle. There are others who rise to the occasion and lead on the basis of practical assessment of risks and benefits. Regardless of the source of strength, given the commonality of this resistance, it can be said that there is in fact a universal standard of the professoriate. The standard is parallel to that identified by Braxton and Bayer (1999). It includes the promise to treat all students with fairness and impartiality. It includes selecting a common hierarchy among differing moral principles. In particular it requires that faculty choose the principle of fairness (to students and colleagues) over the principle of loyalty to family, friends, and ethnic brothers. In this small but important way, certain faculty, even in remote parts of the globe, may lead the way for other local officials in government and business. These "quiet heroes" of the university classroom, those who stand up for their principles without legal or administrative support, in their own way, these resisters are upholding the principles associated with development and freedom. They do this without the possibility of reward; on the contrary, they do this in spite of making enemies and enduring the criticism of their corrupt administrative superiors. They do this for one reason: because it is right (Heyneman 2007b).

On the other hand, simply because there are resisters does not imply that combating the problem can be left to isolated individuals. A more systematic approach is necessary. The chapters in Part III of this volume will deal in detail with specific ways of moving forward on the agenda of reducing corruption and enhancing educational integrity. However, at this point, it may be fruitful to introduce some ideas that can be reflected upon throughout the reading of the remainder of the volume. In particular, there are four measures that seem to be necessary regardless of country or maturity of education systems. Those four measures are (1) structural reforms, which may be necessary to change the environment that makes corruption more common; (2) measures to isolate and prevent corruption behavior; (3) measures to adjudicate cases in which infractions may have occurred; and finally (4) measures to inflict sanctions and effectively translate the implications of those sanctions to the university community and the public at large (Table 2.5).

Structural reform may be a necessity in all countries, but not identically. Structural reform is particularly necessary where mechanisms of land owner-ship and taxation are still developing and where the mechanisms of licensing, accreditation, and higher education selection have been neither modernized nor professionalized. Structural reform includes paying close attention to the quality and honesty of the national standardized entrance examinations (Heyneman 2009b,c); the mechanisms for procurement of textbooks and educational supplies (Heyneman 2006); and better legal clarity in distinguishing between for-profit and not-for profit educational institutions. These issues raise questions of several kinds:

Table 2.5 What Can be Done About Corruption?

Structural Reform	Adjudication and Management	Prevention	Sanction
Autonomous examination agency	Professional boards	Blue ribbon committee evaluations	Criminal penalties for economic and professional corruption
Licensing and certification process separated from higher education	Boards of trustees for each higher education institution	Annual reports on educational corruption	Public exposure
Land ownership by educational institution	School boards	Public access to higher education financial statements	Dismiss all from employment
Tax differentiation between profit-making and non-commercial education institutions	Public ombudsman	Codes of conduct for faculty, administrators, and students	Fines payable to the victim for professional misconduct
Income generated by non-profit educational institutors not subject to taxation	Faculty/student code of conduct boards	Public advertisement of all codes of conduct	Withdrawal of license to practice
		Anti-corruption commissions	
		Free and active education press	

- What structures exist for reducing ethical misconduct and corruption?
- Has there been an "audit" of the university ethical infrastructure?[6]
- As one reads through the chapters in this volume what ideas can be found for structural reform to deal with specific areas of misconduct?

In the case of changes in the mechanisms of *adjudication and management*, it may be necessary to initiate university boards of trust to distance the university from the ministry of education, and to professionalize those boards to avoid them from becoming financially irresponsible and corrupt themselves. It may be required to initiate the office of an educational ombudsman, create codes of conduct boards to hear cases in which infractions may have occurred, and report the frequency and category of those infractions to the university population and the general public.

In terms of *prevention* there need to be codes of conduct for administrators, faculty, and students. They need to be written with clarity and openly displayed on university websites.[7] Active governments might sponsor blue ribbon commissions (consisting of eminent scientists and well-known figures) to assess the problem and issue public reports. A ministry of education might issue public statistics on the frequency and nature of education corruption. It helps too to have an active press interested and informed about corruption issues. There is also an important external role for professional associations and international organizations (Bergan 2009; Sahlberg 2009).

Sanctions may include public exposure of those who have been found guilty, penalties of jail or detention for those who have committed criminal acts, dismissal from employment, fines payable to victims, and the withdrawal of a license to practice. Key to success is the general knowledge that sanctions exist and general respect that rules will be enforced.

Summary

Some might suggest that plagiarism and cheating are more common in the internet era. Some might suggest that bribes for university entrance and to augment one's grades are more common given an overall environment of economic stringency, administrative transition, and the weakness of other societal institutions. The assessment of these influences is correct, but inadequate. The only reasonable barrier to honest conduct of university affairs is the character of the actors themselves. To the extent that they are socially cohesive and have internalized the norms and mores of their functions as teachers and students, corruption can gain no ground. Colleges and universities can help to create such social cohesion and internalize norms and mores and they have an ethical responsibility to do so. There are many universities where corruption is almost unknown and there are millions of students who, if given the opportunity to cheat, won't. To turn around a circumstance from one in which corruption is common to one in which it is unknown requires consistency in action and diligence in policy, but it can be done.

Notes

1. Like any illegal or shameful activity, the measurement of corruption is complicated by respondent embarrassment and fear of sanction. In general, acquiring accurate information on actual participation in corrupt activity is more difficult than acquiring information on the perception that corrupt activity exists and in what amount (Heyneman, Anderson, and Nuraliyeva 2009). For instance, Transparency International ranks countries on the perception of existing corrupt activity. By this method, Romania ranks 69 (out of 91 nations) in terms of corruption perception, Uzbekistan ranks 71 and the Russian Federation ranks 79. See http://www.transparency.org/ (accessed 27 March 2010).
2. "Illegal rent" denotes the tendency to use one's administrative position to collect an illegal income from the public who need the service.
3. Based on Heyneman, Anderson, and Nuraliyeva (2009: 2).
4. In one instance a ministry of education required all universities in the country to suddenly re-apply for accreditation. This was explained to the public as a quality assurance mechanism but was widely interpreted as a shakedown for bribes.
5. Students may have to pay a legal fee for these services. Corruption occurs when employees of a university will not provide the already paid for service without a bribe. In the case of a university library for instance, the librarian "will not find" the book requested without a bribe. In the case of transcript transfer, the administrator will delay the service until a private bribe is collected. In the case of a PhD candidate, the signing of the dissertation will be put "on hold" by the committee chair until a bribe is paid privately.
6. There are three audits of this kind: (1) compliance audits, which assess the degree to which a university adheres to legal codes; (2) cultural audits, which assess the degree to which a university understands how employees and students feel about the standards and the university's approach to maintaining them; and (3) a systems audit, which assesses the degree to which a university has integrated ethnical principles into its organizational structure (Bertram Gallant, Beesemyer, & Kezar 2009: 214).
7. Universities that do not display a code of conduct on their website are suspected as not yet having understood the implications of corruption for the quality of education. The perception of corruption is sufficient evidence to affect the decisions of a potential consumer; therefore, a university that is officially silent about corruption is automatically suspect.

References

Ahlin, C. and Bose, P. (2007) 'Bribery, inefficiency and bureaucratic delay', *Journal of Development Economics*, 84: 465–86.

Anderson, K.H. and Heyneman, S.P. (2005) 'Education and social policy in Central Asia: The next stage of the transition', *Journal of Social Policy and Administration*, 39: 361–80.

Anechiarico, F. and Jacobs, J.B. (1996) *The Pursuit of Absolute Integrity: How Corruption Control Makes Governments Ineffective*, Chicago: University of Chicago Press.

Bakari, S. and Leach, F. (2009) 'I invited her into my office: Normalizing sexual violence in a Nigerian college of education', in S.P. Heyneman (ed.) *Buying Your Way into Heaven: Education and Corruption in International Perspective*, Rotterdam, Netherlands: Sense Publishers.

Bardhan, P. (1997) 'Corruption and development: A review of the issues', *Journal of Economic Literature*, 35: 1320–46

Behrman, J.R. and Birdsall, N. (1983) 'The quality of schooling: Quantity alone is misleading', *American Economic Review*, 75: 928–46.

Bergan, S. (2009) 'The European higher education area as an instrument of transparency?', in S.P. Heyneman (ed.) *Buying Your Way into Heaven: Education and Corruption in International Perspective*, Rotterdam, Netherlands: Sense Publishers.

Bertram Gallant, T., Beesemyer, L.A. and Kezar, A. (2009) 'Creating a culture of ethics in higher education', in J.C. Knapp and D.J. Siegel (eds) *The Business of Higher Education Volume 1: Leadership and Culture*, Santa Barbara, CA: Praeger Publishers.

Blizek, W.L. (2000) 'Ethics and the educational community', *Studies in Philosophy and Education*, 19: 241–51.

Braxton, J.M. and Bayer, A.E. (1999) *Faculty Misconduct in Collegiate Teaching*, Baltimore: Johns Hopkins University Press.

Bruhn, J.G., Zajac, G., Al-Kazemi, A.A., and Prescott, L.D. Jr. (2002) 'Moral positions and academic conduct: Parameters of tolerance for ethics failures', *Journal of Higher Education*, 73: 461–93.

Cizek, G.J. (1999) *Cheating on Tests: How To Do It. How To Detect It. How To Prevent It*, Mahwah, NJ: Lawrence Erlbaum.

Collins, J.M. (2009) 'When schools fail to protect girls: School related gender-based sexual violence in Sub-Saharan Africa', in S.P. Heyneman (ed.) *Buying Your Way into Heaven: Education and Corruption in International Perspective*, Rotterdam, Netherlands: Sense Publishers.

Collins, R. (1979) *The Credential Story: An Historical Sociology of Education and Stratification*, New York: Wiley.

Dale, S.B. and Krueger, A.B. (2002) 'Estimating the payoff to attending a more selective college: An application of selection on observables and unobservables', *Quarterly Journal of Economics*, 117: 1491–527.

Dawson, W. (2009) 'The tricks of the teacher: Shadow education and corruption in Cambodia', in S. P. Heyneman (ed.) *Buying Your Way into Heaven: Education and Corruption in International Perspective*, Rotterdam, Netherlands: Sense Publishers.

Griliches, Z. and Mason, W.M. (1972) 'Education, income and ability', *Journal of Political Economy*, 80: S74–103.

Hallak, J. and Poisson, M. (2007) *Corrupt Schools, Corrupt Universities: What Can Be Done?* Paris: International Institute of Educational Planning.

Hanushek, E. and Wobmann, L. (2007) *The Role of Education Quality in Economic Growth*, Washington, DC: World Bank Research.

Heyneman, S.P. (2000) 'From the party/state to multi-ethnic democracy: Education and social cohesion in the Europe and Central Asia region', *Educational Evaluation and Policy Analysis*, 21: 173–91.

—— (2002/2003) 'Defining the influence of education on social cohesion', *International Journal of Educational Policy, Research and Practice*, 3: 73–97.

—— (2003) 'Education and misconduct', in J. Guthrie (ed.) *Encyclopedia of Education*, Volume 5, New York: Macmillan Publishers.

—— (2004) 'Education and corruption', *International Journal of Education Development*, 24: 638–48.

—— (2005) 'Organizations and social cohesion', *Peabody Journal of Education*, 80: 1–8.

—— (2006) 'The role of textbooks in a modern system of education', in C. Braslavsky (ed.) *Textbooks and Quality Learning for All: Some Lessons Learned from International Experiences*, Geneva: UNESCO/International Bureau of Education.

—— (2007a) 'Buying your way into heaven: The corruption of education systems in global perspective', *Perspectives on Global Issues*, 2: 1–8.

—— (2007b) 'Three universities in Georgia, Kazakhstan and Kyrgyzstan: the struggle against corruption and for social cohesion', *UNESCO Prospects*, 3: 305–18.

—— (2009a) 'Moral standards and the professor: A study of faculty at universities in Georgia, Kazakhstan and Kyrgyzstan', in S.P. Heyneman (ed.) *Buying Your Way into Heaven: Education and Corruption in International Perspective*, Rotterdam, Netherlands: Sense Publishers.

—— (2009b) 'The appropriate role of government in education', *Journal of Higher Education Policy*, 3: 135–57.

—— (2009c) 'The importance of external examinations in education', in B. Vlaardingerbrock and N. Taylor (eds) *Secondary School External Examination Systems: Reliability, Robustness and Resilience*, Amherst, NY: Cambria Press.

—— (2010) 'Changes in higher education in the Post-Soviet Union', in I. Silova (ed.) *The Challenges of Post-Soviet Education Reform: Central Asia in a Global Context*, Greenwich, CT: Information Age Publishing.

Heyneman, S.P. and Todoric-Bebic, S. (2000) 'A renewed sense of purpose of schooling: Education and social cohesion in Africa, Latin America, Asia and Europe and Central Asia', *UNESCO Prospects*, 30: 145–66.

Heyneman, S.P., Anderson, K.H., and Nuraliyeva, N. (2009) 'The cost of corruption in higher Education', *Comparative Education Review*, 51: 1–25.

Josephson Institute (2009) *A Study of Values and Behavior Concerning Integrity: The Impact of Age, Cynicism, and Higher School Character*, Los Angeles, CA: Josephson Institute.

Kalnins, V. (2001) *Latvia's Anti-corruption Policy: Problems and Prospects*, Riga: Soros Foundation.

Kelly, P.C., Agle, B.R., and DeMott, J. (2005) 'Mapping our progress: Identifying, categorizing, and comparing universities' ethics infrastructures', *Journal of Academic Ethics*, 3: 205–29.

Klitgaard, R. (1986) *Elitism and Meritocracy in Developing Countries*, Baltimore: Johns Hopkins University Press.

Kirmani, N. (1986) *Effects of Increased Market Access on Exports From Developing Countries*, Staff Paper No. 31, Washington DC: International Monetary Fund.

Louis, K.S., Anderson, M., and Rosenberg, L. (1995) 'Academic misconduct and values: The department's influence', *Review of Higher Education*, 18: 393–422.

McCabe, D. (1999) 'Academic dishonesty among high school students', *Adolescence*, 34: 681–87.

—— (2005) 'Cheating among college and university students: A North American perspective', *International Journal for Educational Integrity*, 1: 1–11.

McCornac, D.C. (2009) 'Corruption in Vietnamese Higher Education', in S.P. Heyneman (ed.) *Buying Your Way into Heaven: Education and Corruption in International Perspective*, Rotterdam, Netherlands: Sense Publishers.

Maricik, B. (2009) 'Models of corruption and how students could respond: Corruption experienced by the students during their studies in Macedonia', in S.P. Heyneman (ed.) *Buying Your Way into Heaven: Education and Corruption in International Perspective*, Rotterdam, Netherlands: Sense Publishers.

Noah, H.J. and Eckstein, M.A. (2001) *Fraud and Education: The Worm in the Apple*, Lanham, MD: Rowman & Littlefield.

Pinera, S. and Selowsky, M. (1981) 'The optimal ability–education mix and the misallocation of resources within education', *Journal of Development Economics*, 8: 111–31.

Sahlberg, P. (2009) 'The role of international organizations in fighting education corruption', in S.P. Heyneman (ed.) *Buying Your Way into Heaven: Education and Corruption in International Perspective*, Rotterdam, Netherlands: Sense Publishers.

Silova, I., Johnson, M., and Heyneman, S.P. (2007) 'Education and the crisis of social cohesion in Azerbaijan and Central Asia', *Comparative Education Review*, 51: 159–80.

Solmon, L.C. and Wachtel, P. (1975) 'The effect on income of type of college attended', *Sociology of Education*, 48: 75–90.

Stein, R.H. and Baca, M.C. (1981) 'Professional ethics in university administration', *New Directions for Higher Education*, 9: 93–6.

Victor, B. and Cullen, J.B. (1988) 'The organizational bases of ethical work climates', *Administrative Science Quarterly*, 33: 101–25.

Waite, D. and Allen, D. (2003) 'Corruption and abuse of power in educational administration', *The Urban Review*, 35: 281–96.

Wales, T.J. (1973) 'The effect of college quality on earnings from the NBER-Thorndike data', *Journal of Human Resources*, 8: 306–17.

3
Academic Ethics
A Systems Approach to Understanding Misconduct and Empowering Change in the Academy

TRICIA BERTRAM GALLANT AND MICHAEL KALICHMAN

In the previous chapter, Stephen Heyneman posits that corruption is a problem not only for corporations and government, but also for higher education. Heyneman further argues that educational corruption should be of significant concern because when the *means* for achieving higher education *ends* (e.g., providing trained workers, resolving societal ills, and promoting a knowledgeable and educated citizenry) are ethically dubious, then the ends have not been achieved despite artifacts (e.g., the awarding of degrees and diplomas) claiming the contrary. Continuing to ignore the corruption of the means of higher education can result in numerous and pervasive consequences such as the graduation of unethical and unskilled professionals and a loss of public trust in the ability of higher education institutions to fulfill their societal obligations.

This chapter continues with Heyneman's line of argument by offering a conception of the ethical academy, the antithesis to the corrupt academy.[1] While we are not arguing that all colleges or universities are corrupt, we are arguing that there is room for improvement on most campuses and within the education system in general. And a failure to more strategically and intentionally attend to ethics will create fertile ground for corruption to thrive. We say this because context matters—"individual characteristics alone are insufficient to explain" (Victor & Cullen 1988: 103) ethical misconduct and systemic education corruption. Rather, "healthy ethical environments" (Haydon 2004) can and should be created to support ethical choices by individuals, or in Selznick's (1992: 29) words, to bring forth and "sustain 'the better angels of our nature.'"[2] This is a theme you will see threaded throughout this volume, and this chapter sets the stage for that exploration.

Defining Ethics

Before we can define an ethical academy, we would be well served to speak more generally to the topic of ethics. What is ethics and what is it in the context of an organization? For the purposes of this book, we adopt an applied rather than a philosophical approach to ethics. Though not entirely discrete, philosophical or theoretical ethics lies at one end of a continuum and applied ethics at the other, and the continuum ranges from the general to the particular (Almond 1999). Applied ethics asks the question, "What is right or wrong to do in *this* situation?," in other words, what we ought to do given "codes of practice, rules and principles" (Almond 1999: 6). Ethical theories (e.g., ethics of care, utilitarianism, universalizability, justice) underpin the questions of what we ought to do because those theories provide us with the principles (e.g., justice, rights, utility, virtue, community) by which most of us make ethical decisions (Almond 1999: 8) (see chapter 9 for more details). Applied ethics has also been labeled organizational ethics, professional ethics, or, to be even more specific, biomedical ethics, engineering ethics, and so on. For the purposes of this book, we will use the term "academic ethics."

In the applied approach, as we have assumed it, academic ethics can best be described as the study and practice of appropriate ("What should I do?") and inappropriate ("What should I not do?") actions within the context of higher education. More pointedly, the question is, "How should I act, as a student, faculty, staff, administrator, governing board member, alumnus, etc.?"

How do we determine appropriate and inappropriate behaviors? When thinking generally about ethics or the "ethical person," we often think about a person who chooses right actions over wrong actions despite the hardships that might be experienced as a result of that choice. The student who chooses to not cheat on an exam, even if that means she will fail it; the researcher who chooses not to fabricate data, even though it may mean that her experiment has failed to produce the desired findings; the faculty member who chooses to challenge his students in the classroom, despite the risk of receiving poor evaluations; the athletics administrator who does not call the recruit during the "no call" times, even if that means she might lose that player to another campus. We judge "right actions" according to general values such as honesty, respect, and responsibility, or according to laws or tenets such as "do no harm" or "love thy neighbor." In other words, we take philosophical ethical principles and use them to evaluate or judge our own and others' actions. Did that action cause more harm than good? Was that person fair in his behavior? Was the action just? We might think of an ethical person as someone who puts others' needs and interests ahead of her own, or the common good ahead of her personal good.

The context for our actions is relevant because the definition of appropriateness changes based on the circumstances, situation, and expectations; in other words, on "the detailed texture of the situations in which ethical problems arise" (Almond 1999: 3). Others argue that the ethicality of a decision is defined by the "moral obligations" (Victor & Cullen 1988: 101) of the organization or the profession. So, what of the academic context? Many would say that the moral obligations of the college or university are to teach, serve, and conduct research. Decisions about what one should do, then, would be made in relation to these obligations. The import of context for our discussion of academic ethics is high, thus deserving further treatment before we move on to a discussion of the ethical academy.

Academic Ethics

The landscape of academic ethics is defined by the various communities in which academics are situated. To be professionally ethical, one must understand all of the communities of which one is a member. In academic ethics, individuals typically live most immediately within a small group of co-workers, academic collaborators, or fellow students. This smallest unit is nested within a larger unit such as a disciplinary/academic departmental community (e.g., philosophy department, admissions). These organizational units within the university are typically collected together with other similar units in a still larger unit, which is a subset of the college or university, and finally within the educational system writ large. As such, being ethical is not just about what an individual may or may not do based upon personal values, but also about what is expected according to community values.

The nested community context helps to clarify that academic ethical challenges are not solely based on individuals choosing between a right and a wrong, but also between a right and a right (Kidder 2003). What is right for an individual may conflict with what is right for one of the larger communities of which the individual is a part. So, for example, a research lab technician may be faced with having to choose between justly reporting a principal research investigator who is falsifying data and being loyal to the same investigator who forgave the technician's earlier transgressions.

As another example of a right versus right dilemma in academic ethics, picture the common everyday life of the college student who is working not only on her studies but also on the development of friendships and of the self. In such a context, students are often put into a situation in which they must decide between a right and a right. A particularly poignant and relevant example is the decision students often have to make between conveying truth in their academic assignment (i.e., handing in one's own work) and being loyal to a friend who might ask the student for help through the act of copying that academic assignment. To select the "right" or ethical action, the student must emphasize one value over the other. Alternatively, the student can choose to reframe what the values mean. For example, perhaps loyalty to the friend means *not letting him copy the academic assignment* because, in prohibiting that behavior, the student is preventing the friend from being caught for cheating. In this reframing, the student can align the values of truth and loyalty and maintain a sense of ethical agency or principled conduct that is aligned with the ethicality of the organization (Selznick 1992).

It is in this sense that professional (academic) ethics diverts from personal ethics or a sense of personal integrity. At times, professional ethics may require an individual to act in ways that are misaligned with their own sense of what is right or principled. A perfect illustration of this conflict that made international headlines is the case of pharmacists who refused to fill birth control or morning-after pill prescriptions because of personal, moral beliefs.[3] But how might such a conflict between personal and professional ethics extend to higher education and the academy? Could a professor refuse to teach an openly gay student because he personally believes that homosexuality is a moral sin? Could an administrator stop a student from exercising his free-speech rights to talk about the benefits of capital punishment because the administrator views capital punishment as morally wrong? Although these examples might be uncommon or seem unlikely, such conflicts between personal and professional ethics do in fact arise in education. The refusal of teachers to teach Darwinism or the theory of evolution because they personally subscribe to creationism is one such example.

Academic ethics, then, is in part the practice of resolving the ethical dilemmas that arise because we live, work, and study within multiple nested higher education communities that are bound to have conflicting conceptions of what is right.

Facets of Academic Ethics

Three defining facets of academic ethics are determined by the context of the community in which we work, live, and study. These include our obligations to the higher education community and society, our roles as members of that community, and the standards that govern our behavior in academia. The first of these facets is *fulfilling obligations* to society. Each profession has obligations to society, or, to put it another way, society has expectations of professions and professionals. So, for example, society expects medical doctors to do no harm, to treat the sick, and even to cure the diseased.

What does society expect of the academy and its members? Generally, society expects colleges and universities to educate and certify the next generation of professionals and to serve society in other ways (e.g., community education, enrichment, and social programs). More specifically, society expects community colleges to provide open access to anyone who desires an education, to provide support for students with learning deficiencies, and to provide the workforce with the trained professionals needed in market shortages (e.g., nurses, laboratory technicians). On the other hand, society expects research universities to solve social problems, cure societal and individual ills, and uncover truths and advance scientific, economic, social, and political progress. Academic ethics, then, is in part the practice of resolving any conflicts that arise between these, sometimes, competing obligations.

A second facet of professional ethics is *performing roles*. To help the community fulfill its obligations, each member of the organization (aka community) has a role to play. In his book *Academic Duty*, Donald Kennedy (1997), former President of Stanford University, identified eight duties for academics: to (1) teach and (2) mentor, to (3) discover and (4) publish, to (5) serve the university and (6) serve society, to (7) tell the truth, and to (8) be prepared to change and adapt. Students are expected to learn, participate in service/shared governance (to some extent), and demonstrate their learning, knowledge, and abilities to the faculty. Finally, administrators and governing board members are expected to provide the support necessary for the institution to function as a place of learning, research, and service.

Each of these roles is performed in service to the organization and to the organization's obligations to society. So, for example, students must honestly demonstrate their knowledge and abilities so that faculty can effectively evaluate the same. And faculty must honestly and fairly evaluate students so that the institution can honestly and fairly certify that its graduating students have achieved some level of general education as well as expertise in a particular discipline. This honest and fair certification helps the college or university fulfill one of its obligations to society, that of preparing educated and skilled workers and professionals. Understanding the roles that people have within an organization or profession is critical in a conversation about applied ethics because otherwise "no assessment can be made" (Selznick 1992: 28) about an individual's ethicality in relation to those roles. For example, a man who commits adultery might be viewed as an unethical husband, but his ethicality as an engineer would not as readily be questioned.

The third facet of academic ethics is *meeting standards*. In order for organizational members to perform their roles in a manner that will enable the organization to fulfill its obligations, there must be standards for conduct. These shared standards, sometimes referred to as codes of conduct or ethical codes, make explicit to organizational members what is expected of them and what constitutes appropriate and inappropriate behavior. These standards are perhaps most commonly thought of when people think of organizational ethics. Although standards do not constitute ethics themselves, they are symbols for underlying organizational values that define the community and guide ethical behavior.

Standards for ethical conduct, which are often unwritten, may be paired with other written standards for behavior, such as laws or mandates. While not fully consistent (e.g., some unethical behaviors might be fully legal and in compliance), the rules of compliance or behavioral mandates are usually rooted in understandings of ethical behavior. For example, the requirement of researchers to comply with federal mandates against falsification, fabrication, and plagiarism in federally funded research projects is rooted in such values as academic integrity, authorship, originality, and scientific method. Plagiarism is a good example of something that is considered *unethical* in the academy but not always so in daily life. If you are speaking with friends or family and fail to attribute your words to the originator of them, it would be highly unlikely for someone to call you unethical or to exclaim "plagiarist!" However, if a researcher, academic, or student fails to attribute the words or ideas of another, they will be in violation of academic integrity standards, ethics codes, and possibly federal law. In other words, context alters the definition of ethical and unethical conduct.

This is not to say that we subscribe to ethical relativism in the colloquial sense of the term (i.e., "anything goes" or "to each his own" because what is ethical is relative and therefore non-prescriptive). Rather, we posit that although ethicality is not absolute (one right versus one wrong choice), it is plural. There may be many choices but having many choices does not mean that they are equally valid or justifiable as relativism would have us believe (Selznick 1992). Plural ethicality acknowledges that there are competing interests, goods, and rights constantly at play in ethical decision making, often requiring the individual to choose one right or good over another for reasons that may depend on context, situation, involved actors, or desired ends (Kidder 2003).

Defining the Ethical Academy

As a reminder, the main purpose of this book is to help higher education stakeholders move toward an "ethical academy." We have already defined that from which we would like to move away—the corrupt academy as detailed in Heyneman's chapter. We have also already defined what we mean by ethics or academic ethics (the study and practice of appropriate and inappropriate behavior according to the obligations, roles, and standards of the college or university community context). Thus, we should next define what the ethical (versus unethical) academy should look like. The ethical academy, nominally, is one in which individual members (i.e., students, faculty, and staff) are provided a "healthy ethical environment" (Haydon 2004) that supports ethical over unethical or corrupt decision making and conduct. A healthy ethical environment does enhance the likelihood that members will choose rights over wrongs, but also that members will be able to resolve competing community obligations and conflicts between personal and academic ethics standards (or rights versus rights).

We posit that a healthy ethical academy has three main characteristics: individual responsibility, trust, and institutional integrity.

Individual Responsibility

In an ethical academy, institutional members assume individual responsibility to recognize situations characterized by ethical or moral questions. They understand that it is their role to determine if there are ethical standards, organizational obligations, or compliance rules or regulations that should guide their decision making and conduct in such situations. This is critically important because many members of the academy conduct their work unmonitored and unsupervised, especially researchers, teachers, and students. Although there may be externally imposed regulations intended to guide behavior, it is predominantly up to individuals to regulate their behavior in compliance with those externally imposed ethical standards.

An ethical academy also is one comprising individuals who subsume their own short-term interests and goals (e.g., grades, publications, awards) to the moral and ethical obligations of the college or university. The integrity of the ends depends on the integrity of the means and a "subversion of integrity is . . . likely to result from narrowly centered interests and self-serving strategies" (Selznick 1992: 330). Thus, an ethical academy supports and rewards individuals who choose community over self-interests and act in ways that help the college or university fulfill its obligations in a socially responsible way.

The characteristic of individual responsibility and capability for action will vary depending on the member's position within the organization. In particular, college and university students are likely to require more guidance and support in exercising individual responsibility than staff and faculty. However, in the ethical academy, staff and faculty (particularly with adequate support, training, and socialization) will not only model individual responsibility, but will also mentor others, especially students, in doing the same.

Trust

Individual responsibility, or self-regulation, is critical to the realization of the second main characteristic of the ethical academy—trust. Concomitantly, trust is a necessary condition for the privilege of being authorized to self-regulate (rather than to be regulated or monitored by others). Trust is, in very basic terms, the antithesis to opportunism or self-seeking behaviors (Hosmer 1995) such as, in the academy, student cheating, teacher improprieties, research misconduct, and so on. For the purposes of this discussion, we adopt Hosmer's (1995: 399) definition of trust as "the expectation by one person, group or firm of ethically justifiable behavior . . . on the part of the other . . . in a joint endeavor."

Members of the academy (especially of the public academies) and society are engaged in a joint endeavor and thus, without trust, society might not agree to "maintain and empower" colleges and universities to fulfill important societal functions (Brien 1998: 403). The academy is to society, then, as a doctor is to a patient; society (the patient) trusts the academy (the doctor) to share her specialized knowledge and training in ways that will not simply refrain from doing harm but will enhance the society's (patient's) quality of life. When society can no longer trust the academy to do what it promises, to self-regulate, then it can be expected to make demands for external regulation and remove support for maintenance and empowerment. The imposition of external research ethics regulation back in the 1990s is one manifestation of the demise of trust in researchers and the academy. Another is the more recent accountability and assessment movement spearheaded by the federal department of education and Margaret Spellings who seemed to no longer be able to trust that the academy could self-regulate its quality or the achievement of its purpose.[4]

Trust is essential not only for ensuring that the academy maintains its ethics compact with society, but also for ensuring an ethics compact *within* the academy. Researchers must be able to trust one another to conduct their research with integrity, teachers must be able to trust students to do their own work, and staff must be able to trust that institutional leadership will deal fairly and quickly with alleged misconduct. The work performed in the academy is largely individual and conducted in private. Professors teach classes with little oversight or interference from their colleagues or their supervisors. Students do their school work outside of the class, also with minimal or no supervision by their teachers. Even those at the "bottom" of various hierarchies (such as the research lab technician in a large laboratory) function primarily independently with little day-to-day supervision. This is, in most cases, why people enjoy being members of a college or university. There is freedom in being trusted to do one's work. Thus, an ethical academy depends on individual organizational members not betraying that trust. Again, this may be particularly difficult to sustain without the other characteristics of the ethical academy. Students have told us that, if faculty do not want them to cheat, they should not assign them homework to do outside of the classroom, that is, without supervision. The key for sustaining collegial trust is ensuring that people understand what is expected of them (so that they can assume individual responsibility), supporting them in upholding trust, and creating a culture in which trust is seen and modeled at all levels.

Institutional Integrity

For individual members to assume responsibility and trust that others will do the same, the institution itself must be integrous. This means first that the institution always *attempts to do what it promises to do*, that it has congruency and internal consistency. However, a second component of institutional integrity is that the institution responds to problems when they are identified, not first to punish the "bad actors" but to correct systems so as to mitigate factors that may be, in part, responsible for shaping those problems. With respect to the first of the two components, an institution's promises are based on "what the institution is or should be" as defined by its "special functions and values" and "unifying principles" (Selznick 1992: 324). In other words, an institution's promises are based on its obligations to society.

So, in the case of a university or college, it could be said that there are two layers of promises: one that is defined by the functions, values, and principles assigned by society to the institution of higher education, and one that is defined by the functions, values, and principles adopted by the campus itself.

For example, all colleges and universities are expected to educate citizens and train future generations of workers, but an individual campus may decide that its primary mission is to train researchers while another may decide to focus on training trade workers. Selznick (1992: 324) argues that institutional integrity is achieved when an institution defines and upholds the standards that help it reach its "distinctive mission" or "practice."

However, in the ethical academy, the distinctive campus mission or practice should not be at odds with the moral obligations that higher education has to society. The ethical academy, in the words of former Duke University President Nan Keohane (2006), must stand on a "higher moral ground" and maintain its "commitment to duty" despite external forces such as "time constraints, financial problems, governmental regulations, and other social pressures" (Besvinick 1983: 570). The ethical academy is not a perfect academy, but rather it implements structures and processes and works to create and sustain a culture that supports ethical conduct and ethicality above all other choices. So a faculty member, when tempted by research monies to cut corners, has support for constraining misconduct and enhancing his professional ethicality. So an athletic administrator, who is cajoled by her boss to "do whatever it takes" to recruit the latest high school star athlete to the campus, can cite campus norms or policies to dissuade her boss. So the governing board member can question the president who wants to drop the "ethics across the curriculum" initiative to kowtow to parents and students who want only coursework that is thought to be directly tied to economic viability or enhanced job prospects.

With respect to the second component, the honest self-appraisal when standards are not set, met, or upheld, Selznick (1992) offers us the following advice: take a look at the means by which the organization is achieving its ends and assess whether they are enhancing or undermining institutional integrity. As we will see throughout this book, competition, technology, conflicting interests, and other social forces all shape independent judgments about appropriate means for achieving the desired ends, and it is the ethical academy that will dedicate resources to counter those forces through shoring up institutional integrity, trust, and individual responsibility.

A Systems Approach toward the Ethical Academy

Creating a healthy ethical environment depends not only on being clear about the environment that is desired, but also on the problems to be solved, those issues currently polluting the ethical environment. In this book, the authors have chosen to use a common framework for analyzing the misconduct that occurs in the academy and for creating the ethical academy. If the goal is to foster ethical institutions, then we must begin by constructing a clear framework for that purpose.

Framing is the action of asking the question, "what is it that's going on here?"

(Goffman 1974: 8). So, when used purposefully, framing can be a way to analyze and reanalyze organizational realities or problems to make us more cognizant of the complexity of the situation and to generate more creative solutions. Because they are socially constructed, framings are neither right nor wrong but they can be more or less robust; however, the way in which a problem or situation is framed is critical because it shapes the construction of available solutions.

Traditionally, ethical misconduct in the academy has been framed rather simply as a result of individual agency or institutional structures, leading to the propensity to try to fix individuals or control behaviors through structures; neither of which have seemed to work to stem the tide of corruption (Bertram Gallant 2008; Bertram Gallant, Beesemyer, & Kezar 2009). We can say this with confidence because of the data presented in this book and in previously conducted studies. For example, the research has shown that, despite two decades of a focus on educating individuals about research integrity and punishing individuals for research misconduct, the rate of research misconduct has remained virtually unchanged.

Although there are many possible reasons for this lack of movement, none of them supports the argument that an ad hoc focus on individuals is the answer to creating the ethical academy. Consistent with our definition of applied ethics as the study and practice of inappropriate and appropriate behavior in context, our systems framing views the individual agent as nested within context, specifically the college or university, which is nested within the larger academy, which is nested within the larger society.

Figure 3.1 illustrates our premise that individual misconduct or ethical agency is actually a systemic issue, shaped by individual, organizational, educational/academy, and societal factors.[5] This is a sociological interpretation of ethicality that conceives of "every practice and every institution" as "fatefully conditioned by larger contexts of culture and social organization" (Selznick 1992: 29). Forces (e.g., structural, procedural, and cultural) within each system level will naturally shape the structures, procedures, and cultures within the nested levels, and the ethical agency of the individual will shape and be shaped by the entire system. Thus, to understand research misconduct, for example, we must understand how it is shaped by each of these levels. Authors of chapters 4–8 examine these factors in more detail as they relate to specific misconduct issues in the academy. For now, we briefly define each level in turn.

The Individual Level

Although the focus of this book is on systemic approaches to promoting the ethical academy, it is ultimately the individuals who comprise the academy, not the academy *per se*, who act or fail to act with integrity. The individual students, faculty, and staff are certainly embedded in their particular academic organization, subject to the pressures of the educational system itself, and influenced by the society in which they live. However, it is important to also ask about the

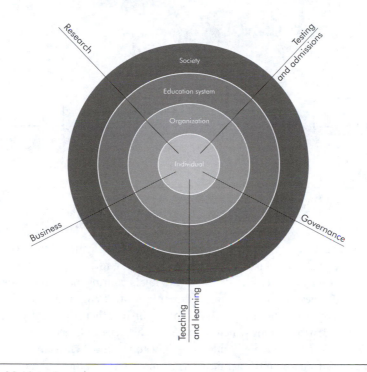

Figure 3.1 A Systems Framework.

individual factors that are likely to enable misconduct in the academy. For the purpose of this discussion, we propose a simple framework for understanding individual behavior as illustrated in Figure 3.2.

Each individual entering the academy arrives with a particular set of knowledge, skills, and attitudes defined by her or his particular history (the environment in which that individual was socialized). And it is this set of knowledge, skills, and attitudes that can be expected to have a profound influence on how an individual will act in the face of the pressures of academia.

Knowledge of what is right, what is wrong, and what is gray is a prerequisite for being able to choose to act with integrity. However, as noted earlier, context changes definitions of right and wrong and so individuals may enter the academy with knowledge that is misaligned or dissonant with the knowledge we want them to acquire and share. In partial recognition of the need to learn new standards and values, it is often the case that first-time offenders, especially students, will be subject to less strict sanctions than someone who is more senior, or a repeat offender. Simply knowing more about academia, or knowing that it is necessary to learn more, is a key first step to acting well.

Skills for analyzing and for addressing an ethical challenge are a prerequisite for arriving at a good decision about how to act. Many skills are relevant to ethical decision making, but one of the most important is what is often referred

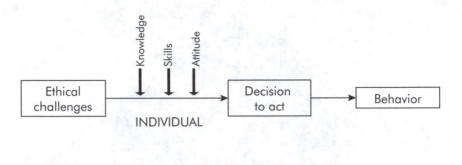

Figure 3.2 Individual Factors Influencing the Decision to Act in Response to Ethical Challenges.

to as "moral reasoning." As a framework for understanding individual conduct, we adapt Rest's theory of moral reasoning. According to Rest's theory (Bebeau, Rest, & Narvaez 1999), ethical decision making is contingent on meeting four distinct challenges: (1) interpreting the situation as involving an ethical dilemma that has multiple possibilities of action which impact others differently (ethical sensitivity); (2) determining which action is the most ethically justifiable (ethical judgment); (3) giving greater value or weight to the most ethically justifiable action over self-interest (ethical motivation); and (4) having the courage, conviction, and determination to choose the right course of action despite hardships, challenges, and frustrations (ethical character). It is worth noting that each of these components is significantly dependent on the more general skill of "critical thinking." The ability to identify a problem, to generate possible solutions, to select among those solutions, and to successfully implement a workable solution are all steps that will be carried out well only when critical thinking skills are sufficiently robust.

Attitudes about what is valued are among the most significant factors defining how we will act. In the face of an "ideal" academic organization and educational system, even an individual fully armed with the requisite knowledge and skills is unlikely to act with integrity if he or she has an attitude that places an unquestioning value on personal success. This is one of the clearest challenges to the ethical academy. If we want to know what the members of our academic institutions are likely to value, it is necessary only to peruse the nature of, for example, business, journalism, politics, professional and amateur sports, and entertainment media. In all cases, the message is clear: the end really does justify the means. Unfortunately, attitudes are notoriously difficult to shape in adult learners. Nonetheless, it is arguable that the single most important factor in defining individual integrity is the individual's attitude toward the importance of acquiring the necessary knowledge and skills to promote the highest standards of conduct (see chapter 9).

The Organization Level

In a groundbreaking book on ethics in the academy, May (1990: 4) posits that individual ethical failures are "symptomatic of organizational dysfunction" and a result of "competing claims within complex institutions." In support of May's organizational framework, other researchers and writers have argued that clearly articulated norms and rules, transparent procedures, distributed power, fair and strong incentive systems, ethical infrastructures, and strong leadership within the organization can support ethical conduct (Bertram Gallant 2006; Hallak & Poisson 2007; Kelley & Chang 2007).

Bruhn and co-authors, while agreeing with May's theory that "ethics failure is a complex individual and organizational phenomenon," add that ethics "operates largely within the realm of *relationships within the academic community*" (Bruhn, Zajac, Al-Kazemi, & Prescott 2002: 481, italics in original). Teachers *teach* in relationship to the students, and teachers *fail to teach* in those same relationships. Students *learn* in relationships to each other, to the teacher, and to their parents, and they *fail to learn* in those same relationships. Administrators *lead* in relationship to the inner life of the school and its members as well as the outer life of politics and the economy, and they *fail to lead* in those same relationships. These relationships between different agents within and outside the organization can create conflicting notions and interests that can make the environment complex and ethical conduct ambiguous (Blizek 2000). May (and his contributing authors) and Bruhn and colleagues emphasize that altering organizational structures, procedures, and cultures (including relationships) may be a more powerful remedy than altering individual behaviors because organizational culture and relationships have "a powerful influence on the behavior and decisions of [individual] organization's members" (Bruhn, et al. 2002: 483).

So even though we can recognize the individual's primary responsibility for "moral choice," it is also clear both in theory and based on evidence that people are profoundly affected by the institutions in which they operate (see, for example, Anderson, Louis, & Earle 1994; Swazey, Anderson, & Louis 1993). Although we might disapprove of an argument that excuses our own bad behavior because of the bad behavior of our institutional leaders, the fact remains that good behavior by institutional leaders is unlikely to be disadvantageous and likely to be beneficial. A student's understanding of plagiarism is shaped by artifacts of the organizational culture, such as the actions of the faculty member who, in his lectures, consistently models and discusses the importance of attributing sources. If a president chooses to divest himself or herself of stock in a socially irresponsible company with which his or her university does business, then this simultaneously serves as a model for acceptable behavior and makes it less likely that the president's behavior will become an excuse for bad behavior by others in the academic community.

An ethical academy has ethics as a strategic institutional priority and has implemented the support structures, processes, and resources as a foundation for this prioritization. This aspect, along with the importance of institutional leadership, will be discussed much later in the book by Adrianna Kezar and Cecile Sam (chapter 10). However, at this point, it is important to note that organizational culture and environment shape individual choices and actions. An ethical academy cannot be achieved without intentional attention to the support of individual ethical conduct. In the complex college or university of the twenty-first century with multiple competing interests and priorities, it cannot be assumed that students, staff, and faculty will intuit what is considered ethical or unethical by the institution and thus teaching and curriculum is critical (see chapter 11 by Keller).

The Education System Level

Factors at the level of the larger education system, including elementary and secondary levels, higher education, and the research system, can also shape or decrease the risk of individual ethical failings and organizational ethical dysfunctions (Eckstein 2003; Hallak & Poisson 2007; Kelley & Chang 2007). These are factors that transcend organizational or campus boundaries and are not unique to a particular organizational culture. State rules about access and admissions, such as those found in the California Master Plan, are examples of educational factors. Others include the competitive research system (see chapter 6), the quest for prestige (see chapter 7), highlighted by the intensified competition in campus rankings and college admissions, and the increasing dependence on standardized testing for educational advancement and organizational survival (see chapter 4).

Clearly the focus on grades in the education system is a major factor in shaping the attention and direction of students (Bertram Gallant 2008). In the twenty-first century, however, grades have become important also to teachers and administrators because public schools receive funding based on performance and performance is measured by test scores and grade point averages (GPAs). Reports of ethical corruption following implementation in the United States of the No Child Left Behind Act have included teachers giving test answers to students, and administrators changing students' answers once the tests are completed (e.g., see Jan 2007; Tyre 2007). Anecdotal and empirical evidence suggests that people will do whatever it takes to get ahead and be "successful," however defined (Callahan 2004). And with grades as the currency necessary to gain access to postsecondary education and graduate education, both of which lead to more lucrative careers than are possible without such certifications, doing whatever it takes to get the grades seems like the logical choice for survival.

Factors at the education system level do not just affect students and K–12 teachers and administrators, but also college and university professors, researchers, and administrators. For example, the competition among coaches to recruit the "best players" to their campuses (perhaps because they receive bonuses in winning seasons, or simply to keep their job for another year) may lead to ethical corruption in our athletic programs (e.g., Moltz 2009). The commercialization of education, in which schools, colleges, and universities are conceived of as businesses and their operations examined in economic terms (e.g., efficiencies, monetary returns), has led to a preoccupation with short-term payoffs (Davis, Drinan, & Bertram Gallant 2009). Thus, researchers may be encouraged to bend research results to fit a funder's motives or administrators may be willing to admit students or give out unearned degrees to influential or potential donors (Jaschik 2008).

The Society Level

The conduct of individuals and institutions occurs against a backdrop of many factors external to the academy and the education system. These include, for example, federal and state regulations, systems of institutional accreditation, professional guidelines, and prevailing standards in the larger community. However, societal factors can also encourage unethical conduct in the academy; these factors include the unethical conduct of other professionals (e.g., politicians, corporate leaders); competition for scarce resources (with educational organizations competing with other states); lack of political and societal effort to control, prevent, and punish corruption; and the increasing sophistication and proliferation of technology (Eckstein 2003; Hallak & Poisson 2007; Kelley & Chang 2007). Hallak and Poisson, for example, found that, in countries rife with political and economic corruption, academic cheating is more prevalent. In other words, societal factors can operate as models of accepted, or at least not unacceptable, behaviors.

Technology may have the greatest impact on unethical conduct, perhaps because it is worldwide and omnipotent, but also because it has caused a blurring of the lines between ethical and unethical conduct (Bertram Gallant 2008). It is almost as if, by making it easier to commit certain acts, the internet and other technologies have thus transformed those acts into "not cheating." For example, because students can now post exam answer keys to the internet, they do not see this behavior as unethical (Bertram Gallant 2008). Or because the internet is "a mutual brain into which we can all tap" (Bertram Gallant 2006), material taken from the internet and used in one's own paper or grant proposal is not seen as plagiarism because the material is not independently owned or individually constructed.

Although it is clear that these societal factors can have a substantial impact on individuals and institutions, it is rarely the case that any one institution, much less an individual, will have the means to significantly alter these external factors. Instead, institutional and individual approaches to shaping ethical conduct will either be unavoidably tempered by or occur in spite of the dictates of these societal factors. However, an awareness of these factors and their possible impact can assist institutions in adapting to, resisting, or lessening their impact. Without this awareness, institutional integrity would be difficult to sustain in the face of external forces. Those interested in stemming corruption and encouraging ethical conduct might, for example, consider how technology can lead to an increase in cheating but can also be used to stem cheating. Plagiarism detection software offers a powerful illustration of this point. Although plagiarism has become easier in the age of the internet, detecting plagiarism has become easier as well.

The Ethical Academy: What Can We Do?

The question begged by this framework is this—can we influence people to act ethically despite *systemic forces that encourage unethical behavior*? Although the answer is not an unequivocal yes, it is clear that there is considerable room to do better than we do now. Given the expectations that society holds for our academic institutions, it is unacceptable for the academy to argue that societal factors are too great to be overcome. We have a moral imperative to strive to develop citizens of sufficient moral and integrous fiber so that they can withstand forceful pressures to act in unethical and dishonest ways.

The focus of this chapter has been to make clear that individual behavior is nested within a framework defined by personal history, relationships within small groups, expectations of departmental communities, organizational culture, the parameters defined by our education system, and the society in which we live. Creating the ethical academy does not mean changing all of these factors, but three clearly lie in the domain of our influence: departmental communities, organizational culture, and the education system. Although a focus on these areas will not change the history of the individuals who have come to our institutions as students, faculty, or staff, a failure to do so will mean a missed opportunity to strengthen today's academy. Conversely, this focus can serve to empower good behavior and discourage bad behavior, not only for today's academy, but also for the future leaders who will help to define the society within which the academy functions.

Notes

1. We would like to acknowledge that we may not have yet convinced the reader that corruption is a problem in education. Part II of the book, we hope, will help to do that by offering specific examples of the corrupt acts that occur in the academy. At this time, we ask the reader for some indulgence as we flesh out the antithesis to the corrupt academy for it is important in the framing of the remainder of the book. In Part II, each chapter will dissect a particular area or function of the college or university that has the potential for or actually causes corruption.
2. It is important to note that this book does not address the morally corrupt or psychologically deviant individuals who behave in unethical or illegal manners regardless of the context in which they are embedded (readers interested in those discussions should consult psychological texts on deviancy). As others have said, "some ethical failure is inevitable" (Allen, 2004, xxv) in all organizations and in all societies. Political scientists such as Patrick Drinan, one of the contributing authors to this volume, focus on how we can maintain an acceptable level of corruption, that is, a level that can be dealt with because it is individually rooted rather than institutionally generated.

3. For more information on this story, see several reports online at http://www.nwlc.org/
    our-issues/health-care-%2526-reproductive-rights/barriers-to-reproductivcare/pharmacy-
    refusals (accessed 19 August 2010) or http://www.washingtonpost.com/wp-dyn/articles/A5490-
    2005Mar27.html or http://abcnews.go.com/Health/Story?id=5542159&page=1 (accessed 1
    June 2010).
4. See http://www2.ed.gov/news/pressreleases/2005/10/10172005.html (accessed 1 June 2010)
    for more information.
5. A version of this framework was originally published in Bertram Gallant (2008).

References

Allen, A.L. (2004) *The New Ethics: A Guided Tour of the Twenty-first Century Moral Landscape*,
New York: Hyperion.

Almond, B. (1999) *Introducing Applied Ethics*, Malden, MA: Blackwell.

Anderson M.S., Louis K.S., and Earle J. (1994) 'Disciplinary and departmental effects on observations
of faculty and graduate student misconduct', *Journal of Higher Education*, 65: 331–50.

Bebeau, M.J., Rest, J.R., and Narvaez, D. (1999) 'Beyond the promise: A perspective on research in
moral education', *Educational Researcher*, 28: 18–26.

Bertram Gallant, T. (2006) 'Reconsidering academic dishonesty: A critical examination of a complex
organizational problem', unpublished doctoral dissertation, University of San Diego.

—— (2008) *Academic Integrity in the Twenty-First Century: A Teaching and Learning Imperative*,
San Francisco: Jossey-Bass.

Bertram Gallant, T., Beesemyer, L., and Kezar, A. (2009) 'A culture of ethics in higher education', in
D. Segal and J. Knapp (eds) *The Business of Higher Education*, Santa Barbara: Praeger.

Besvinick, S.L. (1983) 'Integrity and the future of the university', *Journal of Higher Education*, 54:
566–73.

Blizek, W.L. (2000) 'Ethics and the educational community', *Studies in Philosophy and Education*,
19: 241–51.

Brien, A. (1998) 'Professional ethics and the culture of trust', *Journal of Business Ethics*, 17: 391–409.

Bruhn, J. G., Zajac, G., Al-Kazemi, A.A., and Prescott, L.D. Jr. (2002) 'Moral positions and academic
conduct: Parameters of tolerance for ethics failure', *Journal of Higher Education*, 73: 461–93.

Callahan, D. (2004) *The Cheating Culture: Why More Americans Are Doing Wrong to Get Ahead*,
Orlando: Harcourt.

Davis, S.F., Drinan, P.F., and Bertram Gallant, T. (2009) *Cheating in School: What We Know and
What We Can Do*, Malden, MA: Wiley-Blackwell.

Eckstein, M.A. (2003) *Combating Academic Fraud: Towards a Culture of Integrity*, Paris: International
Institute for Educational Planning.

Goffman, E. (1974) *Frame Analysis: An Essay on the Organization of Experience*, Cambridge, MA:
Harvard University Press.

Hallak, J. and Poisson, M. (2007) *Corrupt Schools, Corrupt Universities: What Can be Done?*, Paris:
International Institute for Educational Planning.

Haydon, G. (2004) 'Values education: Sustaining the ethical environment', *Journal of Moral Education*,
33: 115–29.

Hosmer, L.T. (1995) 'Trust: The connecting link between organizational theory and philosophical
ethics', *Academy of Management Review*, 20: 379–403.

Jan, T. (2007) 'Increased cheating reported on MCAS—Cases of impropriety seen for both students,
teachers', *Boston Globe*, 1 November. Available through LexisNexis (accessed 30 July 2009).

Jaschik, S. (2008) 'Up to 80 degrees at WVU may be suspect', *Inside Higher Ed*, 2 September. Available
at http://www.insidehighered.com/news/2008/09/02/wvu (accessed 30 July 2009).

Kelley, P.C. and Chang, P.L. (2007) 'A typology of university ethical lapses: Types, levels of seriousness,
and originating location', *Journal of Higher Education*, 78: 402–29.

Kennedy D. (1997) *Academic Duty*, Cambridge, MA: Harvard University Press.

Keohane, N.O. (2006) *Higher Ground: Ethics and Leadership in the Modern University*, Durham,
NC: Duke University Press.

Kidder, R.M. (1995; 2nd edn 2003) *How Good People Make Tough Choices: Resolving the Dilemmas
of Ethical Living*, New York: HarperCollins.

May, W.W. (1990) *Ethics and Higher Education*, New York: Macmillan Publishing.

Moltz, D. (2009) 'Rogue compliance officer', *Inside Higher Ed*, 27 May. Available at http://www.
insidehighered.com/news/2009/03/27/ncaa (accessed 30 July 2009).

Selznick, P. (1992) *The Moral Commonwealth: Social Theory and the Promise of Community*, Berkeley: University of California Press.

Swazey J.P., Anderson, M.S., and Louis, K.S. (1993) 'Ethical problems in academic research', *American Scientist*, 81: 542–53.

Tyre, P. (2007) 'To catch a cheat; the pressure is on for schools to raise test scores. Some it seems are willing to resort to anything', *Newsweek*, 15 October. Available through LexisNexis (accessed on 30 July 2009).

Victor, B. and Cullen, J.B. (1988) 'The organizational bases of ethical work climates', *Administrative Science Quarterly*, 33: 101–25.

II

Understanding Ethical Misconduct in Key Areas of Higher Education

4

Undermining Integrity in Standardized Testing and Admissions

Misconduct in the Academic Selection Process

TRICIA BERTRAM GALLANT

As noted by other authors in this volume, higher education is a booming business; as the knowledge economy displaces the industrial economy, the world demand for people with higher education correspondingly accelerates the demand for college diplomas and university degrees thought to be symbolic of education and training. Basic economics informs us that, when there exists *demand*, there will be people who are ready to *supply*, often by any means necessary (especially when demand exceeds supply or the supplies are difficult to obtain).

So, for example, instead of attending a college or university and engaging in the education and training meant to be represented by a diploma, people can choose instead to purchase a diploma from any number of available and accessible "diploma mills."[1] With the click of a button, some basic information, and some money, anyone can buy their educational certificate in a matter of minutes and receive a diploma (even a PhD) within a matter of weeks (Bartlett & Smallwood 2004; Noah & Eckstein 2001). A *USA Today* report estimates that there are "over 400 diploma mills and 300 counterfeit diploma Web sites" in operation around the world (Armour 2003). Some are even operating from within the American prison system (Foley 2010). The purchasing of fraudulent certificates does not seem to be a problem perpetrated by only a few; with charges as little as $50 per diploma, diploma mill operators can earn upward of $50 million per year (Armour 2003).

Why mention the fraud perpetrated by organizations *outside* the academy when we are interested in examining misconduct *within* the academy? I begin the chapter with this illustration for three reasons. First, when businesses pose as educational institutions for fraudulent purposes, their actions do damage the ethical reputation of all colleges and universities, but especially those accredited higher education institutions that offer coursework online, such as the Open

University (Britain) and the University of Phoenix (United States). Second, people with these fake diplomas are able to enter into the academy as our students, faculty, or staff, and thus can affect college and university ethicality should their fraudulent behaviors continue. Third, the increasing pressure of the academic selection process has contributed to the building of the diploma mill industry as people look for ways to bypass requirements such as standardized testing and the admissions process.

The remainder of this chapter is focused on fraud and corruption that occurs within standardized testing and admissions and how this can thwart the realization of the ethical academy. As one of this book's contributors, Stephen Heyneman (2009: 8), pointed out in a previous publication, it is critical to investigate and counter corruption in the academic selection process because:

> The process of academic selection is the linchpin of any education system and overall national cohesion. It represents the essence of the public good. If the system is corrupt, or widely believed to be corrupt, little else in the education system can be successful. Inattention to corruption in selection will place other aspects of a nation's economic and social ambitions at risk.

In this chapter, I rectify the problem of inattention to academic selection corruption by examining it from the systems framework presented earlier. To do this, I first look at the possibilities for corruption in the college readiness process, that is, the business of standardized testing. Then I examine the misconduct believed to be occurring during the college admissions process itself.[2] After presenting the possibilities for corruption, I analyze them according to the systems framework. And finally, I offer some brief policy and practice suggestions for reducing cheating and fraud in these areas and enhancing the ethical academy.

Falsifying College Readiness

College readiness is ascertained primarily by grade point averages (GPAs) and standardized test scores. A tremendous amount of research has been conducted on the cheating and corruption that occurs during the accumulation of GPAs (for a comprehensive overview see Davis, Drinan, & Bertram Gallant 2009). Students, for example, admit to engaging in the following behaviors at least once in a year period: obtaining answers for a test before taking the test (33 percent); using a false excuse to get out of or delay taking a test (16 percent); copying off another's test or allowing someone to copy (10 percent); and using an unauthorized aid during a test (8 percent) (McCabe 2005). Braxton focuses on such classroom cheating and other classroom incivilities in the next chapter. So in this section I focus on the cheating and corruption that occurs on "high stakes" standardized tests such as high school graduation exams, college entrance exams, the Scholastic Achievement Test (SAT), Advanced Placement (AP) Exams, the Graduate Record Examination (GRE), the Graduate Management

Admissions Test (GMAT), the Medical College Admissions Test (MCAT), and the Law School Admissions Test (LSAT).

Standardized tests are often referred to as "high stakes" because their scores can guarantee (or block) access to the legitimate higher education credentials perceived to be necessary for ensuring lifetime economic success and well-being (Clarke & Shore 2001; Hallak & Poisson 2007; Noah & Eckstein 2001; Zemsky 2003). Of course, GPAs also impact access to legitimate higher education credentials. However, because standardized tests are generally seen as "a uniform way to compare students from different . . . backgrounds" (Clarke & Shore 2001: 4) and provide quality assurance that a student is ready for the next level of education (Nichols & Berliner 2007), they are often weighted more heavily in the admissions process. Students may also perceive standardized tests as "high stakes" because prepping for them and taking them is costly, especially if students require extended preparation or take the tests more than once in order to achieve their desired scores.

However, these tests are not only "high stakes" for the students who take them. In some nations and states, standardized test scores serve as public accountability measures—they are used to judge teacher performance, award monetary bonuses, and guarantee continued funding to the school (Cannell 1989; Jacob & Levitt 2003; Nichols & Berliner 2005). For example, in the United States, the Elementary and Secondary Education Act (ESEA) "requires states to test students in third through eighth grade each year and to judge the performance of schools based on student achievement scores" (Jacob & Levitt 2003: 187). The use of standardized test scores in this way, as well as the increasing reliance on standardized test scores as *the only* measures of student learning and progress, naturally creates cheating temptations for all who stand to profit and lose by test scores—students, parents, teachers, and district superintendents. So what forms of cheating do occur on such college readiness tests?

Allow me to start with an anecdote relayed to me by a group of undergraduates attending a competitive research university at which the average incoming student is "better than perfect,"[3] that is, has a grade point average of 4.1 or higher. While speaking with this group of students about cheating, one offered the following story (as I remember it) from her high school experience:

> At my high school, we were given a half hour of "cheating time" on our AP exams. The teacher would distribute the exams and remain in the room "proctoring" for the majority of the time. Then, with a half hour left in the exam, the teacher would leave the room with a comment something like "you're on your own for the last half hour of the exam." Everyone knew that this meant that we were supposed to compare answers, talk, and thus improve our scores.

Even with my experience in the field and my knowledge of the literature, I was shocked by this confession. So I asked the group two questions. First, hoping that the student's experience was an anomaly or perhaps fabricated, I asked the class, "Did anyone else have this experience in high school?" Unfortunately, at least five other students (in a class of twelve) raised their hands and, in drilling further, I discovered that they were all from different schools and districts. Second, I asked the class, "Do you know why a teacher would do this?" and the class responded "Yes because then our scores are raised and he [the teacher] looks better."

Does this anecdote present a rare occurrence of student and teacher cheating on standardized tests? In an empirical test of teacher cheating, Jacob and Levitt (2002: 871) found "thousands of instances of classroom cheating, representing 4–5 percent of the classrooms each year." However, they were examining only the most serious forms of teacher cheating, that is, teachers changing student answers on tests after the tests are complete. Researchers suspect that the range of cheating on standardized tests (from teaching to the test, to leaving the room unproctored, giving extra time to complete the test, giving hints to students during the exam, helping students correct answers during the exam, providing questions and/or answers to students ahead of the test, arranging for proxies to take the test, changing students' answers after the test, and/or manipulating final grades) actually occurs at a much higher percentage than it is possible to observe and quantify (Hallak & Poisson 2007; Jacob & Levitt 2002, 2003; Nichols & Berliner 2005; Noah & Eckstein 2001).

Teaching to the test is probably the most common misconduct perpetrated by teachers on standardized tests and such behavior is a concern if the method allows students to score well without developing the skills and knowledge intended to be represented by the score (Bond 2008). Similar to teaching to the test there is studying to the test, a form of testing corruption that is perpetrated by students but facilitated by teachers and administrators. For example, SAT (required by many American universities as an indicator of college "readiness") or Test of English as a Foreign Language (TOEFL) (a measure of English proficiency for second language learners) scores can be boosted by months of test-taking practice and memorization of vocabulary and math without necessarily improving the students' knowledge or skills (Hammond 2009).

If misconduct on standardized testing is as minor as teaching or studying to the test then we might worry about the validity of the tests but perhaps not about the ethicality of the entire educational system. Unfortunately, we know that standardized testing fraud is widespread and perpetrated at all levels. Students and parents seem willing to pay to shortcut or avoid the testing process altogether, especially if it guarantees higher education admissions (Hallak & Poisson 2007; Noah & Eckstein 2001). For example, in South Africa, tests are sold by employees ahead of time; in China, exam questions are sold or bribes are paid to rig exams; and in the United States, China, and Japan, exam proxies are hired to take the standardized exam for the registered student. Russia, a country that has been concerned about bribery in the admissions process, implemented a Uniform State Exam in an effort to reduce corruption only to discover that corruption continued as "regional test administrators were falsifying high scores for students" (Nemtsova 2009: 5).

Unfortunately, we also know that cheating and corruption do not stop once students have been admitted into the undergraduate portion of the educational pipeline. First, we already know that students cheat regularly on exams and tests while they are undergraduates, and we know that many faculty allow (either indirectly or directly) cheating to occur by not reducing cheating opportunities or even closely monitoring their exam rooms (Davis, et al. 2009). We also know that administrators and the education system itself are complicit in creating environments in which cheating is allowed to proliferate and become normative (Bertram Gallant 2008; Davis, et al. 2009; Whitley & Keith-Spiegel 2002). However, what is occurring further up the educational pipeline, that is, on professional and graduate school admissions exams (e.g., GRE, MCAT, LSAT)?

The stories at graduate and professional level are not substantially different from those we find at the high school or undergraduate level. Perhaps one of the most infamous cases is the cross-country scam that was discovered in the United States in the 1990s. In this scam, an entrepreneur hired people to take GRE, GMAT, and TOEFL tests in New York. The exam answers obtained from these test-takers were encoded into special pencils that were then distributed to customers waiting to take the tests in Los Angeles three hours later (Fiore 1996; Havers 1996). According to the reports, test-takers paid $6000 for this assistance. In addition to highlighting the power of the supply–demand rule and the big business of standardized testing, this tale also illustrates the significant role that technology has played in the shaping and spreading of corruption. Clearly, this particular cross-country scam would have been impossible without technology.

Other testing corruption scams have been accomplished with the use of technology. Transmitters have been attached to computers in a testing center in order to transmit the GRE questions to a "researcher" who would find the answers and then radio them back to the test-taker in the testing center (Carnevale 2002). In another well-publicized scandal of cheating on the GRE, the internet in China, Taiwan, and South Korea was used to transmit answers to the tests as memorized by previous test-takers. The scam was discovered after "some American college deans [expressed concern to the Educational Testing Service, the makers of the exam] that the high verbal scores of some Asian students did not match their English fluency" (Steinberg 2002). A similar scam for the GMAT exam, the one used for admissions into graduate business programs, was uncovered years later. In this scam, questions and answers were posted to scoretop.com and, once discovered, the scores of the found cheaters were abolished and the graduate schools to which they had applied were notified (Sampson 2008). The use of the internet for the trading of test questions and answers has also become popular within the business of professional licensure testing, particularly in the health fields (Smydo 2003).

Clearly the temptations and opportunities for standardized test corruption are as plentiful and leveraged at the graduate/professional level as they are at the high school and undergraduate level.

Manipulating the Admissions Process

Securing a "good" score on a "high stakes" standardized test is only one part of the academic selection process vulnerable to misconduct and corruption. Another part is the admissions process itself, ranging from application preparation to the application process and the decision-making process (who gets accepted and who does not) within the college and university.

College admission, especially to the "select" institutions, is thus considered by many families to be as "high stakes" as the graduation or entrance examinations themselves. And the high stakes are not felt by families alone. High school counselors, especially at private schools, feel under pressure to "produce" university acceptance offers, and college admissions officers feel pressure to recruit and enroll the most "selective" freshmen class (Fallows 2005).

As a result, the college and university admissions process has itself become a big business within the big business of education (Fallows 2005). Within the academy, the number of administrators and professionals hired to manage the admissions process has grown to include admissions counselors, application readers and enrollment managers. And because "students are taught to think about the 'package' of accomplishments they will present to admission committees," the business of admissions actually begins with the preparation of this "accomplishment package" (Fallows 2005: 40). Thus, the number of people who have become "independent admissions advisers" has more than doubled between 2006 and 2009 (Fallows 2005). The fees charged by these consultants reach as high as $40,000 (for a complete admissions consultant package) and they recruit "customers" (the students) as early as the eighth grade (Steinberg 2009). However, students are not the only ones hiring consultants and "talent managers"; colleges and universities themselves are hiring enrollment management consultants who can help them with "strategic market positioning" (Fallows 2005: 41).

The services provided by these admissions consultants (many of whom were previously affiliated with a university or college) have expanded from simply helping applicants determine which schools they should apply to. Those with sufficient funds can hire admissions consultants to write the admissions essay, fill out the application (sometimes with fraudulent data), create or doctor transcripts, manufacture letters of recommendation, and even bribe college and university officials to guarantee admission (Hammond 2009). Part of the problem here may be that the profession and business of admissions consulting is young, and ethics guidelines and regulations are lacking or, at best, loose.[4]

Of course, the admissions consultant is not solely to blame for the fraud perpetrated in the admissions process; after all, there would be no business for consultants if there were not consumers—students and parents willing to submit fraudulent materials. The problem seems so pervasive that internal screening mechanisms for foreign applicants are being implemented in universities to detect faked credentials, letters of recommendation, records, and diplomas (Mangan 2002a). In addition, there are now businesses devoted to validating admissions documents for colleges and universities and

> once they find a fraudulent transcript, the outside evaluators notify the universities the student is applying to, the university he or she claimed to have graduated from, and other evaluation agencies. In some cases, they will also call the Federal Bureau of Investigation, which tracks fraud rings, and the U.S. Immigration and Naturalization Service.
>
> (Mangan 2002b: 20)

Although burdensome and troubling, the estimates are that fraudulent admissions materials represent only about 1 percent of applications (Mangan 2002b), a low figure that may be at an "acceptable level of corruption" *if* the estimated level is accurate and *if* the level is maintained.

Misconduct in the admissions process is also, unfortunately, committed by college and university employees. The admissions scandal in Illinois in 2009 may be the most well known of recent U.S. history, in which the university had a policy to admit students without the proper credentials if they were on a "clout" list, that is, students with connections that would garner the University of Illinois political favors (see chapter 8 for a detailed exploration of this ethical scandal from the perspective of misconduct in governance). Unfortunately, this University of Illinois case is not unique. Shanghai Jiao Tong University in China has also been accused of admitting students without the required test scores because of their political connections (*The Chronicle of Higher Education* 2002). Other incidents of admissions fraud known to occur in many states and countries include university officials taking bribes to admit wealthy students, individuals writing admissions essays or taking entrance exams for applicants, and faculty and staff forging university degrees and records (Eckstein 2003; Mangan 2002a; Xueqin 2001).

Three functional areas related to admissions—academic records, financial aid, and the student visa process—provide additional illustrations of misconduct. For example, in academic records, a massive grade-changing scam was discovered at Diablo Community College (California) in which four student employees were charged with changing the grades of over 400 students in exchange for cash, as much as $600 per grade (DeBolt 2008; Krupnick 2007). This is troublesome because the students used those false grades to gain admissions into several University of California campuses. (Diablo came under fire for allowing student employees access to grades, which many considered a breach of organizational ethics.) In Illinois again, multiple instances of financial aid fraud (falsely reporting income) perpetrated by financial aid officers, parents, and students have been discovered (e.g., see Gose & Young 2001). And in Australia, a number of students fraudulently secured student visas with the help of "college operators or middlemen, such as unscrupulous migration agents or educational agents" who would falsify the paperwork for as much as $20,000 (Das 2009). It seems, then, that there are points at every juncture of the admissions process that are vulnerable to both the temptation and opportunities to cheat.

A Systems Analysis

The illustrations provided in this chapter clearly demonstrate that the student is but one actor in the perpetration of the fraud that occurs throughout the academic selection process. Parents, teachers, administrators, and staff also act in ways that corrupt the academic selection process, and all actors are shaped by the environments that surround them and the forces that originate from those environments. In this section I dissect the problem of corruption in standardized testing and admissions by examining it through the systems framework.

The Individual Level

It is so tempting to blame the individual student, parent, teacher, or administrator who cheats. After all, "they" should know better. Teachers should know better than to walk out of an AP exam to allow the students a half-hour "free-for-all." Administrators should know better than to change the test scores or offer university admissions based on personal or political connections. And students should know better than to pay to have their university admissions packages falsified by a "consultant." However, research over time (starting with Hartshorne & May 1928) has demonstrated that individuals will cheat when provided with the opportunity to do so, especially if there are known end benefits to be gained. Students, for example, may know that they are not supposed to cheat on AP exams, but if the teacher, the authority figure, allows the cheating to occur, what seventeen year old would argue with that? Even if parents and teachers have said "do not cheat," the emphasis on standardized tests or college admissions as keys "to future career success" (Montlake 2006: 18) will encourage many students to cheat when teachers and schools present opportunities for doing so.

Hallak and Poisson (2007) suggest that there are several factors that shape parent, teacher, and administrator misconduct in the academic selection process: low income; lack of understanding of legitimate versus illegitimate actions; allegiances and sympathies to groups of people who may be systematically disadvantaged in testing and admissions preparation; and apathy toward the academic selection process or the organization itself. As an example of the "lack of understanding of legitimate versus illegitimate actions," Hammond (2009: 7) argues that Chinese parents, desperate to have their kids admitted into American universities, believe admissions "consultants" when they tell them that fabricating information and falsifying transcripts is "simply the procedure for applying to U.S. institutions."

There may also be "noble" reasons why teachers and administrators cheat. For example, in the AP exam anecdote presented earlier in this chapter, perhaps the teacher walked out of the room to allow the students to "cheat" because her students cannot afford the private tutoring and AP practice exam sessions that garner unfair advantage to students in richer districts and so she felt her actions were justified as a way to create fairness (or a "level playing field"). However, if the teacher's role is, in part, to ensure the fairness and accuracy of tests, as well as model ethical and moral conduct to her students, than even her passive facilitation of such a cheating opportunity should be, at the very least, considered professional misconduct. Regardless, it seems evident that individual reasons for engaging in corruptive acts can often be related to the larger system of which they are a part.

The Organization Level

Organizations (schools, colleges, or universities) shape individual decisions to engage in unethical behavior. To continue with the AP exam anecdote, what sorts of structures and procedures had the principal put in place to reduce temptations and opportunities for such teacher and student cheating? For example, the principal could have easily put the math teacher in charge of proctoring the English AP exam and vice versa, or hired proctors without a vested interest in the students' scores (if the resources were available). Rather, it seems that the principal in the anecdote above may have turned a blind eye to testing conditions, using a lack of resources as just one excuse.

Individual schools that ignore cheating on routine class tests and assignments may create a situation in which cheating on standardized tests is necessary to maintain the appearance of "successful" students and thus "successful" schools. Schools without the counter-cultural message that unethical means are never justified by the ends may signal to teachers and students that high test scores do matter more than honest test scores (Hallak & Poisson 2007; Haydon 2004). The important point is that an unhealthy ethical environment isolates students, teachers, and administrators and requires them to resolve ethical dilemmas on their own. Alternatively, they may not even perceive problems as having an ethical dimension.

Organizations can also put pressure on members to improve results or performance without simultaneously providing adequate guidance on the appropriate, legitimate, or ethical ways of doing so. Schools and universities, for example, often have very detailed codes of conduct to guide student behavior, but fewer have detailed, accessible, and useable codes of conduct for teachers and administrators (Bertram Gallant, Beesemyer, & Kezar 2009). And when there is an "absence of an overall policy on fraud, with inconsistent or conflicting definitions of academic fraud, no clear understanding by stakeholders of what is legitimate and what is not, lack of supervision, no effective mechanism for detecting and punishing fraud, etc.," there is more likely to be "corrupt behavior" (Hallak & Poisson 2007: 243).

However, even with clear codes of conduct or standards for ethical behavior, there can be an underlying organizational culture that supports misconduct. For example, the admission fraud being perpetrated by students, parents, and admissions consultants in China is enabled by educational organizations that allow and support an entrepreneurial and unregulated culture of transcript creation because they neglect to offer that service themselves and condemn the behavior among their students and parents (Hammond 2009). Organizational culture as a systems force can be seen again in chapter 8 with the analysis of the Illinois admissions scandal; even though the admissions conduct was not aligned with university ethics codes, it was facilitated by the organizational culture and by institutional leadership. In Part III of this volume, Kezar and Sam (chapter 10) will further elaborate on the role that institutional leadership plays in creating healthy ethical cultures on campus.

The Education System Level

Of course, the context of the larger education system is also a factor in shaping the "high stakes" environment that leads to misconduct in testing and admissions. For example, the higher education academy in the United States provides sufficient spaces for all who would like to obtain an undergraduate degree, but there is "tremendous competition among students to gain a spot at a prestigious college" (Avery, Fairbanks, & Zeckhauser 2004: 6). The delineation of some colleges as "prestigious" or "elite" is fueled by university rankings (such as those conducted by the *US News & World Report*), GPA and test scores, university marketing and reputations, and research that demonstrates that graduates from "prestigious" colleges are more likely to obtain prestigious careers and earn higher salaries (Avery, et al. 2004). Thus, for many parents and students, "entry to an elite institution is seen as the [only] route to success" (Avery, et al. 2004: 6), creating a willingness to do whatever it takes to obtain high standardized test scores and create impressive admission packages.

In other countries, such as India, gaining college admissions is actually "high stakes" because there are insufficient spaces for the number of students seeking them (Hallak & Poisson 2007). And when college admission means the difference between a life of poverty and a life of relative comfort, few would pause to wonder why parents and students would engage in cheating and corruption during the academic selection process (Overland 2002).

As mentioned earlier, a lack of regulation and control systems within standardized testing and college admissions organizations can be a shaper of misconduct. However, it is also true that a lack of regulation within the larger academy is partly to blame. Standard regulations and integrity mechanisms at the level of the education system could be implemented in an effort to reduce corruption in the academic selection process. Without such standards and mechanisms, colleges and universities scramble with how best to assess the validity of thousands of application packages each year. The University of California now randomly checks 1 percent of all applications (domestic and international) to verify claims made, but few other systems conduct even such a minor quality check (Krieger 2010). According to Hammond (2009), the American education system needs to play a greater role in communicating with Chinese (and other international) applicants (in order to reduce the sway and power of independent admissions consultants). The academy should also take a look at the validity of standardized tests for measuring what they purport to measure because corruption on those tests can lead to further corruption in the academy as unprepared students face college-level work for which they do not have the skills or abilities (Nichols & Berliner 2007).

The Society Level

Of course, the academy is influenced by the larger society of which it is a part, and there are numerous societal factors that may be shaping misconduct and corruption in the academic selection process. According to Hallak and Poisson (2007: 242–4), these factors include increased competition in the global labor market; the globalization of education so that "students from developing countries are desperate to obtain degrees [fake or real] from universities in developed countries"; poorly funded schools, colleges, and universities that are under pressure to do more with less; "monopolistic power" in the control of education systems in many countries formerly or currently "centrally planned"; and the increasing sophistication of technology that facilitates easy cheating.

For example, we saw earlier in the chapter that cheating on graduate school admissions tests has been facilitated by the existence of the internet and other technologies that enable people to provide future test-takers with questions and answers. We also saw at the very beginning of this chapter that diploma mills are proliferating, not only because of the demand for them but also because technology has made it possible for there to be a sufficient supply for that demand. Principals and teachers cheat on standardized tests because they are poorly funded by the government and even that limited funding is tied to test scores.

If the larger society is corrupt, for example in politics or corporations, or the system is perceived as "unfair," then education corruption is more likely (Altbach 2004; Hallak & Poisson 2007). For example, in countries where college admissions and employment are not meritocratic but based on "social capital," there is greater education corruption (Altbach 2004). In countries where teachers and university administrators are paid menial sums, there can be greater incidences of corruption (Hallak & Poisson 2007). Overall, it seems that "the persistent growth in demand for higher education services coupled with the multiplicity of agencies involved in the market as well as the lack of regularization will sustain the pressure for more distorted practices" (Hallak & Poisson 2007: 244).

Recommendations for Policy and Practice

Although the actual rate of fraud in standardized testing and admissions is estimated to be quite low (under 5 percent by most accounts), the concern is that, left unchecked and unaddressed, it could become more common and pervasive. There is motive, opportunity, supply, and demand. The question is, how do we keep the level where it is or where we deem it to be an acceptable level of corruption, that is, where corruption is more rare than normal? Of course, the main suggestion in this volume is to work toward creating the ethical academy (the steps toward which are detailed in Part III of this volume), but there are immediate changes that could be made throughout the system to enhance detection of fraud, reduce temptations and opportunities, increase the costs associated with fraud, and create standards and regulations for the standardized testing and admissions processes. Specific suggestions from the literature and the field (e.g., Bertram Gallant, et al. 2009; Foster 2008; Hallak & Poisson 2007; Krieger 2010; Montlake 2006; Rampell 2008) include:

- check identities of test-takers;
- randomly check application packages and revoke admissions for fraudulent applicants;
- create whistleblower programs;
- train proctors of standardized tests;
- disallow stakeholders to administer tests;
- set and ensure clarity of rules and standards to reduce confusion and misunderstanding;
- address structural supporters or instigators of fraud by improving pay of some stakeholders and expanding educational opportunities.

Concluding Thoughts

Corruption in the academic selection process may be the most damaging to the integrity of the educational institution because it creates false measures of college readiness and undermines the meritocracy upon which higher education (at least in democratic societies) is supposed to be based. If measures of college readiness are falsified, then we may be admitting students into our undergraduate, graduate, and professional programs who have to resort to continued cheating in order to obtain the degree for which they do not have the requisite knowledge or skills. If there is corruption in the testing and admissions process, then students are being admitted for reasons other than a fair assessment of their knowledge and skills.

Of course, these arguments presuppose that standardized tests, if taken without any corruption, are fair and accurate measures of college readiness, and that the other measures upon which academic selection is based (i.e., applications) are valid and reliable indicators of college readiness or fit. And there certainly is not a consensus that this is indeed the case (Sacks 1997). However, corruption on these measures certainly does not enhance their fairness and a lack of fairness should not be used as justification for additional corruption. As the education system continues to become more global and competitive, the ethicality of the standardized testing and admissions process must be carefully and honestly examined before the level of corruption rises to an unacceptable level.

Notes

1. For more information about diploma mills and some of the governmental attempts to educate would-be diploma seekers, see http://www.ed.gov/students/prep/college/diplomamills/diploma-mills.html (accessed 2 June 2010).
2. The majority of the examples presented in this chapter are derived from an exploration of practice rather than an examination of research because there have been few empirical studies conducted in this area.
3. I put "better than perfect" in quotes to acknowledge that it is a "catchphrase" that I have been using in my work on campus for years before Susan Blum first published the phrase in her 2009 book *My Word! Plagiarism and College Culture* (Ithaca and London, Cornell University Press).
4. The Independent Educational Consultants Association (IECA) is one organization that seems to be attempting to professionalize the occupation. However, not all admissions consultants are members and the IECA offers only loose ethical guidelines rather than regulations or legal rules of compliance. See http://www.educationalconsulting.org/pogp.html (accessed 2 June 2010) for more information.

References

Altbach, P.G. (2004) 'The question of corruption in academe', *International Higher Education*, 34: 7–8.

Armour, S. (2003) 'Diploma mills insert degree of fraud into job market', *USA Today*, 28 September. Available at http://www.usatoday.com/money/workplace/2003-09-28-fakedegrees_x.htm (accessed 12 November 2009).

Avery, C., Fairbanks, A., and Zeckhauser, R. (2004) *The Early Admissions Game: Joining the Elite*, 2nd edn, Cambridge, MA: Harvard University Press.

Bartlett, T. and Smallwood, S. (2004) 'What's a diploma mill?', *The Chronicle of Higher Education*, 25 June. Available at http://chronicle.com/article/Whats-a-Diploma-Mill-/30156/ (accessed 16 January 2010).

Bertram Gallant, T. (2008) *Academic Integrity in the Twenty-First Century: A Teaching and Learning Imperative*, San Francisco: Jossey-Bass.

Bertram Gallant, T., Beesemyer, L.A., and Kezar, A. (2009) 'Creating a culture of ethics in higher education', in J.C. Knapp and D.J. Siegel (eds) *The Business of Higher Education Volume 1: Leadership and Culture*, Santa Barbara, CA: Praeger Publishers.

Bond, L. (2008) 'Teaching to the test: Coaching or corruption', *The New Educator*, 4: 216–23.

Cannell, J.J. (1989) *How Public Educators Cheat on Standardized Achievement Tests: The "Lake Wobegon" Report*. Albuquerque, NM: Friends for Education.

Carnevale, D. (2002) 'High-tech cheating alleged in the GRE', *The Chronicle of Higher Education*, 6 December. Available at http://chronicle.com/article/High-Tech-Cheating-Alleged-in/32003 (accessed 18 January 2010).

Clarke, M. and Shore, A. (2001) *The Roles of Testing and Diversity in College Admissions*, Boston: National Board on Educational Testing and Public Policy.

Das, S. (2009) 'Foreign students could be forced to leave', *The AGE*, 10 June. Available at http://

www.theage.com.au/national/foreign-students-could-be-forced-to-leave-20090609-c28h.html (accessed 18 January 2010).

Davis, S.F., Drinan, P.F., and Bertram Gallant, T. (2009) *Cheating in School: What We Know and What We Can Do*, Malden, MA: Wiley-Blackwell.

DeBolt, D. (2008) 'Jury finds student not guilty of changing his grades', *The Chronicle of Higher Education*, 15 September. Available at http://chronicle.com/blogPost/Jury-Finds-Student-Not-Guil/4238/ (accessed 15 September 2008).

Eckstein, M.A. (2003) *Combating Academic Fraud: Towards a Culture of Integrity*, Paris: International Institute for Educational Planning.

Fallows, J. (2005) 'College admissions: A substitute for quality?', in R.H. Hersh and J. Merrow (eds) *Declining by Degrees: Higher Education at Risk*, New York: Palgrave Macmillan.

Fiore, M. (1996). 'Calif. man arrested for standardized test cheating scam', *The Daily Pennsylvanian*, 30 October. Available at http://www.dailypennsylvanian.com/node/8656 (accessed 27 January 2010).

Foley, R.J. (2010) 'Con man serving time in Wisconsin helped run successful diploma mill', *Los Angeles Times*, 22 February. Available at http://www.latimes.com/news/nationworld/nation/wire/sns-ap-us-diploma-mill-inmate,0,359140.story (accessed 22 February 2010).

Foster, A.L. (2008) 'To reduce fraud, students taking GMAT will get palm scan', *The Chronicle of Higher Education*, 23 July. Available at http://chronicle.com/blogPost/To-Reduce-Fraud-Students/4115 (accessed 23 July 2008).

Gose, B. and Young, J.R. (2001) 'Parents and financial aid advisors charged with federal student-aid fraud', *The Chronicle of Higher Education*, 30 March. Available at http://chronicle.com/article/ParentsFinancial-Advis/15629/ (accessed 23 July 2008).

Hallak, J. and Poisson, M. (2007) *Corrupt Schools, Corrupt Universities: What Can Be Done?*, Paris: International Institute for Educational Planning.

Hammond, B.G. (2009) 'The Chinese are coming, and they need help with the admissions process', *The Chronicle of Higher Education*, 15 November. Available at http://www.chronicle.com/article/The-Chinese-Are-Coming-and/41926 (accessed 15 November 2009).

Hartshorne, H. and May, M.A. (1928) *Studies in Deceit*, New York: Macmillan.

Havers, F. (1996) 'Testing fraud exposed: GRE, GMAT, and TOEFL cheating scam uncovered', *The Yale Herald*, 31 October. Available at http://www.yaleherald.com/archive/xxii/10.31.96/news/gre.html (accessed 18 January 2010).

Haydon, G. (2004) 'Values education: Sustaining the ethical environment', *Journal of Moral Education*, 33: 115–29.

Heyneman, S.P. (2009) 'Introduction: The importance of external examinations in education', in B. Vlaardingerbroek and N. Taylor (eds), *Secondary School External Examination Systems: Reliability, Robustness and Resilience*, Amherst, NY: Cambria Press.

Jacob, B.A. and Levitt, S.D. (2002) 'Rotten apples: An investigation of the prevalence and predictors of teacher cheating', *The Quarterly Journal of Economics*, August, 843–76.

—— (2003). Catching Cheating Teachers: The Results of an Unusual Experiment in Implementing Theory, Brookings-Wharton Papers on Urban Affairs, Washington, D.C.: Brookings Institution Press.

Krieger, L.M. (2010) 'UC sleuths seek proof for glorious claims on admission applications', *The Mercury News*, 1 February. Available at http://www.mercurynews.com/education/ci_14303391?nclick_check=1 (accessed 1 February 2010).

Krupnick, M. (2007) 'Dozens implicated in DVC grade scandal', *Contra Coast Times*, 3 May. Available at http://www.contracostatimes.com/ci_5807980?nclick_check=1 (accessed 3 May 2007).

McCabe, D.L. (2005) 'Cheating among college and university students: A North American Perspective', *International Journal of Educational Integrity*, 1: 1–11.

Mangan, K.S. (2002a) 'UCLA heightens scrutiny of foreign applicants', *The Chronicle of Higher Education*, 27 September. Available at http://chronicle.com/article/UCLA-Heightens-Scrutiny-of-/17144/ (accessed 28 January 2010).

—— (2002b) 'The fine art of fighting fakery', *The Chronicle of Higher Education*, 1 November. Available at http://chronicle.com/article/The-Fine-Art-of-Fighting-Fa/9936/ (accessed 28 January 2010).

Montlake, S. (2006) 'High-tech cheating in Asia's high-stakes exams', *The Christian Science Monitor*, 9 June. Available at http://www.csmonitor.com/2006/0609/p01s02-woap.html (accessed 28 January 2010).

Nemtsova, A. (2009) 'Russia cracks down on fraud in college entrance exam', *The Chronicle of Higher Education*, 1 October. Available at http://chronicle.com/article/Russia-Cracks-Down-on-Fraud/48662/ (accessed 1 October 2009).

Nichols, S.L. and Berliner, D.C. (2005) *The Inevitable Corruption of Indicators and Educators Through High-Stakes Testing*, East Lansing, MI: The Great Lakes Center for Education Research and Practice.

—— (2007) *Collateral Damage: How High Stakes Testing Corrupts America's Schools*, Cambridge, MA: Harvard Education Press.

Noah, H.J. and Eckstein, M.A. (2001) *Fraud and Education: The Worm in the Apple*, Lanham, MD: Rowan & Littlefield.

Overland, M.A. (2002) 'In India, suitcases of money buy admission into college', *The Chronicle of Higher Education*, 2 August. Available at http://chronicle.com/article/In-India-Suitcases-of-Money/11102 (accessed 18 January 2010).

Rampell, C. (2008) 'Association tightens identity verification for medical-school entrance exam', *The Chronicle of Higher Education*, 14 May. Available at http://chronicle.com/article/Association-Tightens-Identi/789/ (accessed 28 January 2010).

Sacks, P. (1997) 'Standardized testing: Meritocracy's crooked yardstick', *Change Magazine*, 29: 24–31.

Sampson, Z.S. (2008) 'MBA exam tester tosses scores over web cheating', *USA Today*, 18 September. Available at http://www.usatoday.com/money/economy/2008-09-10-1829020716_x.htm (accessed 18 January 2010).

Smydo, J. (2003) 'Health fields fight cheating on tests', *Pittsburgh Post-Gazette*, 3 August. Available at http://www.optometry.org/articles/cheating.htm (accessed 10 November 2009).

Steinberg, J. (2002) 'Officials link foreign websites to cheating on graduate admissions exams', *The New York Times*, August 8. Available at http://www.nytimes.com/2002/08/08/us/officials-link-foreign-web-sites-to-cheating-on-graduate-admission-exams.html (accessed 18 January 2010).

—— (2009) 'Before college, costly advice just on getting in', *The New York Times*, 18 July. Available at http://www.nytimes.com/2009/07/19/education/19counselor.html (accessed 18 January 2010).

The Chronicle of Higher Education (2002) 'In China, bribery and fakery lower the value of degrees', 2 August. Available at http://chronicle.com/article/In-China-BriberyFakery/32633 (accessed 18 January 2010).

Whitley, B.E. Jr. and Keith-Spiegel, P. (2002) *Academic Dishonesty: An Educator's Guide*, Mahwah, NJ: Lawrence Erlbaum Associates.

Xueqin, J. (2001) 'Corrupt admissions alleged in China', *The Chronicle of Higher Education*, 14 September. Available at http://chronicle.com/article/Corrupt-Admissions-Alleged-in/18114 (accessed 18 January 2010).

Zemsky, R. (2003) 'Have we lost the 'public' in higher education?', *The Chronicle of Higher Education*, 30 May. Available at http://chronicle.com/article/Have-We-Lost-the-Public-in/21529 (accessed 2 February 2010).

5

Improprieties in Teaching And Learning

JOHN M. BRAXTON

The college classroom is one of the nested communities in which some members of the academy, particularly students and faculty, find themselves (Hirschy & Wilson 2002; Palmer 1998; Tinto 2000). Social forces that facilitate or hinder student learning emerge because of the relationships that faculty and students develop over time (Hirschy & Wilson 2002). Classroom improprieties of both students and faculty function to demarcate such role relationships. Such classroom improprieties include student classroom incivilities and faculty violations of undergraduate college teaching norms. As described later in this chapter, if left unaddressed, both forms of classroom improprieties can corrupt the teaching and learning process and negatively affect the academic and intellectual development of students.

In this chapter, I describe the various forms of student classroom incivilities and faculty teaching norm violations and their effects on students. Bertram Gallant and Kalichman, in chapter 3, assert that academic misconduct occurs within a system comprising four levels, ranging from the individual to the level of society. Student classroom incivilities and faculty teaching norm violations also transpire within such a system. In this chapter, I delineate some possible forces within this system that lead to or constrain such classroom improprieties. In the last section of this chapter, I offer some suggestions for addressing classroom improprieties.

Student Classroom Incivilities

Feldmann (2001: 137) defines student classroom incivilities as actions by students that obstruct "a harmonious and cooperative learning environment in the classroom." In this section, I review three patterns of such classroom incivilities: disrespectful disruptions, insolent inattention, and student cheating.

Disrespectful disruptions are defined as active behavior in which a student or students impede the learning of their peers (Caboni, Hirschy, & Best 2004; Hirschy & Braxton 2004). In contrast, insolent inattention is behavior that reflects a student's lack of desire to learn or participate in classroom activities (Caboni, et al. 2004; Hirschy & Braxton 2004). Student cheating is defined as acts that undermine the integrity of the learning and assessment process (Davis, Drinan, & Bertram Gallant 2009). Each of these types of incivility gives students an opportunity to make judgments about the values, beliefs, and goals of their student peers (Braxton & Jones 2008).

Disrespectful disruptions include such behaviors as repeated interruptions of others during class, talking loudly to another student while someone else in the class is speaking, and receiving cell phone or pages during class. Such behaviors as coming to class high on drugs, sleeping during class, and coming to class intoxicated characterize insolent inattention (Hirschy & Braxton 2004). Facebooking, surfing the web, and twittering during class constitute additional forms of insolent inattention not included in the research by Hirschy and Braxton (2004). Our research suggests that disrespectful disruptions and insolent inattention are relatively uncommon occurrences in private religiously affiliated institutions (Hirschy & Braxton 2004). Student cheating, of course, includes copying homework, using cheat sheets on examinations, plagiarism, and copying during an exam, among many others, and the research on student cheating suggests that it is a common occurrence on college and university campuses with the majority of students committing one act of cheating per year (Davis, et al. 2009).

These patterns of student classroom incivilities negatively affect students who witness such actions in their courses. More specifically, both disrespectful disruptions and insolent inattention wield a negative influence on student perceptions of their academic and intellectual development above and beyond the influence of such possible confounding factors as class standing, gender, faculty and student interactions, and grade point average (Hirschy & Braxton 2004). Academic and intellectual development includes such indicators as perceptions of intellectual growth and a greater interest in ideas. Students who witness other students on their courses cheating on examinations or other graded assignments may also experience negative effects on their level of academic and intellectual development. For example, Jordon (2001) found that engagement in cheating is significantly correlated with a student's belief in the amount of cheating that is being perpetrated by other students as well as a student's witnessing of cheating by others. In an international study of student cheating, Grimes and Rezek (2005) also found that witnessing cheating is highly correlated with engagement in cheating, as did Rettinger and Kramer (2009) in their study.

Additional negative effects of these patterns of student classroom incivilities include student perceptions of communal potential (Braxton & Jones 2008) and students' commitment to their college or university. Communal potential refers to the degree to which students believe that a subgroup of students exists within the social communities of their college or university with whom they share similar values, beliefs, and goals (Braxton, Hirschy, & McClendon 2004). Communal potential plays an indirect role in the college student departure process in residential colleges and universities (Braxton, et al. 2004). Moreover, disrespectful disruptions and insolent inattention also tend to dampen students' commitment to their college or university (Hirschy & Braxton 2004). Student commitment to their college or university stands as a very reliable source of influence on college student persistence as indicated by eleven out of thirteen tests that are supportive of this relationship in residential colleges and universities (Braxton & Lee 2005). By extension, student observations of cheating by classmates on examinations and other graded assignments may also negatively affect both their perceptions of communal potential and their level of commitment to their college or university.

Both junior and senior faculty members experience student incivilities in their classes (Boice 1996). However, women and faculty of color may experience incivilities more often than their white, male faculty counterparts because of student cultural perceptions of women and faculty of color forged by stereotypes and social power (Alexander-Snow 2004).

A Systems Perspective on Student Classroom Incivilities

As previously stated, student classroom incivilities transpire within a system comprising four levels: the individual, the organization, the education system, and society at large. Although some research has been conducted on the forces at all levels that shape student classroom incivilities and cheating, the bulk of the formulations presented in the following subsections remain open empirical questions.

The Individual Level

Some observers of student classroom incivilities view such incidents as manifestations of such student mental health issues as schizophrenia, manic depression, and personality disorders (Amada 1992). Students committing incivilities in the form of disrespectful disruptions may have such mental health issues. Students suffering from alcoholism or drug abuse may exhibit insolent inattention in the form of coming to class high on drugs or intoxicated.

Other students committing incivilities may lack motivation for a particular class or for attending college in general. Some students may also have little or no commitment to the college or university they are attending. Their lack of interest and commitment finds expression in disrespectful disruptions, insolent inattention, or cheating.

Students who experience difficulty in coping with the transition from high school to college may also commit incivilities. Bray and Del Favero (2004) assert that going to college confronts students with the need to cope with both self-discovery and fitting into student peer groups. Students who fail to cope may diminish their interest in their course work resulting in apathy and disinterest. Apathy and disinterest can lead to classroom incivilities.

Students with poor or failing grades in a course may also engage in incivilities and cheating. Bray and Del Favero (2004) point to anomie theory as a possible explanation. To elaborate, individuals experience strain when they perceive that they are unable to achieve goals or ends set by society through the means designated to the achievement of such goals (Merton 1968). Both students and faculty in colleges and universities place a high value on the achievement of good grades, an achievement students expect to attain. However, some students either fail a course or receive poor grades. Such students experience a strain marked by alienation and formlessness. These feelings result in student classroom incivilities and, as some research has shown, cheating (Haines, Diekhoff, LaBeff, & Clark 1986; McCabe & Trevino 1997).

The Organization Level
Bertram Gallant (2008) places student peer culture and the community of the classroom in the organizational level of the system within which academic misconduct and by extension classroom improprieties occur. Norms represent a central characteristic of peer groups (Kuh & Whitt 1988). Norms prescribe or proscribe behaviors (Hechtor & Opp 2001; Merton 1968, 1973). Consequently, student peer cultures exert an influence on student classroom incivilities through norms espoused regarding such behaviors. The findings of one study conducted in private research university with its undergraduate admissions selectivity classified as most competitive suggest that undergraduate college students proscribe with considerable disdain those incivilities associated with insolent inattention (Caboni, et al. 2004). In comparison, such undergraduate students regard disrespectful disruptions as mildly inappropriate behaviors (Caboni, et al. 2004). This configuration of findings suggests that the student peer culture works to deter students from insolent inattention, but wields a more modest influence on the deterrence of disrespectful disruptions. In other institutional settings, the norms of student peers may not deter classroom incivilities, but may encourage incivilities. Likewise, peer norms also influence student academic dishonesty as students who perceive that their peers frequently cheat tend to cheat themselves (McCabe & Trevino 1997).

Moreover, students who perceive that their classroom peers will likely punish or sanction them for disrespectful disruptions, insolent inattention, or cheating will be less likely to engage in such incivilities. Such sanctions or punishments might include ostracism of the offending individual by class members and directly confronting the offending student during or after class. This is perhaps why honor code schools report less cheating—peer pressures to not cheat seem to work better than pressures from others such as parents or teachers (McCabe & Trevino 1997). These formulations resonate with deterrence theory, a sociological theory identified by Bray and Del Favero (2004) to help account for classroom incivilities and by other researchers (e.g., Haines, et al. 1986; McCabe, Butterfield, & Trevino 2006; McCabe & Trevino 1993; Michaels & Miethe 1989) to help account for student cheating. Deterrence theory asserts that behavior is deterred by the probability of being punished or sanctioned for such behavior (Akers 1997; Gibbs 1975).

For some students, their incivilities may represent attempts to gain respect and social support from some student peers. Two sociological theories delineated by Bray and Del Favero (2004) suggest such a possibility: rational choice theory and social bond theory. Rational choice theory depicts a decision-making process by which individuals decide to engage in inappropriate behaviors (Akers 1997; Piliavin, Gartner, Thornton, & Matsueda 1986). This decision-making process takes into account both punishments/sanctions and rewards for engaging in such behaviors. Social bond theory (Hirschi 1969) posits the role of attachment among individuals. Thus, students who perceive that they will gain respect from peers as rewards for classroom incivilities will engage in such improprieties. Moreover, students who have strong attachments to their student peers and believe that they will receive social support from them for incivilities will also commit acts of classroom incivilities.

Like student peer groups, faculty members as principal agents of the community of the classroom also play a part in the occurrence of student classroom incivilities. Faculty members encourage or discourage student incivilities in their classes in three ways. First, faculty who commit incivilities toward students in their classes incur incivilities by students in their classes. Boice (1996) observed such a connection in his study of classroom incivilities. Social exchange theory provides a vehicle for understanding this connection, a sociological theory delineated by Bray and Del Favero (2004) as a possible explanation for classroom improprieties. According to the formulations of this theory, course learning can be viewed as an exchange between the faculty member and students in the class. Mutuality and reciprocity define the relationship embedded in such an exchange (Blau 1994; Homans 1974). Bray and Del Favero (2004) assert that student classroom incivilities result from a reduction in mutuality in the form of an exchange. In this case, mutuality takes the form of both faculty and students alike behaving in an appropriate way in the classroom.

Second, faculty members who fail to punish or sanction students who engage in cheating, disrespectful disruptions, or insolent inattention also encourage incivilities of this sort in their classes. This contention finds theoretical support in deterrence theory. As indicated above, this theory posits that the probability of being punished or sanctioned for acts of incivility deter such behavior (Akers 1997; Gibbs 1975). Faculty sanctions or punishments could range from talking privately to the offending individual after class to demanding before the whole class that offending students stop their uncivil behavior.

Third, faculty members who treat the students in their classes with respect as individuals, as well as equitably, provide an incentive for students to also behave in a civil manner. Rational choice theory, as previously discussed, provides an explanation for this contention. In this case, the reward received by students comes in the form of faculty respect for them as individuals and fair treatment.

The Education System Level
Incidents of student classroom incivilities tend to vary by institutional type and size. Boice (1996: 479) concludes from his observational study of classroom incivilities that incivilities are "more common than uncommon." He found a similar pattern in other large public universities. In contrast, he noted fewer incidents of student classroom incivilities in institutions with a teaching orientation and smaller classes. Moreover, using a four-point scale to indicate how frequently students observed such incivilities during the academic year (0 = never, 1 = rarely, 2 = occasionally and 3 = frequently), Amy Hirschy and I (2004: 105) report a mean of 1.14 with a standard deviation of 0.54 for disrespectful disruptions and a mean of 0.53 with a standard deviation of 0.69 for insolent inattention. These means suggest that classroom incivilities in religiously affiliated colleges and universities are not common occurrences. The pattern that Amy Hirschy and I observed in these teaching-oriented colleges and universities parallels Boice's (1996) observation that incivilities were not common in the teaching-oriented university in which he also observed classes.

Apart from between institutional differences, the institutional dimension plays a role in classroom incivilities in other ways. For example, state and local laws and institutional policies pertaining to alcohol and drug abuse may deter students from engaging in insolent inattention if they fear being reported to institutional officers by students and faculty. Fear of consequences or the greater the costs also deter students from cheating (Passow, Mayhew, Finelli, Harding, & Carpenter 2006). Deterrence theory (Akers 1997; Bray & Del Favero 2004; Gibbs 1975) provides a theoretical lens for this assertion, as the fear of punishment deters students from engaging in classroom incivilities.

Although the majority of colleges and universities have policies to explain and prohibit student cheating (Bertram Gallant & Drinan 2006), few colleges and universities promulgate policies that specifically delineate classroom incivilities such as disrespectful disruptions as student decorum that results in some form of punishment. To elaborate, Bayer (2004: 83) offers the observation that codes and student handbooks "generally do not even mention proper classroom decorum and courtesies such as turning off cell phones, allowing others to speak, not entering the class late, or leaving early in a disruptive manner." He drew this observation from his inspection of student codes of conduct or student handbooks posted on the websites of a convenience sample of fifteen public and private non-sectarian collegiate institutions. The absence of institution policy places direct responsibility on individual faculty members to handle incidents of disrespectful disruptions.

The Society Level

Some observers assert that incivility constitutes a problem of society (Twale & De Luca 2008). One author (Truss 2005) notes that such feelings as disrespect, selfishness, and rudeness prevail in the United States. Other authors (e.g., Callahan 2004; Eckstein 2003) note that cheating and corruption are also quite common in society as people attempt to gain what they want by whatever means necessary. These incivilities find expression in the classroom behaviors of college students as they are also members of the larger society.

The ascending role of technology in society also encourages student classroom improprieties. Because of the prevalence of student laptop computers in college and university classrooms, students can appear to be taking class notes while surfing the internet, facebooking, and twittering. Technology, of course, also makes it easier for students to cheat and may be changing the ways in which students view knowledge and information and thus their definitions of cheating behaviors (Bertram Gallant 2008).

Faculty Teaching Norm Violations

Norms are prescribed or proscribed patterns of behavior (Merton 1973). Put differently, norms provide guides for the choices that faculty make in their teaching. Because of the high degree of autonomy that faculty hold in their teaching, norms safeguard the welfare of students as clients of teaching role performance (Braxton & Bayer 1999).

In our book *Faculty Misconduct in Collegiate Teaching* (1999), Alan Bayer and I describe an empirically derived normative structure for undergraduate college teaching. We derived this normative structure from the perceptions of 949 faculty members holding academic appointments in five types of colleges and universities (research I universities, comprehensive universities and colleges I, liberal arts colleges I and II, and two-year colleges) and four academic disciplines (biology, chemistry, mathematics, and psychology). This normative structure consists of seven inviolable and nine admonitory norms. Inviolable norms are behaviors that academics believe warrant severe sanctions and admonitory norms are those behaviors that academics believe should be avoided but not severely sanctioned (Braxton & Bayer 1999).

One of the seven inviolable norms that we identified pertains to departmental and colleague relationships; the other six pertain to students as clients of undergraduate teaching role performance. I will briefly describe these six norms that, when violated, constitute classroom improprieties by individual faculty members: (1) condescending negativism: treatment of both students and colleagues in a condescending and demeaning way; (2) inattentive planning: a lack of planning of a course (e.g., required texts not routinely ordered in time for the first class session, and a course outline or syllabus not prepared for the course); (3) moral turpitude: prohibits depraved, unprincipled acts by faculty; (4) particularistic grading: the uneven or preferential treatment of students in the awarding of grades; (5) personal disregard: a disrespect for the needs and sensitivities of students (profanity in class, poor hygiene by faculty); and (6) uncommunicated course detail: the failure of faculty members to inform students of important particulars about a course during the first day of class (changing class location to another building, changing class meeting time without consulting students, students not informed of the instructor's policy on missed or make-up examinations.

Each of these six inviolable norms resonates with espoused ethical principles for undergraduate college teaching. Three of the inviolable norms—condescending negativism, moral turpitude, and personal disregard—embody the ethical principles of "respect for persons" (Smith 1996) and "respect for students as individuals" (Reynolds 1996; Svinicki 1994). Moral turpitude and particularistic grading symbolize the ethical principle of equal consideration of students in advisement, teaching, and grading (Cahn 1986; Markie 1994). The professional obligation to plan courses posited by Cahn (1986) exemplifies the inviolable norms of inattentive planning and uncommunicated course detail.

Of the nine admonitory norms we empirically identified, three safeguard the welfare of students as clients of teaching role performance: inadequate communication, inadequate course design, and insufficient syllabus. The admonitory norm of inadequate communication censures faculty who fail to provide students with details about their course. The proscribed norm of inadequate course design rebukes faculty who prepare poorly for a course. The failure to provide students with a syllabus for a course characterizes the proscribed behaviors of the norm of insufficient syllabus. Like the six inviolable norms, these three admonitory norms also symbolize ethical principles of teaching. Cahn's (1986) ethical principle that stipulates an obligation for academics to plan their courses finds expression in these three admonitory norms.

These normative orientations of members of the professoriate place moral boundaries around the professional choices individual college and university faculty members make in their teaching (Braxton & Bayer 1999). Nevertheless, some violations of these norms occur. Norm violations by faculty members take place because norms and behaviors are never perfectly correlated (Merton 1976; Zuckerman 1988). Merton (1976: 40) refers to this disjuncture as a "painful contrast" between normative expectations for behavior and actual behavior. Given the likelihood of norm violations by individual faculty members, what detrimental effects on students result? Teaching norm violations by faculty members harm the academic and intellectual development of undergraduate college students above and beyond the influence of such possible confounding factors as class standing, gender, faculty and student interactions, and grade point average (Braxton, Bayer, & Noseworthy 2004).

The harm to the welfare of students that results from norm violations of individual faculty members indicates a need for the social control of such deviance. Deterrence, detection, and sanctioning of norm violations constitute the mechanisms of social control (Zuckerman 1977, 1988). Students bear the primary responsibility for the detection of teaching norm violations given that faculty members seldom observe the classroom behavior of their colleagues except in the case of appraisals for tenure and promotion decisions (Braxton & Bayer 1999).

However, colleagues and I (Braxton, Bayer, & Noseworthy 2002) assert that undergraduate students may be unlikely agents of social control for violations of the six inviolable norms. To elaborate, faculty members in teaching-oriented colleges and universities regard the behaviors that make up the six inviolable normative patterns with a high level of disdain. However, undergraduate college students in teaching-oriented, religiously affiliated colleges and universities view only moral turpitude with similar levels of disdain (Braxton, et al. 2002). For the other five normative patterns, students perceive them as admonitory. Accordingly, undergraduate students may likely detect and report violations of the norm of moral turpitude but not violations of the other five inviolable norms.

Despite such pessimism regarding students as agents of social control, students tend to take action when they label classroom incidents of misconduct as most grievous (Braxton & Mann 2004). Braxton and Mann (2004) found that more than half of such students took direct action by either talking to the offending faculty member or reporting the incident to a dean or a department chairperson.

A Systems Perspective on Faculty Teaching Norm Violations

The six inviolable norms and three admonitory norms protective of students as clients of teaching role performance place moral borders around the professional choices that individual college and university faculty members make in their teaching (Braxton & Bayer 1999). Despite the existence of a normative structure, violations of norms occur as norms and behaviors are never perfectly related (Merton 1976; Zuckerman 1988). Consequently, a systems perspective on faculty teaching norm violations takes into account factors that induce normative conformity as well as factors that provoke norm violations. Some research has focused on topics pertinent to faculty teaching norm violations; however, most of the formulations presented in the following subsections remain open empirical questions.

The Individual Level

Twale and De Luca (2008) contend that incivility and bullying by college and university faculty are on the rise. Bullying, an act of incivility, includes such behaviors as showing intolerance or disrespect to others (Appleton, Briggs, &

Rhatigan 1978). Thus, faculty bullies might routinely violate such inviolable teaching norms as condescending negativism, moral turpitude, and personal disregard.

Violations of these three norms, the other three inviolable norms, and the three admonitory norms may also result from the lack of internalization of these norms by offending faculty members (Braxton & Bayer 1999). Conversely, faculty conformity to these normative orientations occurs because of the internalization of these norms by individual faculty members (Braxton & Bayer 1999).

Personal controls also induce conformity to these undergraduate college teaching normative patterns (Braxton & Bayer 1999; Reiss 1951). In contrast, norm violations occur when personal controls lack the strength to induce conformity (Reiss 1951). Such faculty characteristics as gender, administrative experience, and tenure constitute personal controls (Braxton & Bayer 1999). The level of disdain that faculty voice indexes the strength of such personal controls. As a consequence of the pattern of findings regarding the level of disdain voiced for various normative configurations, Alan Bayer and I (1999) posit that women faculty members are less likely than their male counterparts to violate such teaching norms as condescending negativism, personal disregard, and inadequate communication. We also assert that faculty who have served or are currently serving as an academic dean or a department chairperson are less likely than faculty without administrative experience to violate the proscriptive norm of personal disregard. Moreover, Alan Bayer and I also contend that tenured faculty members are less likely to violate the admonitory proscriptive norm of inadequate course design.

Another perspective on faculty violations of teaching norms holds that the theories of teaching embraced by some faculty include the belief that students grow and develop through being treated in a condescending and demeaning way. Such condescending treatment creates in students a level of anxiety that motivates them to perform better in answering questions in class and in producing written graded work.

The Organization Level
Like student classroom incivilities, the organizational dimension pertains to the community of the classroom. In the case of faculty, however, the organizational dimension includes the role that department colleagues play in inducing normative conformity or normative violations.

In the community of the classroom, students play an important role. To elaborate, undergraduate college teaching stands as a highly public activity primarily seen by students (Braxton & Bayer 1999). Put differently, faculty teaching behaviors are highly visible to undergraduate students. Thus, violations of the six inviolable and three admonitory norms by faculty in their courses are highly observable by students in them. Such observability also varies as a function of class size, as the observability of behaviors increases with decreases in class size (Braxton & Bayer 1999; Horowitz 1990).

Because of the observable nature of possible teaching norm violations, student course ratings provide a way for students to anonymously report such violations. Alan Bayer and I (1999) contend that many course rating items delineate behaviors indicative of violations of the six inviolable norms and the three admonitory norms. As a consequence, students can punish faculty through poor ratings on such items. As with student classroom incivilities, the possibility of poor student course ratings or reports of grievous faculty misconduct to a dean or department chairperson functions as a deterrent to teaching norm violations because of the high probability of being punished for such behaviors (Braxton & Mann 2004; Bray & Del Favero 2004). Conversely, students can reward faculty for treating them with respect as individuals, treating them equitably, and adequately preparing for a course through positive ratings on course evaluation instruments that contain pertinent items. The possibility of rewards for conformity with norms fits with the postulations of rational choice theory, a theory previously delineated in this chapter.

As previously discussed in this chapter, faculty teaching norm violations also occur as a consequence of student classroom incivilities, a relationship noted by Boice (1996). Bray and Del Favero (2004) assert that student classroom incivilities and by extension faculty teaching norm violations occur because of a reduction in mutuality in social exchanges in the classroom. The expected mutuality finds expression in both faculty and students behaving in appropriate ways in the classroom.

Departmental colleagues also play a role in deterring faculty teaching norm violations. If individual faculty members perceive that their departmental colleagues are conforming to the norms of undergraduate college teaching, then such individuals are also more likely to avoid the behaviors prohibited by these six inviolable and three admonitory normative patterns. To elaborate, research shows that conformity to the norms of science by individual faculty members varies as a function of their perception of the degree to which their disciplinary colleagues conform to these norms (Braxton 1990). Alan Bayer and I extend this pattern of findings to the case of college teaching norms (Braxton & Bayer 1999).

However, the rules of professional etiquette that govern relationships among colleagues may provide little or no deterrence to faculty violations of teaching norms. The rules of professional etiquette stipulate that public or private criticisms of colleagues should be avoided (Freidson 1975). The rules of professional etiquette also ordain that harm should not come to the reputations and careers of colleagues (Freidson 1975). Because of the rules of professional etiquette, departmental colleagues will take little or no action for teaching norm violations by individual faculty colleagues.

The Education System Level

Melinda Mann and I (2004: 39) concluded from our study of faculty teaching norm violations observed by undergraduate college students in religiously affiliated colleges and universities that such violations "are neither rampant nor non-existent." Although the rate is unknown, violations in research-oriented universities may be more frequent. This assertion stems from a hypothesis generated by Alan Bayer and me (1999). We posit that incidents of teaching norm violations occur more frequently in research-oriented universities than in teaching-oriented colleges and universities (comprehensive universities and colleges I, liberal arts colleges I and II, and two-year colleges). We derived this hypothesis from our pattern of findings which indicated that faculty in research-oriented universities tend to voice less contempt for such teaching norms as condescending negativism, inattentive planning, personal disregard, and excommunicated course detail than their academic counterparts in teaching-oriented institutions. Furthermore, faculties in such universities allocate admonitory status to two of these normative orientations: condescending negativism and inattentive planning.

The extent to which colleges and universities have clearly articulated sanctions or punishments for teaching norm violations remains unknown. Consequently, the influence of the possibility of sanctions as a deterrent to violating teaching norms also remains an open empirical question. Nevertheless, the postulations of deterrence theory (Akers 1997; Gibbs 1975) suggest that the likelihood of teaching improprieties decreases with increases in the probability of being punished or sanctioned for such inappropriate actions. Put more clearly, sanctions function as a deterrent when known and communicated (Ben-Yehuda 1985; Tittle 1980).

The Society Level

Truss (2005) asserts that such feelings as disrespect, selfishness, and rudeness prevail in the United States. College and university faculty members are members of the larger society marked by such incivility. However, the work of faculty generally sets the professoriate apart from lay society. Nevertheless, the climate of incivility in larger society can find some expression in the teaching behaviors of faculty members who teach undergraduate college students. Disrespect and rudeness characterize faculty who engage in behaviors that violate the proscriptive norms of condescending negativism and personal disregard.

Recommendations for Policy and Practice

The recommendations for institutional policy put forth may serve as deterrents to some student and faculty classroom improprieties. Unfortunately, both student classroom incivilities and faculty violations of teaching norms will continue to occur. This stark reality stems from Merton's (1976: 40) "painful contrast between normative expectations for behavior and actual behavior." Consequently, actions taken for classroom improprieties become critically important. The policies delineated serve both as deterrents and as bases for action.

I offer four recommendations, each of which I regard as equally important. These recommendations are as follows:

1. Colleges and universities should promulgate statements of students' rights and responsibilities. Bayer (2004) and Bayer and Braxton (2004) have previously advanced this recommendation. However, its repetition reinforces its importance. Student rights should encompass expectations that students should have for how faculty conduct their courses. The six inviolable norms and the three admonitory norms described in this chapter could serve as a basis for the delineation of the rights and expectations that students should have for faculty classroom decorum. Such delineation provides a basis for undergraduate students to identify improper conduct by faculty members. Put differently, statements of rights and expectations for classroom decorum enable students to more clearly detect improprieties by faculty in the classroom. Moreover, such statements would encourage students to report incidents of faculty classroom improprieties to a department chair or some other administrator (Bayer 2004). Actions for faculty teaching norm violations depend on the report of such incidents by students who have personally witnessed them.

    Likewise, responsibilities of students for their own classroom decorum require delineation. To be sure, student classroom incivilities should provide the basis for such a demarcation. For example, student responsibilities for classroom decorum should include not talking on cell phones during class, not interrupting other students during class, and not talking loudly to other students while the professor or other students are speaking. Other responsibilities include not coming to class intoxicated or high on drugs. Such formal statements function to circumscribe such behaviors as inappropriate and detrimental to the learning environment of the college classroom. Statements of student responsibilities should also encourage students to present their displeasure with incivilities by their classmates to their course instructors.

    Student handbooks and community codes might include statements of student rights and responsibilities. Statements of student rights and responsibilities might also take the form of a stand-alone document. Such statements function as mechanisms of deterrence and detection with detection being a catalyst for action.

2. Colleges and universities should promulgate codes of conduct for undergraduate college teaching. This recommendation has been previously suggested (Bayer & Braxton 2004; Braxton & Bayer 1999, 2004); nevertheless,

it bears repeating because of its importance in deterring and detecting faculty teaching norm violations.

Braxton and Bayer (2004) put forth ten tenets that a code of conduct should include. Colleges and universities considering the development of a code of conduct for undergraduate college teaching should review these tenets for possible inclusion. Regardless of the frequency of incidents of teaching norm violations that occur in an institution, the promulgation of a code of conduct constitutes a proactive step in both the deterrence and detection of such classroom improprieties by faculty members (Braxton & Bayer 2004). Codes of conduct provide a robust basis for the delineation of possible sanctions. A section of the *Faculty Handbook* of Tusculum College delineates a set of faculty responsibilities to students (Tusculum College 2009). These responsibilities resonate with some of the tenets of the code of conduct promulgated by Braxton and Bayer (2004).

3. Colleges and universities should establish teaching integrity committees. Like the previous two recommendations, this recommendation has also been previously advanced (Bayer & Braxton 2004; Braxton & Bayer 1999, 2004); however, its critical importance justifies its repetition.

    The purpose of such a committee would be to attend to reported incidents of teaching norm violations by individual faculty members. Such reports could come from a variety of constituents ranging from students who witness incidents to the president of a college or university. The complications inherent in incidents of teaching norm violations require a collective response. Complications include the harm done to students by the violation, the frequency of the types of violation during the term of the course, and whether the violation fits a pattern of repeated violations.

    Suggestions on the deliberations of teaching integrity committees are offered by Braxton and Bayer (1999, 2004). The existence of such a committee would function as a deterrent to teaching norm violations. More importantly, such a committee provides a context for both reporting and sanctioning teaching improprieties.

4. Colleges and universities should delineate sanctions for student classroom incivilities and teaching norm violations by faculty. Such sanctions should be clearly communicated in student handbooks and in faculty manuals. Sanctions function as punishments for both forms of classroom behavior and, as such, also deter such improprieties (Akers 1997; Ben-Yehuda 1985; Gibbs 1975; Tittle 1980). The preservation of harmonious classroom learning environments constitutes the underlying rationale for the delineation of sanctions.

    The termination of the offending faculty member stands as the most severe sanction for a teaching norm violation (Braxton & Bayer 2004). Less severe sanctions include a warning or a reprimand, public censure, no salary increase, reduction in salary, peer monitoring of the class of the offending individual, and required counseling (Franke 2002).

Sanctions for classroom incivilities committed by students also require delineation. Institutional statements of student rights and responsibilities should include such sanctions. Repeated incidents of coming to class intoxicated or high on drugs (insolent inattention) could result in suspension or dismissal from a college or university. Many colleges and universities already have student conduct boards that deal with student cheating and other misconduct that occurs outside of the classroom, and these same boards could also handle reports of classroom incivilities made by students and faculty. Extreme and repeated incidents of various forms of disrespectful disruptions could also result in suspension or dismissal.

Colleges and universities might also permit faculty to dismiss students from their courses who frequently and egregiously commit acts of incivilities. Such a possible action by faculty would require the development of institutional policy. Permitting such action would provide faculty with a strong sanction or punishment for such students.

An Over-arching Recommendation for Institutional Practice

In addition to these recommendations for institutional policy, I present an over-arching recommendation for institutional practice: colleges and universities should strive to develop strong teaching cultures. Teaching cultures place a high value on college teaching (Paulsen & Feldman 1995). Espoused values, norms, and rules for behavior define an organization's culture (Schein 1992). Tierney (1988: 3) asserts that culture manifests itself in "what is done, how it is done, and who is involved in doing it." Thus, culture operates as social glue that controls the behavior of its members.

Strong teaching cultures resonate with one condition for educationally effective colleges and universities empirically identified by Kuh, Kinzie, Schuh, Whitt, and Associates (2005: 65): "an unshakeable focus on student learning." Such a focus finds expression in the priority that student personal development and learning receive. Such a priority is authentic and actively pursued. Accordingly, faculty and staff are committed to student learning and enact pedagogical practices that facilitate student learning. This condition leads to higher than expected levels of student engagement and graduation rates (Kuh, et al. 2005) A teaching culture that exhibits "an unshakable focus on student learning" creates a positive classroom learning environment that students work hard to maintain through the development of strong student norms that proscribe classroom incivilities. As a consequence, incidents of classroom incivilities by students become rare events.

Clear expectations for faculty to make professional choices in their teaching role performance that enhance student course learning emanate from a strong teaching culture (Braxton 2008). One such professional choice by individual faculty members involves avoidance of those teaching behaviors that violate the six inviolable and three admonitory norms that pertain to students. In strong teaching cultures, violations of teaching norms by faculty rarely occur.

Statements of student rights and responsibilities, codes of conduct for undergraduate college teaching, teaching integrity committees, and the delineation of sanctions for student classroom incivilities and teaching norm violations by faculty members flow from strong institutional teaching cultures. Likewise strong teaching cultures provide a robust context for the implementation and serious enactment of such institutional policies.

Paulsen and Feldman (1995) delineate eight characteristics derived from the research literature that portray a teaching culture. Of these eight characteristics, two stand as particularly important. The first characteristic involves the commitment and support of high-level administrators of the institution to teaching. Such administrators communicate the high value that the institution places on teaching and give high visibility to efforts focused on the improvement of teaching. Second, frequent interaction and the existence of a community among faculty about issues pertaining to teaching characterize a strong teaching culture. Paulsen and Feldman (1995) assert that intrinsic rewards from teaching emerge from frequent opportunities for faculty to talk with their peers about teaching. The presence of a community organized around college teaching constitutes another aspect of this particular defining characteristic. The sharing of ideas about teaching and intellectual stimulation around teaching transpire within such a community (Aitken & Sorcinelli 1994).

Colleges and universities striving to develop strong teaching cultures should work toward the embodiment of these two key characteristics. The other six defining characteristics described by Paulsen and Feldman (1995) also merit attention.

Concluding Thoughts

Given Merton's (1976) contention that norms and behavior are never perfectly correlated, it is unrealistic to expect the total eradication of incidents of student classroom incivilities and teaching norm violations by faculty members. However, the development of strong teaching cultures and the enactment of the recommendations for institutional policy outlined in this chapter go a long way toward substantial reductions in the frequency of such incidents to the point that such occurrences become a rarity. The opportunities for undergraduate college students to achieve success depend to some degree on it.

References

Aitken, N. and Sorcinelli, M. (1994) 'Academic leaders and faculty developers: Creating an institutional culture that values teaching', in E. C. Wadsworth (ed.) *To Improve the Academy: Resources for Faculty, Instructional, and Organizational Development*, Stillwater, OK: New Forum Press.

Akers, R. (1997) *Criminological Theories: Introduction and Evaluation*, 2nd edn, Los Angeles: Roxbury.

Alexander-Snow, M. (2004) 'Dynamics of gender, ethnicity, and race in understanding classroom incivility', in J. Braxton and A. Bayer (eds) *Addressing Faculty and Student Classroom Improprieties*, San Francisco: Jossey-Bass.

Amada, G. (1992) 'Coping with the disruptive college student: A practical model', *Journal of American College Health*, 40: 203–15.

Appleton, J., Briggs, D., and Rhatigan, J. (1978) *Pieces of Eight: The Rites, Roles, and Styles of the Dean, by Eight Who Have Been There*, Portland: NASPA Institute of Research and Development.

Bayer, A. (2004) 'Promulgating statements of student rights and responsibilities', in J. Braxton and A. Bayer (eds) *Addressing Faculty and Student Classroom Improprieties*, San Francisco: Jossey-Bass.

Bayer, A. and Braxton, J. (2004) 'Conclusions and recommendations: Avenues for addressing teaching and learning improprieties', in J. Braxton and A. Bayer (eds) *Addressing Faculty and Student Classroom Improprieties*, San Francisco: Jossey-Bass.

Ben-Yehuda, N. (1985) *Deviance and Moral Boundaries*, Chicago: University of Chicago Press.

Bertram Gallant, T. (2008) *Academic Integrity in the Twenty-first Century: A Teaching and Learning Imperative*, San Francisco: Jossey-Bass.

Bertram Gallant, T. and Drinan, P. (2006) 'Institutionalizing academic integrity: Administrator perceptions and institutional actions', *NASPA Journal*, 44: 61–81.

Blau, P. (1994) *Structural Contexts of Opportunities*, Chicago: University of Chicago Press.

Boice, B. (1996) 'Classroom incivilities', *Research in Higher Education*, 37: 453–86.

Braxton, J. (1990) 'Deviancy from the norms of science: A test of control theory', *Research in Higher Education*, 31: 461–76.

—— (2008) 'Toward a theory of faculty professional choices in teaching that foster college student success', in J. Smart (ed.) *Higher Education: A Handbook of Theory and Research*, Rotterdam, Netherlands: Springer.

Braxton, J. and Bayer, A.E. (1999) *Faculty Misconduct in Collegiate Teaching*, Baltimore, MD: Johns Hopkins University Press.

—— (2004) *Addressing Faculty and Student Classroom Improprieties*, San Francisco, Jossey-Bass.

Braxton, J. and Jones, W. (2008) 'The influence of student classroom incivilities on communal potential', *NASPA Journal*, 45: 425–51.

Braxton, J. and Lee, S. (2005) 'Toward reliable knowledge about college student departure', in A. Seidman (ed.) *College Student Retention: Formula for Student Success*, Westport, CT: ACE/Praeger.

Braxton, J. and Mann, M. (2004) 'Incidence and student response to faculty teaching norm violations', in J. Braxton and A. Bayer (eds) *Addressing Faculty and Student Classroom Improprieties*, San Francisco: Jossey-Bass.

Braxton, J.M., Bayer, A.E., and Noseworthy, J.A. (2002) 'Students as tenuous agents of social control of professorial misconduct', *Peabody Journal of Education*, 7: 101–24.

—— (2004) 'The influence of teaching norm violations on the welfare of students as clients of college teaching', in J. Braxton and A. Bayer (eds) *Addressing Faculty and Student Classroom Improprieties*, San Francisco: Jossey-Bass.

Braxton, J., Hirschy, A., and McClendon, S. (2004) *Understanding and Reducing College Student Departure*, San Francisco: Jossey Bass.

Bray, N. and Del Favero, M. (2004) 'Sociological explanations for faculty and student classroom incivilities', in J. Braxton and A. Bayer (eds) *Addressing Faculty and Student Classroom Improprieties*, San Francisco: Jossey-Bass.

Caboni, T., Hirschy, A., and Best, J. (2004) 'Student norms of classroom decorum', in J. Braxton and A. Bayer (eds) *Addressing Faculty and Student Classroom Improprieties*, San Francisco: Jossey-Bass.

Cahn, S. (1986) *Saints and Scamps: Ethics in Academia*, 1st edn, Totowa, NJ: Rowman & Littlefield.

Callahan, D. (2004) *The Cheating Culture: Why More Americans Are Doing Wrong to Get Ahead*, Orlando: Harcourt.

Davis, S.F., Drinan, P.F., and Bertram Gallant, T. (2009) *Cheating in School: What We Know and What We Can Do*, Malden, MA: Wiley-Blackwell.

Eckstein, M.A. (2003) *Combating Academic Fraud: Towards a Culture of Integrity*, Paris: International Institute for Educational Planning.

Feldmann, L. (2001) 'Classroom civility is another of our instructor responsibilities', *College Teaching*, 49: 137–40.

Franke, A. (2002) 'Faculty misconduct, discipline, and dismissal'. Paper presented at the Annual Meeting of the National Association of College and University Attorneys, New Orleans, LA.

Freidson, E. (1975) *A Study of Professional Social Control*, New York: Elsevier.

Gibbs, J. (1975) *Crime, Punishment, and Deterrence*, New York: Elsevier.
Grimes, P. and Rezek, J.P. (2005) 'The determinants of cheating by high school economics students: A comparative study of academic dishonesty in transitional economies', *International Review of Economics Education*, 4: 23–45.
Haines, V.J.., Diekhoff, G.M., LaBeff, E.E., and Clark, R.E. (1986) 'College cheating: Immaturity, lack of commitment, and the neutralizing attitude', *Research in Higher Education*, 25: 342–54.
Hechter, M. and Opp, K. (2001) *Social Norms*, New York: Russell Sage Foundation.
Hirschi, T. (1969) *Causes of Delinquency*, Berkeley, CA: University of California Press.
Hirschy, A. and Braxton, J. (2004) 'Effects of student classroom incivilities on students', in J. Braxton and A. Bayer (eds) *Addressing Faculty and Student Classroom Improprieties*, San Francisco: Jossey-Bass.
Hirschy, A. and Wilson, M. (2002) 'The sociology of the classroom and its influence on student learning', *Peabody Journal of Education*, 77: 85–100.
Homans, G. (1974) *Social Behavior: Its Elementary Forms*, Orlando, FL: Harcourt, Brace, Jovanovich.
Horowitz, A. (1990) *The Logic of Social Control*, New York: Plenum Press.
Jordon, A. (2001) 'College student cheating: The role of motivation, perceived norms, attitudes, and knowledge of institutional policy', *Ethics & Behavior*, 11: 233–48.
Kuh, G. and Whitt, E. (1988) *The Invisible Tapestry: Culture in American Colleges and Universities*, Washington, DC: Association for the Study of Higher Education.
Kuh, G., Kinzie, J., Schuh, J., and Whitt, E. (2005) *Student Success in College: Creating Conditions That Matter*, San Francisco: Jossey-Bass.
McCabe, D.L. and Trevino, L.K. (1993) 'Academic dishonesty: Honor codes and other contextual influences', *Journal of Higher Education*, 64: 522–38.
—— (1997) 'Individual and contextual influences on academic dishonesty: A multicampus investigation', *Research in Higher Education*, 38: 379–96.
McCabe, D.L., Butterfield, K., and Trevino, L.K. (2006) 'Academic dishonesty in graduate business programs: Prevalence, causes, and proposed action', *Academy of Management, Learning & Education*, 5: 294–305.
Markie, P. (1994) *A Professor's Duties: Ethical Issues in College Teaching*, Lanham, MD: Rowman & Littlefield.
Merton, R. (1968) *Social Theory and Social Structure*, New York: The Free Press.
—— (1973) *The Sociology of Science: Theoretical and Empirical Investigations*, Chicago, IL: University of Chicago Press.
—— (1976) 'The sociology of social problems', In R. Merton and R. Nisbet (eds) *Contemporary Social Problems*, New York: Harcourt Brace.
Michaels, J.W. and Miethe, T.D. (1989) 'Applying theories of deviance to academic cheating', *Social Science Quarterly*, 70: 870–85.
Palmer, P. (1998) *The Courage to Teach: Exploring the Inner Landscape of a Teacher's Life*, San Francisco: Jossey-Bass.
Passow, H.J., Mayhew, M.J., Finelli, C.J., Harding, T.S., and Carpenter, D.D. (2006) 'Factors influencing engineering students' decisions to cheat by type of assessment', *Research in Higher Education*, 47: 643–84.
Paulsen, M. and Feldman, K. (1995) *Taking Teaching Seriously: Meeting the Challenge of Instructional Improvement*, Washington, DC: George Washington University.
Piliavin, I., Gartner, R., Thornton, C., and Matsueda, R. (1986) 'Crime, deterrence, and rational choice', *American Sociological Review*, 51: 101–19.
Reiss, A. (1951) 'Delinquency as the failure of personal and social controls', *American Sociological Review*, 16: 196–207.
Rettinger, D.A. and Kramer, Y. (2009) 'Situational and personal causes of student cheating', *Research in Higher Education*, 50: 293–313.
Reynolds, C. (1996) 'Making responsible academic ethical decisions', in L. Fisch (ed.) *Ethical Dimensions of College and University Teaching: Understanding and Honoring the Special Relationship Between Teachers and Students*, San Francisco: Jossey-Bass.
Schein, E. (1992) *Organizational Culture and Leadership*, 2nd edn, San Francisco: Jossey-Bass.
Smith, R. (1996) 'Reflecting on the ethics and values of our practice', in L. Fisch (ed.) *Ethical Dimensions of College and University Teaching: Understanding and Honoring the Special Relationship Between Teachers and Students*, San Francisco: Jossey-Bass.
Svinicki, M. (1994) 'Ethics in college teaching', in W.J. McKeachie and B.K. Hofer (eds) *McKeachie's Teaching Tips: Strategies, Research, and Theory for College and University Teachers*, Boston: Houghton Mifflin.

Tierney, W. (1988) 'Organizational culture in higher education: Defining the essentials', *Journal of Higher Education*, 59: 2–21.

Tinto, V. (2000) 'Linking learning and leaving: Exploring the role of the college classroom in student departure', in J. Braxton (ed.) *Reworking the Student Departure Puzzle*, Nashville, TN: Vanderbilt University Press.

Tittle, C. (1980) *Sanctions and Social Deviance: The Question of Deterrence*, New York: Praeger Publishers.

Truss, L. (2005) *Talk to the Hand: The Utter Bloody Rudeness of Everyday Life*, New York: Gotham Books.

Tusculum College. (2009) *Faculty Handbook*, Greeneville, TN: Tusculum College.

Twale, D. and De Luca, B. (2008) *Faculty Incivility: The Rise of the Academic Bully Culture and What To Do About It*, San Francisco: Jossey-Bass.

Zuckerman, H. (1977) 'Deviant behavior and social control in science', in E. Sagarin (ed.) *Deviance and Social Change*, Beverly Hills, CA: Sage Publications.

—— (1988) 'The sociology of science', in N. Smelser (ed.) *Handbook of Sociology*, Thousand Oaks, CA: Sage Publications.

6

Research Misconduct and Misbehavior

MELISSA S. ANDERSON

Research is a fundamental activity of the university sector in higher education. Advancement of knowledge for its own sake and for the betterment of humankind is the creative core of universities' contribution to society. The authority of universities in presenting new knowledge and other innovations to the world is grounded in the integrity of the research system.

The research system, like the academy in general (see chapter 3), functions on the basis of trust. Researchers work at the frontiers of their academic disciplines, often beyond the expertise of all but a few others in the world. Indeed, their goal is to stretch beyond the limits of knowledge to discover new things. Part of the social contract between scientists and the public is that, in exchange for the public's trust, researchers will do their work properly. No regulatory system could be devised to anticipate every ethical conundrum that may arise in the pursuit of new knowledge. Researchers' behavior must earn and sustain the public's trust.

These assumptions are reinforced by the training and socialization that scientists[1] receive. Research that is "good" is both scientifically and ethically sound; good research cannot be scientifically solid but ethically wrong. Journals reinforce this principle by retracting articles that are scientifically valid but which were produced under ethically inappropriate conditions, such as conflict of interest or compromise of human–subjects requirements. The principle is so fundamental to science that researchers frequently express disbelief in scientific misbehavior (e.g., Koshland 1987). They assume that every researcher has personal integrity and a strong sense of right and wrong. Scientists employ careful review procedures to control entry into the profession and keep out miscreants.

The scientific community does not, however, leave all matters of ethical conduct up to individuals' righteousness. A system of mechanisms exerts considerable control over researchers' behavior. The scientific method itself provides guidance on steps that need to be taken for scientific findings to be deemed legitimate. The research community supports self-regulation through professional norms that represent a collective understanding of appropriate behavior in the community (Anderson, Ronning, De Vries, & Martinson 2010; Braxton 1986; Resnick 2007). Peer review and replication of experiments are more concrete aspects of self-regulation, fundamental to ensuring the integrity of science. In addition, in the United States, a highly articulated, formal regulatory system enforces proper behavior through mandated training, institutional assurance of compliance, reporting systems for ethical improprieties, whistleblowing, protections for whistleblowers, inquiries, investigations, and sanctions.

Still, problems persist.

In keeping with the focus of this book on contextual influences on academic improprieties, in this chapter I illustrate the connection between research misbehavior and the research environment, at various levels. I begin with a brief review of the forms that research misbehavior can take. I then examine four misconduct cases, each in light of its most salient contextual features.

Forms of Research Misbehavior

Improper behavior in scientific research takes two basic forms. In the United States, *misconduct* is formally defined by the *Federal Policy on Research Misconduct* as "fabrication, falsification, or plagiarism in proposing, performing, or reviewing research, or in reporting research results" (Office of Science and Technology Policy 2000). According to the policy, a finding of misconduct requires that "there be a significant departure from accepted practices of the relevant research community; the misconduct be committed intentionally, or knowingly, or recklessly; and the allegation be proven by a preponderance of evidence." Though the policy technically applies only to research funded by the federal agencies that have adopted the definition, most university and professional association policies explicitly identify fabrication, falsification, and plagiarism as forms of misconduct. Investigations that confirm misconduct lead to severe sanctions against the scientists involved, such as debarment from federal funding for a specified period of time. At the institutional level, a formal finding of misconduct may lead to dismissal. At either level, the scientists may be required to repay money used to support the fraudulent work.

The second form of problematic behavior is *questionable research practices* (Steneck 2004) or *misbehavior* (De Vries, Anderson, & Martinson 2006). These behaviors fall outside the formal definition of misconduct yet pose potential or actual threats to the integrity of science. They include, for example, violations of human subject regulations, inappropriate assignment of authorship (by inclusion or omission), disregard for proper research protocols, and inappropriate management of conflicts of interest. Carelessness and negligence fall into this category when they introduce error into the scientific record; the emphasis here is on preventable error, not on honest mistakes or human imperfection.

Using materials purchased under one grant to do work on another grant may be inappropriate or even illegal, but the practice is common. Certifying that all requirements of a regulation have been met without taking the time to verify every point is a familiar consequence of workload pressures. Another misbehavior, generally tolerated, is glossing over regulatory details when, for example, local and national regulations are mutually contradictory, or when compliance might, in certain cases, actually pose a greater threat to research subjects than non-compliance. These various questionable research practices are particularly troublesome, because they are rather common (Anderson, Horn, Risbey, Ronning, De Vries, & Martinson 2007; Martinson, Anderson, & De Vries 2005) and can have serious consequences.

Though most scientists have a clear sense of what does and what does not qualify as misbehavior in their own work contexts, the rules can become much less clear in interdisciplinary or international research contexts. Regulations and standards are not always aligned across diverse contexts. International research teams need to be attentive to and compliant with the most stringent regulations and policies that apply to any of their members.

In most cases, the exact origins of research misconduct and other question-able behaviors are difficult to uncover, amid the many interactions of factors at various contextual levels. As Bertram Gallant and Kalichman note in chapter 3, the origins of inappropriate behavior are variously associated with failings of individuals, organizations, the academy, or society. The roles of these contextual levels in permitting or enabling bad behavior are examined below through analysis of cases.

Cases of Research Misconduct

One could argue that every contextual level is implicated, in some way, in cases of research misconduct. That viewpoint, however, obscures the nature of each level's contribution to misbehavior. The cases presented here have been chosen to bring into sharper focus the environmental forces operating at each level of this volume's conceptual framework. In each of the four cases reviewed in this section, one particular level has an easily identified, powerful influence. The focus on one level per case is not meant to suggest, however, that the other levels are entirely without effect.

The Individual Level

Misbehavior is attributed to a number of different individual-level factors. There is evidence that decisions to misbehave are associated with personality traits, such as narcissism, at least in tests of hypothetical responses (Antes, et al. 2007; Mumford, et al. 2006). Evidence of this connection supports the belief that those who misbehave "must have something wrong with them," as a colleague put it to me. Some blame misbehavior on deficits in moral development. The argument here is that some people simply never learned how to behave properly and therefore do not fully recognize ethical or moral aspects of situations (Rest & Narváez 1994). From this perspective, people who misbehave are seen as deficient or delayed in their recognition of moral dilemmas, ability to reason about various alternatives and their consequences, and selection of a course of action that is grounded in a well-developed moral sense. Personal weakness is also seen as contributing to misbehavior. One may have a strong moral grounding but be unwilling or unable to match decisions and actions to high ethical standards. The lack of "backbone" may make some people particularly susceptible to temptation. Some scientists see miscreants as "taking the easy way out," to maintain the appearance of productive careers, instead of doing the hard work necessary for scientific advancement.

The following misconduct case illustrates the role of individual-level factors. It is a case of data fabrication that occurred at my own institution. It was relayed to me by the faculty member involved, who is no longer at my university. This faculty member was reviewing preliminary statistical results with her graduate research assistant. They had collected some, but not all, of the data for their project. Geographic representation was a critical aspect of the data collection, and the professor noted that one particular area was substantially under-represented. She commented, "We need more data from that area."

The next time they met, the graduate assistant brought in updated analyses, which showed satisfactory representation from all geographical areas. They had not yet, however, collected additional data. The student had simply changed the geographical indicators in the preliminary data set.

There is no way to know for certain why the graduate assistant falsified the data. It is possible that the student himself would not be able to explain why. The case nevertheless provides an opportunity to review some of the reasons why people misbehave even in the absence of strong contextual pressures. The student may have had a casual disregard for ethical practices. The change of data may have reflected his ignorance as to where one should draw the line between acceptable and unacceptable behavior. Perhaps he thought that the professor's comment was a directive that he was obliged to obey. Maybe he thought of data manipulation as a normal practice in the academy. Maybe he was amoral. Maybe he was lazy.

It is possible that contextual forces (such as competitive pressure) were playing a role in this situation, but they were not obviously relevant in this case. The dominant dynamic was the individual's decision to falsify data in response to a casual comment from his professor, without prior verification of the professor's intent. It is clear that he made no effort to cover up the misconduct. At the second meeting, the professor could clearly see what he had done. The student had not recognized anything at any contextual level—organization, education system, or society—that would prevent or deter his manipulation of the data.

In fact, of course, he was wrong. The professor was appalled by his actions and made him realize the gravity of his misconduct. What is more, the machinery to support exposure was in place: she could have notified the institutional compliance officer, who would have initiated an inquiry, which would have led to an investigation and sanctions. Supported by a federal grant, the student could have been subject to federal sanctions and media exposure. At all levels, procedures exist to ensure good behavior and deal with bad behavior.

The Organization Level

At the organizational level, behavior is influenced by incentives, rewards, and punishment. Institution-level employment sets the conditions for the work environment: salary, promotion, responsibilities, workspace, colleagues (including students), and so on. To receive both tangible and intangible benefits, researchers must perform well in ways that the institution rewards, and expediency can be a distinct advantage. Sometimes an institution's oversight is weak or its systems are so loosely monitored that they can be easily manipulated. Organizational inattention to scientists' behavior may be due to neglect of supervisory responsibility or to organizational overload and stress. If a scientist perceives a rather wide tolerance for questionable behavior, a low likelihood of being caught, and mild or non-existent sanctions for the few who are caught, it may seem worthwhile to take a risk, particularly if the associated payoff is substantial.

A recent case illustrates the role of the organization as a contextual factor in misconduct. Pattium Chiranjeevi is a professor of chemistry at Sri Venkateswara University in India. His publication record was regarded as excellent, until it was determined to be fraudulent. He was found guilty of plagiarism or falsification in over seventy journal articles in a four-year period (Schulz 2008). His strategy was to find obscure papers on the internet and submit them for publication under his own name, often adding others' names as well. In some cases the papers were wholly plagiarized, perhaps with a change in a critical word, such as the name of a chemical. He sometimes submitted the plagiarized works to several journals at the same time.

Chiranjeevi involved his students in his scheme. One university source said that the scientist "used to start his day by asking his students, 'Well, what have you downloaded today?'" (Jayaraman 2008: 7). He relied on a former student who was on a postdoctoral fellowship in Seoul, Korea, and another collaborator in Singapore who sent him materials that he could then submit under his own name (Jayaraman 2008).

Had the organizations involved been more attentive, they would have discovered clues that the papers were not legitimate. Some papers described experiments carried out on equipment that did not exist at Chiranjeevi's institution. In others, the science was simply wrong; the institutional inquiry committee found that some chemical reactions described "were impossible" (Jayaraman 2008). A news report quoted an institutional source as saying, "The chemistry in most of his papers is illogical—the chemistry itself is wrong" (Schulz 2008: 37). Other indications that something was amiss were the sheer quantity of papers and the co-author lists that sometimes stretched to fifty-six co-authors, including people from a wide variety of different disciplines.

What enabled Chiranjeevi to extend this fraud so far was his ability to exploit organization-level weak points, both at his university and at the journals. He benefited from his institution's inattentiveness in overseeing his work, his productivity, and his mentoring of students. None of his work came under systemic scrutiny because he had never received government funding (Service 2008) and he did not report all of his papers to his university (Jayaraman 2008). Implicating his students ensured that they would not turn on him, particularly given the power differential between faculty and students.

Many research organizations give similar leeway to their faculty, trusting that they will fulfill their responsibilities in ethically appropriate ways. It is clear that once Chiranjeevi's work came under scrutiny, his results appeared unbelievable and his methods of production were quickly exposed, suggesting that better oversight might have uncovered the misconduct much earlier. Research organizations, however, have little incentive to take proactive steps to expose misbehavior among their researchers; to the contrary, they have every reason to avoid all association with misconduct and the public embarrassment that it causes. Some commentators applauded Sri Venkateswara University for sanctioning Chiranjeevi, precisely because they saw the university's response as atypical (Service 2008).

Chiranjeevi was also adept at exploiting the weaknesses of the organizations (associations or publishing houses) that issue scientific journals. These organizations have made articles available online in formats that are simple to modify. Resubmission under a different name can be the work of a few minutes, and neither the original publisher nor the receiving publisher typically has ready access to information that would reveal the plagiarism. Bruce Wiersma, the editor of *Environmental Monitoring and Assessment*, which published some of Chiranjeevi's plagiarized papers, noted that "the problem with peer review is that it is an honor system . . . There is no fail-safe. If people want to break the honor system, there is nothing you can do" (quoted in Schulz 2008: 38).

There are also practical weaknesses in journals' review procedures, notably, organizational overload that can be exploited to inappropriate ends. Another journal editor noted that "Chiranjeevi's tactic was to flood journals with manuscript submissions in the hopes of wearing down editors who would eventually publish some of his work" (Schulz 2008: 37). A chemistry professor commented that the journals are "snowed under" with manuscripts (Jayaraman 2008). Also, journals sometimes have a difficult time finding reviewers who are able to provide timely reviews and who have enough expertise in the specific science to make well-informed judgments.

Until recently, journals have had no reliable way to verify that a scientist did the work represented in a paper or even contributed to the paper at all. At best, journals have required authors to specify their roles in the work under consideration, which is still a matter of self-report. Also, papers outside the "hot" areas of science seldom attract much attention (or, indeed, readership). It is no accident that all of Chiranjeevi's plagiarized papers were in relatively obscure areas. Now, however, journals are adopting procedures to protect themselves from fraud, such as submitting manuscripts to plagiarism-checking programs and examining images for inappropriate tampering. Publishers have strong incentives to expose misconduct before it taints their journals. By contrast, universities face quite different incentive structures and have not taken similar steps to expose misconduct in their midst.

The Education System Level

At the level of the academy—that is, higher education institutions and affiliated organizations as a whole—misbehavior may be influenced by a kind of systemic perversity that is present in all highly complex systems. For example, governmental and institutional regulations may sometimes be mutually contradictory. A scientist's commitment to support his or her students and postdoctoral fellows can be compromised by the need to adhere to the details of academic visas. Restrictions on materials bought with grant funds pose a choice between using the materials in other ways, in violation of the restrictions, or wasting the materials, sometimes at considerable cost. Hapless scientists, caught in these situations, sometimes acknowledge their misbehavior by saying things like, "Of course I lied. Wouldn't you?"

The academy also exerts more direct pressures on researchers that may increase the likelihood of misbehavior, chief among them being competitive pressures. Science is, in large part, a competitive system. Scientists compete for funding, journal space, appointments, positions of influence, and, most of all, recognition. Competitive pressures exist largely at the level of the academy, as one's primary competitors are usually (though not always) employed at another institution. The competition itself is played out within networks of people working in a particular field, across universities, scientific funding agencies, academic associations, and professional communities. The education system encourages and rewards competitive success and, some maintain, fosters behaviors that stretch the rules to competitive advantage. Institutional and disciplinary sorting mechanisms favor those who know how to work the system. From graduate school to the top of the scientific pyramid, those who advance are the ones whose personal ambition and drive best fit the system's insatiable quest for originality and innovation.

The case of Eric Poehlman highlights the influence of competition in the academy. It is well known because it developed into a criminal case of research misconduct, yielding him a one-year prison sentence and lifetime debarment from federal research funding (Kintisch 2006).

Dr. Eric Poehlman was a physiologist carrying out research in the areas of obesity, menopause, and aging at the University of Vermont. His results from a clinical study showed no support for his hypothesis that, as people age, their levels of low-density lipoprotein increase and their levels of high-density lipoprotein decrease. A technician in the lab noticed that the results were different after Poehlman took the data set home, supposedly to correct mistakes due to erroneous data entry. The technician found that, not only did the results now support the hypothesis, but also the only data that had been changed were those that contradicted the hypothesized trend (Interlandi 2006).

This incident triggered attention to other previous irregularities and, eventually, a full investigation. At one point, Poehlman sued the University of Vermont to keep it from notifying the U.S. Office of Research Integrity of the misconduct investigation. Eventually, he admitted to falsifying seventeen grant applications to the U.S. National Institutes of Health (NIH) and fabricating data in ten journal articles (Dalton 2005). The $2.9 million of research funding that he received in the 1990s was associated with research that turned out to be fraudulent. For example, his findings that postmenopausal weight gain was less among women who were administered hormone replacement therapy were, in fact, based on data he had fabricated; those findings supported his successful application for over a half-million dollars in NIH grant funding. According to the U.S. attorney in Burlington, Vermont, during the investigation Poehlman "destroyed electronic evidence ... presented false testimony, presented false documents, and influenced other witnesses to provide false documents" (Goldberg & Allen 2005: sidebar).

The Poehlman case is unusual in its scope and outcomes, but it is otherwise typical of many instances of research misconduct and less egregious forms of misbehavior. Scientists' success is measured in terms of their publications, grants, and the attention that their work attracts in the academy. An ambition-driven scientist will seek to maximize his or her role as a principal investigator and primary author ("corresponding author") using collaborations to advance without allowing them to obscure the impact of singular achievement. Success yields reputation and prestige, which are compounded like interest over time. As Robert Merton (1968) noted long ago, the Matthew Effect[2] ensures that further rewards go to those who have accumulated previous rewards. The problem, of course, is that this effect and other realities of professional advancement (such as increasingly limited slots as one rises in the achievement pyramid) create a situation in which rewards are not necessarily proportional to effort. Competitive pressure, which is a condition of survival in the early stages of a career, does not necessarily wane over time for the truly ambitious researcher.

It appears that Eric Poehlman responded to academic incentives and pressures by trying to enhance his chances of competitive success. Like many others implicated in major scandals, Poehlman had a stellar reputation, a substantial publication record, and many prizes to his name. Indeed, once the investigation began, he accepted an endowed research position at the University of Montreal. In a statement to the judge at his federal trial, he wrote that he was "motivated by my own desire to advance as a respected scientist" and that he misrepresented his data "to increase the odds that the grant would be awarded" (quoted in Kintisch 2006: 3). At the time of his sentencing, an article in *The New York Times* noted that "Poehlman had definitely stepped on some toes and made a name as an aggressive self-promoter, but this was nothing remarkable for a successful researcher" (Interlandi 2006: 36). The article further noted that he took responsibility for his actions but appeared to place some of the blame on the competitive education system. He told the court, "I had placed myself, in all honesty, in a situation, in an academic position which the amount of grants that you held basically determined one's self-worth," and "Certainly there is this point of having a grant because it raises your esteem and raises your standing vis-à-vis your colleagues" (quoted in Interlandi 2006: 54). His colleagues suggested that he "buckled to an exaggerated perception of the pressure to publish papers and win grants to keep his laboratory going" (Goldberg & Allen 2005: 10).

Clearly, most scientists do not respond to competitive pressure in the education system by engaging in misconduct. There is evidence, however, that lesser misbehaviors are significantly more prevalent under conditions of high perceived competition (Anderson 2008). How much misbehavior is directly attributable to the competitive pressures in the academy is unknown.

The Society Level

Misbehavior in research is not often attributed to social factors. At most, misconduct among scientists might be compared to that of other professionals. The difference is, of course, that not all other sectors are subject to the kind of social contract described above, whereby public funding is based on public trust, which in turn is based on appropriate conduct as defined and assured by scientists themselves. There is, however, one notable instance in which scientific misbehavior may be linked to social factors: when the scientist is caught up in national or international acclaim and expectations. In this case, the momentum of publicity and social pressure might induce misbehavior or encourage cover-up of ethical lapses that could accumulate and eventually be exposed in a very public way.

The case of Woo Suk Hwang at Seoul National University in South Korea is one of the best-known cases of scientific misconduct in recent years. Hwang is a celebrated researcher in the stem cell field. In a paper published in *Science* in 2004, Hwang and his collaborators claimed to have cloned thirty human embryos and extracted stem cells from one of them (Hwang, et al. 2004). A year later, in another *Science* paper, the researchers announced that they had established eleven embryonic stem cell lines from human skin cells (Hwang, et al. 2005). The papers attracted worldwide attention because they represented progress toward the goal of developing therapeutic technologies from cells that could be induced to develop into a wide variety of cell types. Hwang and his colleagues were not the first to claim cloning of human embryos, but their work clearly represented a substantial advancement of the related science. They also produced the world's first cloned dog, named Snuppy (Lee, et al. 2005).

Soon after the publication of the first *Science* article, an investigation by the journal *Nature* raised ethical questions about improprieties in the consent procedures used in obtaining human ova, including reliance on eggs from female junior members of the research team and monetary payments to other donors. The high profile nature of the topic, the extraordinary achievement that the articles represented, and the initial ethical questions opened up Hwang's work to special scrutiny. Subsequent investigations confirmed the improprieties related to consent and also turned up fabrication of data and publication of duplicate images. In 2006, Hwang was indicted on charges of embezzlement, fraud, and violation of South Korean bioethics law. The charge of fraud was based on Hwang's bid for research funds on the basis of fabricated data.

The most prominent contextual factors associated with this case are at the level of society. Hwang's work proceeded in the context of national praise and high expectations. He was working in arguably the "hottest," most competitive field of science, given its tantalizing potential for cures for a wide range of human diseases. Any significant progress in the field is likely to attract both scientific and media attention, and Hwang's apparent success represented stunning progress.

Such success was particularly sweet for South Korea. Herbert Gottweis (2007: slide 6) has argued that Hwang offered "the scientific solution for the state's political program of industrial transformation through biotechnology." Biotechnology was linked to the promise of economic growth and prosperity at the national level. It represented an avenue to national advancement that depended not on past political hegemony but on scientific knowledge, which could be had through biotechnology investment and the brilliance of a researcher like Hwang. It also represented a specific advantage for Asian countries that permitted scientific work with human stem cells, beyond what their counterparts in the United States were able to do under restrictions on federal government funding in this field.

South Korea did more than dream, however. It supported his work through "an alliance between government, politicians, and the media" (Gottweis 2008: slide 14). Financial support flowed from the government and specifically from the president's office. The World Stem Cell Hub was established by the South Korean government for Hwang's work and global collaboration. Headed by Hwang, it proudly identified itself (in English) as the "Hope of the World, Dream of Korea" (photo in Gottweis 2007). The Korean Bioethics and Biosafety Act, enacted in January 2005, gave special consideration to those whose stem cell work and publications preceded the Act; Hwang was the only person who fell into this category (Gottweis 2007). In a media extravaganza, Hwang himself became known as the "King of Cloning," a handsome media darling. In 2005, the Korean government issued a postage stamp showing a stem cell superimposed with five stages in silhouette: a figure seated in a wheelchair, the figure rising, stepping, leaping, and then hugging someone, perhaps Hwang.

The high-stakes nature of stem cell research and the national hopes for economic development and prosperity were important contextual factors in Hwang's rise and fall. His real successes (e.g., the derivation of some stem cell lines, the birth of Snuppy) were extended fraudulently and supported by improper methods. The funding he was awarded on the basis of past success was expanded in part through the momentum of national attention and celebrity status. Under such circumstances, admission of either error or intentional wrongdoing would be difficult, as would correction and retraction. Of course, at the same time, the high-profile visibility of the research made exposure of wrongdoing more likely.

The fates of two characters connected to this story illustrate the social import of this case. In 2006, a truck driver who believed in Hwang's research despite the exposed misconduct and who had distributed literature urging the scientist to continue his work, immolated himself (*Nature News* 2005). He represents, in extreme, the dashed hopes of the Korean people. By contrast, in October 2009, at the conclusion of a three-year trial, Hwang himself was found guilty of embezzlement and illegal payments for human ova, but received only a suspended two-year sentence (Akst 2009). He continues to work in the field, at a different South Korean research site. His contrition and the value of his work earned him the court's leniency.

Concluding Thoughts

The cases presented above suggest that research misbehavior needs to be considered in relation to contextual forces prevalent in the research environment. Like most wrongdoing, research misconduct is influenced by contextual factors at several levels. It exposes weaknesses and fault lines in research systems that miscreants know how to use to their own advantage. No social system, especially one so vast as international scientific research, is perfect, and there will always be people who figure out how to advance within the system by devious means. Moreover, undue competition and perceived injustice in the research system may be intensifying pressures that empirical evidence has linked to misbehavior (Anderson 2008; Martinson, Anderson, Crain, & De Vries 2006).

As the above cases illustrate, research misconduct is typically associated with incentives that have positive, functional roles but which can promote bad behavior when exploited to deviant ends. Rewards for individual initiative, such as a supervisor's approval of a graduate assistant's work, provide incentives, but they can skew behavior inappropriately. Organizational oversight and peer review are the surest defenses against bogus science, but Chiranjeevi and others have learned how to take advantage of institutional overload. Competition is an important element of a meritocratic sorting mechanism based on achievement and good ideas, but systemic weaknesses provide opportunities to those, like Poehlman, who are willing to take advantage of them. Governments offer incentives to scientists to boost national economic standing, but researchers like Hwang can falsely cultivate unreasonable and inappropriately high expectations.

The social contract that has undergirded public support of science for decades has acknowledged, first, that most scientific research activities are beyond the public's capacity for oversight and, second, that public funding is provided on the basis of trust. This specific trust linked with expertise imposes a grave obligation on scientists: they must earn and maintain the public's trust, which makes their work possible, without having to or even being able to prove in detail to the lay public that they have done everything right. The catch, of course, is that scientists can and do prove their trustworthiness to their peers who understand the details of the work. Peer review serves as a kind of republic of accountability: scientists are designated overseers of each others' work, as representatives of the public welfare.

Given the conditions and the incentives at various layers of the research environment, how is scientific integrity to be maintained? The simplest answer is that people need training and mentoring to know what they are and are not supposed to do, but that response is not particularly useful. It would be difficult to find a researcher who doesn't know that it's wrong to fabricate data, plagiarize, and so on, and training and mentoring have been shown to have ambiguous relationships with misbehavior, at best (Anderson, et al. 2007).

Scientists often express dismay when they hear about a case of misconduct. In blunt terms, they tend to view the miscreant as simply "dumb" because he or she (1) did something that is "just plain wrong," and (2) ignored the consequences of that action. These assessments are useful, in that they suggest the forces that keep an individual's behavior in check: a sense of right versus wrong, and a dread of exposure and punishment.

These two familiar restraints on behavior have social analogues at the level of the scientific community. The first is professional integrity, a shared sense of what is acceptable or unacceptable behavior for scientific researchers. This sense is supported by professional norms, codes of ethics, exemplary leaders in the profession who are widely emulated, worthy mentors and teachers, inspiring messages from professional associations and their leaders, and repeated messages in print and presentations about ideals and standards of behavior. The second social analogue is oversight. The regulatory machinery that has been built up over the past twenty years in the United States is both a reminder and a deterrent. Laws, university policies, regulations, reporting requirements, journal policies, compliance offices, confidential reporting mechanisms for suspected misconduct, legal and regulatory precedents, mechanisms for investigation and sanction, and training all raise researchers' awareness that misbehavior is likely to be discovered, disclosed, and punished.

And yet, there will always be some level of intentional misbehavior. There will always be behavior that straddles the line between acceptable and unacceptable conduct. There will always be new methods and new approaches at the frontier of research whose ethical implications have not been fully appreciated or tested. Countering these tendencies is not a matter of simply telling people not to engage in inappropriate behavior. It is important to consider the role of the research environment at various levels in enabling or promoting misbehavior and to find ways to eliminate or temper its unfortunate effects. Doing so will support the responsible conduct of research and the integrity of the scientific enterprise.

Notes

1. In this chapter, I use the terms "researcher" and "scientist" interchangeably, in acknowledgement of the dominance of scientific research in terms of scope, funding, and public awareness. More to the point, most attention within and outside the academy has been captured by scientific misconduct, though non-scientific fields have had their share of cases of ethically questionable behavior.
2. The "Matthew Effect" references the following quotation from the biblical *Book of Matthew*: "For to all those who have, more will be given, and they will have an abundance; but from those who have nothing, even what they have will be taken away" (chapter 25, verse 29, New Revised Standard Version).

References

Akst, J. (2009) 'No jail time for Hwang', *The Scientist NewsBlog*, 26 October. Available at http://www.the-scientist.com/blog/print/56117/ (accessed 3 November 2009).

Anderson, M.S. (2008) 'The contrary research environment: What is RCR instruction up against?' Paper presented at the National Academies workshop on Ethics Education and Scientific and Engineering Research: What's Been Learned? What Should Be Done?, Washington DC, August. Available at http://www.nae.diamax.com/Programs/CEES14954/CEESActivities/EthicsEducationandScientificandEngineeringResearchWorkshop/MelissaAndersonPresentation.aspx (accessed 1 June 2010).

Anderson, M.S., Horn, A., Risbey, K.R., Ronning, E.A., De Vries, R., and Martinson, B.C. (2007) 'What do mentoring and training in the responsible conduct of research have to do with scientists' misbehavior? Findings from a national survey of NIH-funded scientists', *Academic Medicine*, 82: 853–60.

Anderson, M.S., Ronning, E.A., De Vries, R., and Martinson, B.C. (2010) 'Extending the Mertonian norms: Scientists' subscription to norms of research', *Journal of Higher Education*, 81, 366–93.

Antes, A.L. Brown, R.P., Murphy, S.T., Hill, J.H., Waples, E.P., Mumford, M.D., Connelly, S., and Devenport, L.D. (2007) 'Personality and ethical decision making in research: The role of perceptions of self and others', *Journal of Empirical Research on Human Ethics*, 2: 15–34.

Braxton, J.M. (1986) 'The normative structure of science: Social control in the academic profession', in J.C. Smart (ed.) *Higher Education: Handbook of Theory and Research, Volume II*, New York: Agathon Press.

Dalton, R. (2005) 'Obesity expert owns up to million-dollar crime', *Nature*, 434: 424.

De Vries, R., Anderson, M.S., and Martinson, B.C. (2006) 'Normal misbehavior: Scientists talk about the ethics of research', *Journal of Empirical Research on Human Research Ethics*, 1: 43–50.

Goldberg, C. and Allen, S. (2005) 'Researcher admits fraud in grant data: Ex-Vermont scientist won nearly $3m from US', *Boston Globe*, 18 March. Available at http://www.boston.com/news/nation/articles/2005/03/18/researcher_admits_fraud_in_grant_data?mode (accessed 12 November 2007).

Gottweis, H. (2007) 'Hwang-gate: Lessons for science governance'. Paper presented at the First World Conference on Research Integrity, Lisbon, Portugal, September 2007.

—— (2008) 'South Korea's Hwang-gate: Mass media and research ethic'. Paper presented at the

BIONET Ethical Governance of Biological and Biomedical Research: Chinese European Co-operation Workshop for Journalists, Changsha, March 2008.

Hwang, W.S., Ryu, Y.J., Park, J.H., Park, E.S., Lee, E.G., Koo, J.M., Jeon, H.Y., Lee, B.C., Kang, S.K., Kim, S.J., Ahn, C., Hwang, J.H., Park, K.Y., Cibelli, J.B., and Moon, S.Y. (2004) 'Evidence of a pluripotent human embryonic stem cell line derived from a cloned blastocyst', *Science*, 303: 1669–74.

Hwang, W.S., Roh, S.I., Lee, B.C., Kang, S.K., Kwon, D.K., Kim, S., Kim, S.J., Park, S.W., Kwon, H.S., Lee, C.K., Lee, J.B., Kim, J.M., Ahn, C., Paek, S.H., Chang, S.S., Koo, J.J., Yoon, H.S., Hwang, J.H., Hwang, Y.Y., Park, Y.S., Oh, S.K., Kim, H.S., Park, J.H., Moon, S.Y. and Schatten, G. (2005) 'Patient-specific embryonic stem cells derived from human SCNT blastocysts', *Science*, 308: 1777–83.

Interlandi, J. (2006) 'An unwelcome discovery', *New York Times*, 22 October. Available at http://www.nytimes.com/2006/10/22/magazine/22sciencefraud.html?scp=1&sq=interlandi%20an%20unwelcome%20discovery&st=cse (accessed 17 March 2010).

Jayaraman, K. (2008) 'Chemistry's "colossal" fraud', *Chemistry World*, 25 March. Available at http://www.rsc.org/chemistryworld/News/2008/March/25030801.asp (accessed 5 October 2009).

Kintisch, E. (2006) 'No deal: Researcher Eric Poehlman was sentenced to prison today for fabricating research', *ScienceNOW Daily News*, 28 June. Available at http://news.sciencemag.org/sciencenow/2006/06/28–01.html (accessed 17 March 2010).

Koshland, D.E. Jr. (1987) 'Fraud in science', *Science*, 235: 141.

Lee, B.C., Kim, M.K., Jang, G., Oh, H.J., Yuda, F., Kim, H.J., Shamim, M.H., Kim, J.J., Kang, S.K., Schatten, G., and Hwang, W.S. (2005) 'Dogs cloned from adult somatic cells', *Nature*, 436: 641.

Martinson, B.C., Anderson, M.S., and De Vries, R. (2005) 'Scientists behaving badly', *Nature*, 435: 737–8.

Martinson, B.C., Anderson, M.S., Crain, A.L., and De Vries, R. (2006) 'Scientists' perceptions of organizational justice and self-reported misbehaviors', *Journal of Empirical Research on Human Research Ethics*, 1: 51–66.

Merton, R.K. (1968) 'The Matthew effect in science', *Science*, 159: 56–63.

Mumford, M.D., Devenport, L.D., Brown, R.P., Connelly, S., Murphy, S.T., Hill, J.H., and Antes, A.L. (2006) 'Validation of ethical decision making measures: Evidence for a new set of measures', *Ethics and Behavior*, 16: 319–45.

Nature News. (2005) 'Timeline of a controversy', nature.com, December 19, doi:10.1038/news051219–3. Available at http://www.nature.com/news (accessed 1 June 2010).

Office of Science and Technology Policy (2000) *Federal Research Misconduct Policy*, Washington, DC: Office of Science and Technology Policy. Available at http://ori.dhhs.gov/policies/federal_policies.shtml (accessed 7 March 2010).

Resnick, D.B. (2007) *The Price of Truth: How Money Affects the Norms of Science*, New York: University Press.

Rest, J.R. and Narváez, D. (eds) (1994) *Moral Development in the Professions: Psychology and Applied Ethics*, Hillsdale, NJ: Lawrence Erlbaum.

Schulz, W.G. (2008) 'A massive case of fraud: Journal editors are left reeling as publishers move to rid their archives of scientist's falsified research', *Chemical and Engineering News*, 86: 37–8.

Service, R.F. (2008) 'Chemist found responsible for ethical breaches', *Science*, 319: 1170–1.

Steneck, N.H. (2004) *ORI Introduction to the Responsible Conduct of Research*, Washington, DC: U.S. Government Printing Office.

7

Ethical Challenges and the Aspirational University

Fund-Raising and Spectator Sports

J. DOUGLAS TOMA AND MARK KAVANAUGH

As Americans have come to understand higher education in terms of gains for individuals and contributions to local economic development, as opposed to solely the advancement and dissemination of knowledge for the overall good of society, universities and colleges are increasingly seeking resources in new markets and viewing outputs as commodities. Having embraced the neo-liberal conception of the university, they are de-emphasizing their traditional academic core in favor of seeing revenues at their more agile peripheries; expanding management capacity and the influence of managers; and restructuring the composition of the faculty to lower instructional costs. In addition to seeking efficiencies and revenues, they are also making significant investments: subsidizing researchers (who themselves are increasingly focused upon individual gain); aggressively recruiting accomplished students; and obsessing over essentially meaningless measures, such as those associated with rankings (Bok 2002; Kirp 2004; Slaughter and Rhoades 2004). As a result, institutions are less able to control spending and have become more expensive (Ehrenberg 2002; Geiger 2004; Zemsky, Wegner, & Massy 2005).

They are racing ahead to develop capacity in fund-raising, assuming that these investments will yield direct returns. Universities and colleges are further enhancing their commitment to intercollegiate athletics toward improving their competitive position in areas such as student recruitment and external affairs. We focus on the ethical challenges that have emerged or have been exacerbated in the present entrepreneurial climate in these two areas: fund-raising and spectator sports. We begin by offering various illustrations of how universities have acted in ethically unsound ways in both, responding to various pressures associated with the commercialization of academe. These pressures reside across levels in the systems framework proposed by the editors: grounded in emergent neo-liberal societal norms, similar across an industry in which aspirations and strategies tend to be generic, operating within given institutions, and requiring individuals to act in ways that protect values.

In next introducing the contexts for fund-raising in U.S. higher education, considering also the direct and indirect uses of spectator sports in it, we suggest that institutions across types have similar ambitions and pursue a standard set of strategies toward realizing them, interested in getting to "the next level," as they commonly express it (Toma 2008). These strategies involve attracting talent, whether students or faculty, with fund-raising enabling institutions to endow the scholarships and endowments needed to do so, and athletics perceived to support external relations. As the stakes associated with universities and colleges engaged in what amounts to an open market being so high, the potential for ethical challenges is heightened, whether it is a "have" protecting its position or an "almost have" or "have not" seeking to make up ground quickly.

Spectator sports operate in an environment even more connected with commercial influences and professional impulses than does the broader university—and we discuss ethical aspects of increases and disparities in spending on athletics to make the point. (It is essential to differentiate between spectator sports that attract broad outside interest and involve significant financial investments, as with football and men's basketball at the largest universities, and all other forms of competition, which are more akin to a student activity.) The integrity associated with the amateur ideal that continues to define athletics apart from spectator sports—teams such as swimming and tennis at larger institutions and even football at smaller ones—is overwhelmed by market pressures when applied in the context of Southeastern Conference football or Big East men's basketball. Exacerbating the challenges associated with spectator sports is the structural and normative divide common between athletics and the remainder of the university, with its distance from the academic core of the institution making spectator sports an extreme case.

Fund-raising is usually more connected than spectator sports with the broader university or college. Major gifts to the university tend to be for academic purposes, thus involving the president or a dean in the process. (There is some relatively low-stakes fund-raising that occurs in alumni affairs, as through direct mail and call centers to solicit for annual funds.) Also, many fund-raisers hold appointments within schools and colleges, and even those who do not still must be able to articulate academic values in making a case for support to prospective donors. But despite being more embedded in the academic mainstream, fund-raisers—and the presidents and deans they serve—are under considerable pressure to regularly deliver the private donations needed by institutions as they compete in various markets for talent. They also engage sufficiently with external constituents to internalize some of their norms—notions that are not always consistent with traditional academic values.

These values remain important even in an American society now defined by neo-liberal notions, in a higher education industry that is increasingly market driven, at institutions concerned with generating revenue and prestige (the two thought to be mutually reinforcing), and with individuals ever more pressured to deliver resources. Integrating fund-raising and spectator sports more completely into the broader university encourages these areas to balance commercial pressures with the ideals long associated with academe. In doing so, ethics becomes more holistic, cutting across institutions and doing so in a more consistent fashion. But the guardians of traditional academic values also need to appreciate the changed context of the American university and recognize the realities of the marketplace. Ethical questions are relatively straightforward within a society, industry, and institution—and among individuals—that are only driven by values (or, conversely, merely by profit). The commercial realities of contemporary higher education complicate matters, as traditionally defined within academe, such as living in community, fulfilling obligations, performing roles, and meeting standards. If the essence of creating an ethical academy is in the recognition of the environment in which it operates, it is essential to consider the external pressures to which fund-raising and spectator sports so draw attention.

Ethical Challenges in Fund-Raising and Spectator Sports

In offering selected illustrations of how the increasingly entrepreneurial nature of the contemporary university only exacerbates pressures toward acting in ethically unsound ways in fund-raising and, especially, spectator sports, we appreciate that professional practice in both areas is generally marked by adherence to values. The Council for the Advancement and Support of Education (CASE) and the Association of Fundraising Professionals (AFP) codify a set of ethical principles, as with addressing conflicts of interest and the profiling of potential donors. The National Collegiate Athletic Association (NCAA) rules on recruitment and eligibility have express enforcement mechanisms and penalties for non-compliance. But codes and rules—and even enforcement—only go so far. In both fund-raising and athletics, ethics are dependent upon deeply internalized values—at society, education system, organization, and individual levels—such as the amateur ideal, which still predominates in the Olympic sports.

In both fund-raising and athletics, larger institutions commonly employ foundations and other arms-length organizations designed to receive and manage private funds. One purpose of foundations is to augment the state salary of presidents and coaches, turning a figure in the hundreds of thousands into one in the millions. There are similar foundations devoted to research or real estate, particularly at public institutions at which there are limits on the uses of state funds. Under NCAA rules, an athletics association needs to have sufficient contacts with the broader university or college, with citations for lack of institutional control accompanied by severe penalties. There are also reporting requirements and other rules governing foundations within institutions, as with those grounded in compliance with tax laws.

But there is commonly more secrecy and less oversight associated with foundations than is the norm in higher education, especially at public institutions. Slaughter, Feldman, and Thomas (2009) and Kavanaugh (2009) say the same about funded research. At private institutions, there can be even less transparency, as with the illustration of endowment investments at Yale, sometimes in enterprises with Yale connections, being released to only a few senior administrators.[1] Foundations and athletics associations can also be strongly influenced be a handful of leading donors. There are the examples of Boone Pickens at Oklahoma State (OSU) and Phil Knight at Oregon making massive donations and having significant influence.

Oklahoma State presents an interesting illustration of an institution, acting within these foundations and in the context of athletics, being increasingly creative and aggressive, pushing closer to ethical lines. In 2007, the OSU athletics program funded a $280 million endowment for its athletics program by establishing $10 million life insurance policies on twenty-eight of its leading athletics boosters, borrowing $20 million to do so. The university intended the endowment to fund athletics scholarships and facilities upgrades. The effort eventually prompted litigation, filed early in 2010, with OSU seeking repayment of $33 million in premiums from the insurer.[2] Similarly, planned giving is increasingly prominent in fund-raising, whereby donors name institutions as beneficiaries in their wills. There is federal legislation proposed to limit charitable uses of life insurance policies and increasing scrutiny by state insurance regulators—and the ethics associated with institutions profiting from the death of a donor are uncertain. There is also the question of the institution borrowing $20 million and paying $10 million annually in premiums, with no guarantee of any return. Perhaps the most significant ethical concern is associated with a university bolstering athletics through such investments, instead of its academic program. Nevertheless, resource-hungry athletics programs immediately expressed interest in the Oklahoma State model—and planned giving, in general, is a growth area in fund-raising.

Another ethically ambiguous area involves exclusive contracts between institutions and corporations. Larger athletics programs derive significant revenue from these, with advertisements for local businesses, regional companies, and national corporations ubiquitous within sports venues. In 2006, the athletic program with the largest budget, Ohio State, earned $7 million in royalties (as through licensed apparel), advertisements, and corporate sponsorships (Toma 2009a). (Such possibilities are much more limited outside of the leading programs.) Following the trend in professional sports, universities are increasingly selling to corporations naming rights to arenas and stadiums, as with the Comcast Center at the University of Maryland and Papa John's Cardinal Stadium at the University of Louisville.

There are also the cola wars, with Pepsi and Coca-Cola entering into contracts to be the provider of sodas and water for institutions, including at their stadiums and arenas. The landmark deal was between Penn State and PepsiCo in 1992 for twelve years and $14 million. In 2008, Coke and the University of Minnesota system renewed their contract for ten years, with the five institutions receiving $38 million. The corporation secured pouring rights and signage at the new TCF Bank Stadium on the Twin Cities campus (the naming rights came with a $35 million, twenty-five-year deal), in addition to operating vending machines and providing beverages at dining facilities and concession stands managed by Aramark. (Campus bookstores are increasingly managed by a few large providers, such as Follett and Barnes and Nobel, as are dining services, with Sodexo-Marriott as the other main competitor.) There are also relationships with fast food providers, these having become a staple at food courts. Additionally, athletics programs from the largest to the smallest partner with apparel companies, such as Nike and Adidas, with Michigan moving in 2007 from the former to the latter for $60 million over eight years.

As universities and colleges across types have signed these deals, they have attempted to mitigate ethical concerns, as with Minnesota dedicating Coca-Cola revenues to student activities. But such contracts do tend to raise questions and even prompt protests, such as over the labor policies of the apparel companies in the developing world. There are also health-related arguments against fast food and sodas. These arrangements may also create conflicts of interest, as with potential overlaps between trustees and corporations involved (Kavanaugh 2009; Slaughter, et al. 2009). There are similar challenges associated with industry– university partnerships in fields such as pharmaceutical research, for example sponsors reserving the right to review research results. Relatively little writing in higher education has addressed such issues, however (Kavanaugh 2009).

There is more scholarly attention given to corruption in intercollegiate athletics. Problems with violence and cheating arose over a century ago, with the latter continuing despite regular reform efforts, most recently with the Knight Commission (Thelin 1994). Revenue pressures and prestige seeking associated with the present salaries and facilities arms races have only exacerbated such concerns. A fundamental ethical challenge in spectator sports is "under the table" inducements, often from sources outside of the control of the university, to attract (and retain) particularly desirable athletes. Athletes in the spectator sports often have standardized test scores that are well below the median for undergraduates. There is a similar ethical challenge in the Ivy League and at elite liberal arts colleges, as there is a pronounced admissions advantage for athletes, as well as recruited varsity athletes comprising up to one-third of students on many smaller campuses (Bowen & Levin 2005; Shulman & Bowen 2002). There is also writing, arriving at mixed conclusions, on the impact of participation on the cognitive and affective development of athletes (Gayles & Hu 2009). When such outcomes are negative, suggestions that universities are exploiting athletes are more persuasive.

A related ethical challenge is keeping students who are elite athletes but struggle as students eligible, under NCAA rules, for competition. This can involve tracking them into more "manageable" majors—most large universities have an academic department that enrolls large numbers of athletes—up to outright fraud associated with their academic work. A former tutor revealed late in 2009 that Florida State had designated an unusually large proportion of student athletes as learning disabled—more than one-third of the football team and three-quarters of the basketball team—enabling them to access classroom accommodations, such as note-takers and untimed tests (ESPN 2009). There are regular allegations that tutors employed by athletics programs write papers for athletes or otherwise aid them in cheating, with whistleblowers having reported intimidation and harassment.[3] There also tends to be more overt homophobia and sexual harassment in athletics, although it is important not to generalize (Wolf-Wendel, Toma, & Morphew 2001).[4]

Such problems can be disposed of discreetly through settlement payments, especially given the quasi-private nature of some athletics associations. There is also the challenge in athletics of hiding losses—not capturing on budget spreadsheets the true costs associated with athletics, such as the value of a scholarship or spending on capital projects and facilities maintenance. All but the most prominent athletics programs receive subsidies, often significant ones, from the general budget of the institution (Lederman 2010). As these funds could be spent for academic purposes, universities have a strong incentive to "hide the ball," as they can and do avoid discussion of a difficult ethical question. As institutions cope with economic crises through furloughs and budget cuts, such difficulties are only exacerbated. There are also buyouts, sometimes in the millions of dollars, given annual salaries in that range, to dismissed coaches with years left of their contract. There is the reverse challenge of institutions exploiting sometimes dubious "for-cause" grounds to dismiss coaches and thus avoid a buyout based on morals clauses in contracts, as with Cincinnati dismissing basketball coach Bob Huggins in 2005 or Texas Tech firing football coach Mike Leach late in 2009.

There are several other ethical questions associated with spectator sports. For instance, coaches are regularly removed for poor win–loss records on the field or court, even if the athletes for whom they are responsible are successful in the classroom—while the opposite is almost never the case. There continue to be imbalances between spending on spectator sports and budgets for Olympic sports, even when the former do not generate revenue (the usual justification for differences at larger programs).[5] Similarly, even with Title IX, women remain under-represented in administrative roles in athletics and women's sports continue to be underfunded at many institutions. Also, institutions defer to television in scheduling football and men's basketball games at times that require athletes to miss classes and are disruptive to campus routines, as with the weeknight football games that are becoming increasingly regular. Another ethical question is associated with so-called guarantee games—a smaller program taking a large payment to visit a large one—that usually result in a humiliating defeat, but enable the athletic department receiving the payment to stay afloat financially. Finally, there is significant giving to athletics at the institutions with the most prominence in spectator sports, predominately tax-deductable annual payments to secure premium tickets and skybox access. For instance, football ticket priority accounts for approaching one-third of the funds raised annually by the University of Georgia.[6] Whether giving here siphons off private support of academic purposes—or actually encourages it—is an open question.[7]

As our selection of these illustrations suggests, spectator sports is a more ethically challenging environment than fund-raising. The usual strategy in organizing fund-raising in higher education is to develop a "pyramid" structure. The base of the pyramid is modest donations solicited for annual funds.[8] Another type of fund-raising involves grants from corporations and foundations to support research or programmatic initiatives, with institutions entering into an application process with the funder, and larger grants often involving developing close relationships. Apart from research fraud, there are few issues with such fund-raising, limited to those such as alumni associations partnering with credit card companies receiving a percentage of "affinity" cards—thus associating themselves (not even all that indirectly) with the practices of these corporations.

Major gifts, atop the pyramid, can be more controversial. These involve building a deep connection with a prospective donor, leading to a proposal for an investment in a priority at the institution. Donors usually designate such gifts for a particular purpose, such as supporting a building project or endowing a professorship, student scholarship, or lecture series.[9] Donations to endowment have particular value, as they provide some of the qualities of a nest egg for an institution. Like admissions numbers and research funding, endowment is also a marker of institutional prestige. The same is true of the dollar figure attached to capital campaigns, which are periods of five years or so during which institutions especially emphasize fund-raising.

But how much influence major donors have over institutions can present interesting ethical questions. For instance, does a donor ever have sufficient leverage to secure admission for a relative who would otherwise be denied an offer? Do universities or colleges sometimes develop a program, scholarship, or professorship in a given area not based on real institutional needs (or even strategic ends), but because the donor desired it? Another ethical issue is the tendency of donations to cluster in the already most prosperous areas of institutions, such as law and business schools—in the same way that fund-raising tends to be the most developed at wealthier universities and colleges.

Fund-raising is, nevertheless, increasingly essential in higher education, especially to enable the aspirations of institutions. State appropriations to public institutions have declined in relative terms, with society having made a value judgment to shift responsibility to individuals (Zusman 2005). Other revenue sources, such as tuition and fees or auxiliary enterprises, do not make up the difference, even though increasing as a percentage of budgets (McGuinness

2005). Meanwhile, costs are escalating, with the institutional aspirations on which we concentrate in the next section requiring investments reliant upon fund-raising in areas such as tuition discounting, recruiting faculty, and research infrastructure. (Fixed costs—as in benefits, technology, and energy—have also increased.) Cost savings have been difficult to achieve, even with institutions aggressively professionalizing management, shifting to contingent faculty, and outsourcing functions such as maintenance, bookstores, and dining (Collis 2004).

Aspirations and Resources

Fund-raising and spectator sports are occurring in the context of institutions fixating on their upward mobility—and are influenced by societal, educational system, organizational, and individual impulses. Through becoming more like universities and colleges at "the next level" within the industry, institutions hope to gain the legitimacy and autonomy that come with greater prestige (DiMaggio & Powell 1983). Also through increasing prestige they attempt to minimize the influence of external entities within society on which they rely for support. Doing so involves enhancing their independent resource base through means such as endowed funds, as opposed to state appropriations and student tuition (Pfeffer 1982; Pfeffer & Salancik 1978). Individuals associated with any university or college also invest ego in "their" institution, wanting others to hold it in esteem and knowing there are both tangible and intangible benefits if they do, as writing on organization identification and brand equity contends (Dutton, Dukerich, & Harquail 1994; Toma, Dubrow, & Hartley 2005).

Positioning for prestige is such a necessity—an obsession really—across much of American higher education for reasons anticipated by these theories. Legitimacy and autonomy are particularly attractive outcomes, as the resources perceived to accompany these make it easier for an institution—and those affiliated with it—to accomplish more. Because there is neither a set status hierarchy nor formal structural barriers within U.S. higher education, moving up is an available option for an institution. There are just enough examples of doing so—winning the lottery, in effect—to convince institutions to undertake the effort needed. They perceive that with sufficient fund-raising, anything is possible. Institutions across types accordingly tend to arrive at a common aspiration, despite vast differences in respective resources available to them. And if increasing in reputation requires stretching traditional values, such as ones associated with access for less affluent students, institutions are increasingly willing to accept that.

Universities and colleges that are even marginally selective in admissions attempt to operationalize these ambitions at the institutional level through a rather generic set of strategies (Toma 2008). Each is dependent upon raising funds in excess of those required to maintain standard operations. Foremost among these strategies is student recruitment, which institutions have professionalized and expanded. They recognize the importance of the characteristics of entering students, namely the average standardized test score of the admitted class, in rankings such as those by *U.S. News and World Report* each year. (They also understand that other key variables, such as research funding or endowment amount, which are also connected with fund-raising, are more difficult to strengthen.) Standardized scores tend to correlate with affluence, so the student composition of universities and colleges has changed, with state flagships drawing more suburban students and fewer from rural areas, for instance (Everson, Dixon-Roman, McArdle, & Michna 2010). There are thus societal impacts associated with institutional aspirations. Enrolling accomplished students can also have the additional benefit of enhancing net revenue for institutions, as occurs with those paying full tuition at private universities and colleges and out-of-state students at public ones (Ehrenberg 2002).

But recruiting elite students can also be expensive, requiring that institutions discount tuition regardless of family need. Universities and colleges have also launched or enhanced innovative or unusual academic programs, study abroad opportunities, service learning efforts, honors options, and undergraduate research initiatives (Toma 2008). They are also concentrating more on marketing, advertising aggressively in targeted areas. Institutions are also seeking advantage in attracting the students (and faculty and administrators) they desire by updating the infrastructure devoted to collegiate life. Necessities such as dormitories, dining halls, and gymnasia have become amenities—luxury apartments, upscale food courts, and deluxe fitness centers (Toma 2008). Institutions are also constructing academic buildings, especially science buildings, in another construction arms race. In addition, research universities continue to hire noteworthy faculty and invest in needed infrastructure to build their research programs (Clotfelter 1996; Ehrenberg 2002). Each of these strategies is expensive, with most connected in some manner with enhanced private support.

Once again, institutions have learned to accept that these strategies, while consistent with neo-liberal societal norms and connected with positioning within the higher education industry, may distract from fulfilling traditional obligations and upholding longstanding values. For instance, universities and colleges have invested in facilities and programs connected with prestige while allowing academic programs within their core to struggle. If defining ethics as recognizing community, fulfilling obligations, performing roles, and meeting standards, these aspirations and strategies may well constitute a breach. They cause institutions to focus externally within an industry, as opposed to becoming better by their own standards; prompt them to overlook traditional constituents and purposes; and value meaningless measures such as rankings.

The Uses of Spectator Sports

Universities and colleges are engaged in similar strategic efforts in intercollegiate athletics, improving facilities, "upgrading" to Division I, and adding programs, commonly assuming sometimes considerable debt in doing so (Sweitzer 2009; Toma 2003, 2009b).[10] The University of Michigan, for instance, has invested in a $226 million renovation and expansion of Michigan Stadium, adding eighty-two luxury boxes and 3,000 premium seats. Georgia State, UNC Charlotte, South Alabama, and Texas-San Antonio are launching football programs in the Football Championship Subdivision (FCS, formerly Division I-AA), the class below the Football Bowl Subdivision (FBS, formerly Division I-A), in which Michigan competes. These institutions cite the need to provide their students with a collegiate touchstone, football being a critical marker of a "real" large American university. Several smaller colleges have added Division III (non-scholarship) football toward furthering alumni and community relations and enhancing student recruitment, especially of the men who will attend the college primarily to participate on the team (Feezell 2009). Institutions have answered inevitable questions about investing in athletics while allowing the academic core to erode, by indicating that, although traditional values (community, obligations, purposes, and standards) remain important, market realities are more pressing.

Toma (2003) suggests the strategic advantages that institutions derive from large-scale college football,[11] employing it to advance the resource acquisition that serves various broader institutional agendas. They thus employ something essentially divorced from their academic purposes to advance these same functions, reconciling the attendant disconnects with various ends justifying means arguments. Football contributes to advancing the campus community and collegiate atmosphere that is expected of all institutions, including the largest universities. It also is useful in fostering the effective external relations needed in attracting resources from increasingly skeptical local sources—resources that allow universities not only to maintain, but also to build. Remaining unanswered are values-based questions, as someone from the European tradition might ask, such as whether collegiate life is all that important relative to the academic core of institutions, and whether funds raised are mostly devoted to initiatives at the margins of institutions. As the collegiate ideal and institutional ambitions—like football itself—are so embedded in the American conception of higher education, perhaps suggesting another reality is merely an intellectual exercise.

Spectator sports also provide institutions that are essentially local in their reach with what amounts to a national brand, adding distinctiveness and significance to campuses with few other areas of real national prominence (Fisher 2009; Harris 2009). The names and symbols associated with spectator sports (along with geography) are what distinguish otherwise interchangeable large universities (and otherwise indistinguishable states) on a national level. The benefits that accompany a recognized brand, termed brand equity, are consequential (Toma, et al. 2005). Spectator sports are also accessible (and even relevant) to broad audiences, particularly in ways that many activities are not (say, research in the humanities). It is what many outsiders know and like about an institution, making insiders out of local communities that extend statewide, causing them to want to deepen and announce their affiliation (Dutton, et al. 1994; Toma, et al. 2005). Universities can then leverage these positive perceptions and connections in fund-raising (as they also do in government relations and student recruitment). Even at the universities with the most prominent athletics programs, fund-raising extends well beyond leveraging football, of course. Most prospective donors making major gifts are primarily interested in the academic welfare of an institution. Football games may provide an excuse to invite them to campus during the Fall, but it is hardly what motivates their giving to endow scholarships or professorships.

Haves, Almost-Haves, and Have-Nots

Apart from the several more intangible benefits associated with collegiate life and external relations, institutions and supporters also invest in spectator sports in the interest of winning. Winning is perceived by institutions to enhance each of these strategic advantages, whether campus community, local appeal, or national identity.[12] But there is also an inherent attractiveness to athletics success—one that encourages supporters, in particular, to contribute aggressively in its pursuit, perceiving that investments in salaries and facilities can translate into victories.

Because prominent athletics programs commonly function autonomously within large universities, certainly more than do academic units, with individual boosters and corporate partners exerting significant influence from outside, institutional controls over resources and spending can be difficult to impose. Boosters and partners are unlikely to appreciate academic values, at least to the extent that faculty and administrators do—and athletics administrators and coaches are commonly not completely connected with the rest of the institution. Although the NCAA regulates relationships with student athletes, seeking to eliminate corruption in areas such as recruiting and coursework, fund-raising activities in athletics occur with no real outside oversight.

Spending on athletics has increased significantly over the past few years, as the area is experiencing an arms race akin to that in building student amenities and hiring prominent researchers. Between 2004 and 2008, the median operating budget among the 120 FBS athletics programs increased by 46 percent, to $41 million (Art & Science Group 2009), far outpacing increases in spending elsewhere at institutions, with budgets at leading programs approaching or exceeding $100 million.[13] Programs are not only investing in facilities, such as Michigan Stadium and lavish practice complexes, but an intensely competitive environment is also influencing salaries. The University of Texas set the market price for head football coaches late in 2009, agreeing to pay Mack Brown $5 million annually (entirely from athletics revenue). In justifying the amount, Texas argued that football revenues have quadrupled under Brown, from $21.3 million in 1997, when the coach made $750,000, to $87.5 million in 2008 (*Associated Press* 2009).[14] (There are similar arguments made in recruiting prominent researchers to universities—the investment will be made back in increased external funding.) Another justification is that athletics is increasingly results driven, with unsuccessful coaches more quickly relieved of their responsibilities. Whether such a high-risk, high-reward approach is consistent with ethical behavior is a question readily dismissed, if ever even considered.

Given its abundant athletics revenues, such spending is possible at Texas. But as in annual fund-raising, endowments, and research funding, there are considerable differences in possibilities and outcomes among haves, almost-haves, and have-nots. It is the equivalent of a race to a common finish line with every runner beginning at a markedly different starting point—which constitutes an ethical question in itself. For instance, leading flagship state universities, such as Michigan, North Carolina, and Virginia, raise around $250 million annually and $900 per student per year in private funds. Meanwhile, other flagships, such as Michigan State, N.C. State, and Virginia Tech, which are ranked in the twenties and thirties among public universities, generate about one-third of those figures. Comprehensives, such as Central Michigan, East Carolina, and Kent State, are typically below 10 percent.[15] Similar categories emerge in reviewing the percent of institutional budget drawn from fund-raising, as well as endowment per student, and endowment as a percentage of the overall budget (Toma 2010a). The same distribution occurs in research funding. It is not surprising that the *U.S. News and World Report* rankings parallel fund-raising prowess, as initiatives funded by private dollars can influence the factors that the annual survey measures, particularly the endowments needed to fund scholarships and professorships.

Disparities in athletics are similar (Toma 2009a). Among the 330 programs eligible to compete in the annual Division I basketball tournaments for men and women, the largest programs spend thirty times more than the smallest ones. Among the sixty-six programs in Bowl Coalition Series (BCS) conferences (and Notre Dame), the programs at the bottom tend to spend about one-third of those at the top—over $120 million at Alabama compared with closer to $40 million at Cincinnati. Among all 120 FBS athletics programs, those mostly comprehensive universities in the smaller conferences such as the Mid-American spend one-sixth or so (around $20 million). In revenue raised outside of subsidies to athletics from institutional transfers and student fees, the difference is more like 30:1, as essentially all of the Mid-American conference athletics budgets come from subsidies, as does one-half of the $40 million athletics budget at Rutgers.

The difference between the haves, almost-haves, and have-nots tends to be the capacity to generate revenue through ticket sales and private donations, television revenues and conference distributions, and sponsorships and royalties. For example, Georgia raises nearly $30 million annually in private giving, which exceeds the entire budget of any of the non-BCS conference institutions, and Florida earns $10 million from selling local media rights. (Such financial data have only recently become available, furthering transparency and enabling analysis—an important step in improving ethical behavior (Suggs 2009). Conference television contracts are similar in proportion. The Southeastern Conference (SEC) now receives $205 million annually, divided among the twelve league members, from CBS and ESPN-ABC for broadcasting rights. In contrast, the Mountain West Conference television deal is closer to $12 million per year, while the Western Athletic Conference contract is around $4 million and the Mid-American Conference is about $1.5 million.[16]

Athletics revenue and spending are thus akin to disparities on the academic side of institutions—there are haves, almost-haves, and have-nots, with the distribution across institutions within the industry roughly similar in both realms. And as in various academic competitions, the haves in athletics almost always win. The national champions in football since the launch of the BCS in 1998—Alabama, Florida, Louisiana State, Texas, Southern California, Ohio State, Miami, Oklahoma, Florida State, and Tennessee—are in the top fifteen or twenty in resources devoted to athletics (with the exception of Miami). Institutions may enter the season with the same goal, but are not competing on a level field financially. Nevertheless, because the market for televised football—as for students, faculty, research funding, fund-raising, etc.—has no structural barriers to have-nots (and almost-haves) participating fully, complaints are unusual.[17] The process is open, even if the results tend to favor a few leaders. But is equality of opportunity sufficient if results are so divergent, consistently favoring one group?

However, pressures are similar across the industry, as are temptations to cut ethical corners, whether institutions are working to maintain or advance their position. For instance, it is difficult to counter the criticism—an ethical one, really—that provosts and deans are cutting budgets while athletics is either awash in money or subsidized by institutions. Reform is simply unrealistic, as presidents indicate in the Knight Commission report, with the only option they identify being the pursuit of the additional revenues needed to continue to compete (Art & Science Group 2009). It is just such pressure associated with fund-raising and spectator sports that should raise red flags for those concerned with building an ethical academy. The situation is the same with the prestige race across institutions—opting out is inconceivable (Toma 2010b). When there is neither a set status hierarchy nor formal structural barriers, there is always the hope of winning the lottery and increasing impressively in stature. But just because aspirations and strategies are appealing does not mean they are ethically sound.

Concluding Thoughts

Whether in fund-raising or spectator sports, institutions are sometimes stretching in ethically uncomfortable ways as they race to stay ahead or catch up in the increasingly intense battle for resources and prestige. These challenges are likely to grow only more pronounced as appropriations continue to decline and endowments only slowly recover after the 2008 stock market crash. An interesting question is whether athletics, which has commercialized more apparently and perhaps more extensively—and in which ethical challenges are more pronounced—is suggestive of where the university is headed in fund-raising (and funded research)? Also, are ethical challenges inevitable, as institutions are not regulated and acting ethically in both fund-raising and spectator sports is primarily dependent upon individuals? (Even industry-wide NCAA rules on recruitment and eligibility can be difficult to enforce.) In other words, is it too difficult to maintain a consistent ethical stance amidst the pressures associated with spectator sports—and which may be creeping into fund-raising across institutions?

The premise of this volume is that ethics need to become more holistic within institutions, with everyone considering what it really means in an academic setting to live in community, fulfill obligations, perform roles, and meet standards. Fund-raising and spectator sports offer a critical reminder that across institutions traditional academic values increasingly coexist with the realities of the marketplace, with commercial pressures complicating ethical questions. With many, if not most, of the challenges we identify above, one could substitute phrases such as "funded research" or "student recruitment" for "fund-raising" or "spectator sports." As costs escalate and traditional revenue sources dwindle, institutions have become more entrepreneurial across functions, shifting attention from their cores to what they perceive to be more agile peripheries. That core may be a college of arts and sciences, an annual fund, or the amateur ideal, with the periphery being convenience-focused academic programs, "exotic" gift instruments, and extreme investments in athletics personnel and infrastructure. The pressures to depart from traditional academic values across institutions are increasingly similar to the incentives to cut corners in fund-raising or athletics (Toma & Kramer 2009).

Notes

1. *The Chronicle of Higher Education* reports on this in a September 2, 2005 story.
2. *The Chronicle of Higher Education* addresses the OSU insurance program in 2007 articles dated March 16, May 4, and May 25, following up on February 4, 2010. In its October 26, 2007 edition *The Chronicle* reports on the influence of large donors at Oregon and interviews Red McCombs, who has donated $100 million to Texas, Minnesota, and Southwestern; and in its October 30, 2008 edition it reports on Pickens handling investment strategy at Oklahoma.
3. *The Chronicle of Higher Education* reports on such a scandal at LSU in its May 17, 2002 issue. An October 6, 2009 story in *The Chronicle* considers a SUNY-Binghamton adjunct professor allegedly fired for not fixing athletes grades.
4. A $3.5 million settlement for sexual harassment in athletics at Fresno State is the subject of an October 15, 2007 *The Chronicle of Higher Education* piece.
5. There is even a trend toward sports discontinued for budget reasons being continued through private support.
6. *The Chronicle of Higher Education* reports in its January 23, 2009 edition that fifty-six of the seventy-three institutions in the six major athletic conferences (counting the Big East basketball-only programs) raised $1.1 billion in private support for athletics in 2007–8.

7. *The Chronicle of Higher Education* addresses this issue in an October 5, 2007 article.
8. There is research on whether winning (or losing) in spectator sports influences these gifts, but results are mixed (Anctil 2009; Frank 2004).
9. Different institutions designate what constitutes a major gift differently. A public research university with decent fund-raising by national standards might set the baseline at $25,000, payable over up to five years, whereas an elite private liberal arts college or research university that raises far more money annually may have a higher threshold.
10. *The Chronicle of Higher Education* considers problems associated with assuming debt related to athletics in its September 29, 2009 and July 27, 2007 issues.
11. At most institutions and involving the Olympic sports at even the largest institutions, athletics is primarily a student activity, not an extravaganza of interest to a massive audience of spectators. Spectator sports are the exception, occurring in only a few sports at around 150 universities.
12. There is also evidence, sometimes anecdotal, that athletics success increases undergraduate applications, as *The Chronicle of Higher Education* reports occurred at George Mason following its unexpected Final Four appearance in 2006 (March 28, 2008) (Toma and Cross 1998).
13. A May 1, 2009 *The Chronicle of Higher Education* article considers increases in athletics spending relative to that on academic programs.
14. In 2009, Tennessee broke the $1 million mark for paying an assistant football coach—and salaries at leading programs, especially in the Southeastern Conference, are increasing rapidly.
15. *The Chronicle of Higher Education* compares athletics resources at neighboring Michigan and Eastern Michigan in a September 8, 2006 story. It reported on the increasing gaps between haves and have-nots a decade ago on November 17, 2000—differences that have only increased.
16. In its August 31, 2009 edition, *The Chronicle of Higher Education* covers the increasing financial advantages that the SEC has over competitors nationally.
17. The one exception is the Bowl Championship Series, which allocates slots in the four leading bowl games, and the national championship game, which is weighted toward teams in the six major conferences.

References

Anctil, E. (2009) 'Institutional advancement and spectator sports: The importance of television', in J.D. Toma and D.A. Kramer (eds) *The Uses of Intercollegiate Athletics: Opportunities and Challenges for the University*, San Francisco: Jossey Bass.

Art & Science Group, LLC. (2009) *Quantitative and Qualitative Research with Football Bowl Subdivision University Presidents on the Costs and Financing of Intercollegiate Athletics: Report of Findings and Implications*, Miami, FL: Knight Commission on Intercollegiate Athletics. Available at http://www.knightcommissionmedia.org/images/President_Survey_FINAL.pdf (accessed 16 March 2010).

Associated Press. (2009) 'Brown to receive $5b a season', ESPN, 10 December. Available at http://www.espn.com (accessed 10 December 2009).

Bok, D.C. (2002) *Universities in the Marketplace: The Commercialization of Higher Education*, Princeton, NJ: Princeton University Press.

Bowen, W.G. and Levin, S.A. (2005) *Reclaiming the Game: College Sports and Educational Values*, Princeton, NJ: Princeton University Press.

Clotfelter, C. (1996) *Buying the Best: Cost Escalation in Elite Higher Education*, Princeton, NJ: Princeton University Press.

Collis, D. (2004) 'The paradox of scope: A challenge to the governance of higher education', in W.G. Tierney (ed.) *Competing Conceptions of Academic Governance: Navigating the Perfect Storm*, Baltimore: Johns Hopkins University Press.

DiMaggio, P.J. and Powell, W.W. (1983) 'The iron cage revisited: Institutional isomorphism and collective rationality in organizational fields', *American Sociological Review*, 48: 147–60.

Dutton, J.E., Dukerich, J.M., and Harquail, C.V. (1994) 'Organizational images and member identification', *Administrative Science Quarterly*, 39: 239–63.

Ehrenberg, R. (2002) *Tuition Rising: Why College Costs So Much*, Cambridge, MA: Harvard University Press.

ESPN. (2009) 'Seminoles helped by "LD" diagnosis', 18 December. Available at http://www.espn.com (accessed 18 December 2009).

Everson, H.T., Dixon-Roman, E., McArdle, J.J., and Michna, G. (2010) 'Is the SAT a wealth test? Modeling the influences of family income on black and white students' SAT scores', unpublished paper. Available at http://www.docstoc.com/docs/23806587/Is-the-SAT-a-Wealth-Test (accessed 16 March 2010).

Feezell, T. (2009) 'Adding football and the "uses" of athletics at NCAA Division II and Division III institutions', in J.D. Toma and D.A. Kramer (eds) *The Uses of Intercollegiate Athletics: Opportunities and Challenges in Positioning Universities*, San Francisco: Jossey-Bass.

Fisher, B. (2009) 'Athletics success and institutional rankings', in J.D. Toma and D.A. Kramer (eds) *The Uses of Intercollegiate Athletics: Opportunities and Challenges in Positioning Universities*, San Francisco: Jossey-Bass.

Frank, R.H. (2004) *Challenging the Myth: A Review of the Links Among College Athletic Success, Student Quality, and Donations*, Miami, FL: John S. and James L. Knight Foundation. Available at http://www.knightfoundation.org/research_publications/detail.dot?id=178207 (accessed 16 March 2010).

Gayles, J. and Hu, S. (2009) 'Athletes as students: Ensuring positive cognitive and affective outcomes', in J.D. Toma and D.A. Kramer (eds) *The Uses of Intercollegiate Athletics: Opportunities and Challenges in Positioning Universities*, San Francisco: Jossey-Bass.

Geiger, R. (2004) *Knowledge and Money: Research Universities and the Paradox of the Marketplace*, Stanford, CA: Stanford University Press.

Harris, M.S. (2009) 'Institutional brand personality and advertisements during televised games', in J.D. Toma and D.A. Kramer (eds) *The Uses of Intercollegiate Athletics: Opportunities and Challenges in Positioning Universities*, San Francisco: Jossey-Bass.

Kavanaugh, M.S. (2009) 'Interests in conflicts: A legal analysis of university conflicts of interest', unpublished doctoral dissertation, University of Georgia.

Kirp, D. (2004) *Shakespeare, Einstein, and the Bottom Line: The Marketing of Higher Education*, Cambridge, MA: Harvard University Press.

Lederman, D. (2010) 'Sports subsidies soar', *Inside Higher Ed*, 19 January. Available at http://www.insidehighered.com/news/2010/01/19/subsidy (accessed 19 January 2010).

McGuinness, A.C. (2005) 'The states and higher education', in P.G. Altbach, R.O. Berdahl, and P.J. Gumport (eds) *American Higher Education in the Twenty-First Century: Social, Political, and Economic Challenges*, Baltimore: Johns Hopkins University Press.

Pfeffer, J. (1982) *Organizations and Organization Theory*, Marshfield, MA: Pitman.

Pfeffer, J. and Salancik, G.R. (1978) *The External Control of Organizations: A Resource Dependence Perspective*, New York: Harper and Row.

Shulman, J.L. and Bowen, W.G. (2002) *The Game of Life: College Sports and Educational Values*, Princeton, NJ: Princeton University Press.

Slaughter, S. and Rhoades, G. (2004) *Academic Capitalism and the New Economy: Markets, State and Higher Education*, Baltimore: Johns Hopkins University Press.

Slaughter, S., Feldman, M.P. and Thomas, S.L. (2009) 'U.S. research universities' institutional conflict of interest policies', *Journal of Empirical Research on Human Ethics Research*, 4: 3–20.

Suggs, W. (2009) 'Old challenges and new opportunities for studying the financial aspects of inter-collegiate athletics', in J.D. Toma and D.A. Kramer (eds) *The Uses of Intercollegiate Athletics: Opportunities and Challenges in Positioning Universities*, San Francisco: Jossey-Bass.

Sweitzer, K. (2009) 'Institutional ambitions and athletic conference affiliation', in J.D. Toma and D.A. Kramer (eds) *The Uses of Intercollegiate Athletics: Opportunities and Challenges in Positioning Universities*, San Francisco: Jossey-Bass.

Thelin, J.R. (1994) *Games Colleges Play: Scandal and Reform in Intercollegiate Athletics*, Baltimore: Johns Hopkins University Press.

Toma, J.D. (2003) *Football U.: Spectator Sports in the Life of the American University*, Ann Arbor, MI: University of Michigan Press.

—— (2008) 'Positioning for prestige in American higher education: Case studies of strategies at four public institutions toward "getting to the next level" '. Paper presented at the Association for Research on Higher Education (ASHE) Annual Meeting, Jacksonville, FL, November 2008.

—— (2009a) 'The business of intercollegiate athletics', in D. Siegel and J. Knapp (eds) *The Business of Higher Education*, Santa Barbara: Praeger.

—— (2009b) 'Why U.S. universities and colleges are positioning for prestige: Legitimacy and dif-ferentiation in the Atlanta market'. Paper presented at the Consortium for Higher Education Research (CHER) Annual Meeting, Porto, Portugal, September 2009.

—— (2010a) ' "Haves," "almost-haves," and "have-nots": Segmentation across U.S. research and comprehensive universities in research funding, fund raising, and athletics budgets'. Paper presented at the Consortium for Higher Education Research (CHER) Annual Meeting, Oslo, Norway, June 2010.

—— (2010b) 'Strategy and higher education: Isomorphism and differentiation in positioning for prestige', in M. Bastedo (ed.) *Organizing Higher Education*, Baltimore: Johns Hopkins University Press.

Toma, J.D. and Cross, M.E. (1998) 'Intercollegiate athletics and student college choice: Understanding the impact of championship seasons on undergraduate applications', *Research in Higher Education*, 39: 633–61.

Toma, J.D. and Kramer, D.A. (2009) 'Editors' notes', in J.D. Toma and D.A. Kramer (eds) *The Uses of Intercollegiate Athletics: Opportunities and Challenges in Positioning Universities*, San Francisco: Jossey-Bass.

Toma, J.D., Dubrow, G., and Hartley, J.M. (2005) *The Uses of Institutional Culture: Strengthening Identification and Building Brand Equity in Higher Education*, San Francisco: Jossey-Bass.

Wolf-Wendel, L.E., Toma, J.D., and Morphew, C.C. (2001) 'There's no 'I' in team . . . And other lessons from intercollegiate athletics in creating community from difference', *Review of Higher Education*, 24: 369–96.

Zemsky, R., Wegner, G.R., and Massy, W.F. (2005) *Remaking The American University: Market-Smart And Mission-Centered*, New Brunswick, NJ: Rutgers University Press.

Zusman, A. (2005) 'Challenges facing higher education in the twenty-first century', in P.G. Altbach, R.O. Berdahl, and P.J. Gumport (eds) *American Higher Education in the Twenty-First Century: Social, Political, and Economic Challenges*, Baltimore: Johns Hopkins University Press.

8

Corruption at the Top

Ethical Dilemmas in College and University Governance

NATHAN F. HARRIS AND MICHAEL N. BASTEDO

The wake of corporate scandals in the past decade has renewed interest in clarifying the fiduciary responsibilities of college and university governing boards. Although the Sarbanes–Oxley Act, which increases the accountability of corporate boards, does not apply to non-profit organizations, its influence has extended beyond *Fortune 500* companies into the boardrooms of the nation's colleges and universities. The Association of Governing Boards (AGB), for example, has prioritized clarifying the fiduciary and ethical responsibilities of trustees in order to protect and enhance the public's trust (AGB 2006, 2009; Leslie & MacTaggart 2008). AGB advises boards to conduct "ethical audits" of institutional governance to promote "the four duties of fiduciary responsibility"— loyalty, care, obedience, and good faith—and to ensure that boards have defined procedures for managing ethical dilemmas (Leslie & MacTaggart 2008: 13–14). AGB also recommends that colleges and universities formulate "statements of expectations" for current and prospective board members, establish voluntary recusal and dispute resolution procedures for conflicts of interest, appoint chief ethics officers, and encourage leaders, particularly presidents and board chairs, to espouse ethical standards in public forums and behind closed doors.

The American Council on Education (ACE) also affirms the role of colleges and universities as the "stewards of the public trust." Yet the ACE cautions that the increasingly complex network of relationships among the academy, businesses, and governments can blur distinctions between ethical and unethical behavior. "New economic demands and emerging forms of financial and academic relationships . . . mean that even the most scrupulous collegiate leader sometimes needs guidance to discern the most ethical course of action" and "how to manage" inevitable conflict of interests (ACE 2008: 1). In response to these challenges, ACE offers institutions "basic precepts" (e.g., requiring financial interests disclosures) and questions to consider (e.g., potential institutional conflicts of interest) when creating conflict of interest policies.

The recommendations of ACE and AGB to conduct ethical audits and establish conflict of interest policies help guide trustees and administrators wanting to define, and uphold, high ethical standards. Who, for example, can argue against discussing potential conflicts of interest confronting trustees and administrators during board or cabinet meetings, or identifying relationships that might constitute conflicts of interest for the institution? From our perspective, the ACE and AGB recommendations begin to reflect a more nuanced conceptualization of ethical misconduct that threatens governance practices: colleges and universities are embedded in increasingly complex networks of interdependent, and potentially competing, relationships that can create ethical hazards; institutional representatives such as trustees, senior administrators, and faculty navigate and leverage these relationships that intersect the "inner life" and "outer life" of their institutions while pursuing strategic institutional objectives; and through their interactions in these relationships, trustees, senior administrators, and faculty determine how, and whether, their colleges and universities uphold ethical standards.

Despite the usefulness of these recommendations, they offer an incomplete solution for explaining and understanding how unethical misconduct can originate, proliferate, and sustain itself throughout the governance structures of colleges and universities. To echo an assertion articulated in chapter 3, these types of recommendations mischaracterize ethical misconduct as solely representing individual failings that can be fixed by adopting more stringent ethical regulations. Although rules are important, they are only one facet of the solution to establishing ethical governance practices. Instead, in this chapter, we conceptualize and examine ethical misconduct in institutional governance as a systems phenomenon, and espouse a greater appreciation for the environmental context that creates potential ethical hazards for trustees, administrators, and faculty. We first emphasize the salience of leadership and relationships in understanding ethical misconduct in institutional governance, highlighting themes presented throughout this volume and in organizational research. We then illustrate these themes in a case study of a recent admissions scandal at the University of Illinois, and offer recommendations to colleges and universities for establishing ethical governance practices.

Reconceptualizing Misconduct in Institutional Governance

The systems framework presented in this book reflects a broader trend toward developing more complex conceptualizations of organizational misconduct, including more nuanced perspectives on academic ethics and corruption in education. We want to briefly underscore two elements of this broader trend with respect to institutional governance: relationships and leadership. First, unethical behavior is not only a series of individual failings, but also the product of social interaction. Second, it is within this network of relationships where individuals enact ethical—or unethical—behavior. This is particularly true for interpreting ethical hazards confronting trustees and senior administrators situated at the "boundaries" of colleges and universities; these leaders engage diverse groups of internal and external stakeholders who may espouse competing institutional priorities and different ethical standards.

Organizational research outside of higher education echoes these central themes. Scholars increasingly reject conceptualizations of organizational misconduct as being the outcome of deviant individual attributes such as a lack of integrity, moral identity, empathy, or self-control, or even psychopathology (Ashforth, Gioia, Robinson, & Trevino 2008; Brief, Bertram, & Dukerich 2001; Palmer 2008). Organizational research on ethical misconduct, for example, illustrates the important role of leadership and relationships in the proliferation of ethical misconduct. Senior managers initiate unethical actions after either engaging in "mindful and rational" cost–benefit calculations concerning the risks and rewards of unethical behavior, or assessing the beliefs, norms, and values influencing their organization's culture and environment (Palmer 2008). They then leverage their formal authority to direct employees lower in the organizational hierarchy to pursue unethical actions, thus proliferating misconduct (Palmer 2008).

After leaders leverage their authority to enact unethical actions, unethical behavior becomes institutionalized or embedded in organizational cultures and structures (Palmer 2008). Ashforth and Anand (2003: 11), for example, describe how institutionalization and routinization desensitizes employees to misconduct because these processes remove "discrete (strategic) decision points" that might trigger "reflective thought" among employees, fostering mindlessness about the ethicality of actions. Brief and colleagues (2001: 481) describe a common characteristic of institutionalization: "members of the offending organization simply persist in their adherence to directives that, on their surface, carry no obvious moral or ethical implications." Misconduct, therefore, becomes embedded in a series of interdependent processes: individuals become "locked in by dense task connections such that the whole sustains each part; one is swept along by the momentum of the *system*" (Ashforth & Anand 2003: 12).

The socialization of new employees illustrates another example of the role of leaders and relationships in organizational misconduct. Through socialization, new employees are exposed to attitudes and actions supporting unethical behavior (Palmer 2008). Through processes such as co-optation, incrementalism, and compromise, the attitudes of new employees about certain behaviors change from abhorrent to acceptable; in co-optation, for example, new employees are induced and persuaded to change their attitudes about unethical behavior (Ashforth & Anand 2003). Brief and colleagues (2001: 485) also highlight how the use of "euphemistic labeling" by leaders can rationalize the actions of leaders or staff as serving the organization's best interest rather than breaking ethical norms: "the use of emotionally sterile or positively valenced terminology" influences the "meanings organizational inhabitants assign ethically ambiguous behavior, thereby perpetuating a collective culture of pernicious activity."

These insights reveal several important implications for examining ethical misconduct in institutional governance. First, individuals do not always understand the scope of their nefarious actions; although observers may identify a progression of unethical behavior after the fact, individuals engaged in such actions do not typically appreciate how a series of smaller decisions culminate in an egregious example of unethical behavior (Palmer 2008). In a similar vein, Ashforth and Anand (2003) suggest that individuals might not notice unethical behaviors because of the mindlessness stemming from institutionalization. Moreover, individuals can obscure the unethical nature of actions by rationalizing them as being in the best interest of their organization (Bastedo 2009).

Second, a variety of mechanisms help to shape the initiation, proliferation, institutionalization, and socialization of misconduct. Organizational structures and processes such as the division of labor, for example, fragment information flow within organizations; individuals in one department may not possess information that elsewhere in the organization might expose misconduct. Palmer (2008: 115) quotes a frustrated manager who questioned the sale of fabricated insurance policies saying he "knew something was wrong," but "did not know the total picture." Moreover, the division of labor diffuses responsibility and accountability; individuals in one part of the organization may suspect unethical actions elsewhere in the organization, but may not feel authorized, or even obligated, to reveal their concerns. Organizational routines can also perpetuate unethical behavior. Instead of focusing on the ends of performance—and realizing that all may not be what it seems—managers often focus on efficiently completing the tasks of their work.

In other words, leaders assume a critical role in discouraging, or encouraging, ethical misconduct (for more on this theme, see chapter 10). Senior leaders assume explicit roles in devising and implementing unethical behavior, but they also serve as role models of how individuals should respond to unethical behavior (Ashforth & Anand 2003). Presidents, provosts, and deans, for example, send clear signals to community members when they reward, condone, or ignore misconduct. The difference between explicit and implicit sanctioning of unethical behavior may be quite subtle: "the implicit message received from the top may be that much more weight is attached to job completion than to legal or ethical means of accomplishment" (Yeager 1986: 110). Ashforth and colleagues (2008: 673), for example, characterize Arthur Andersen's collapse as a failure of leadership that ultimately created a permissive ethical culture: "Management's message to employees might have been implicit, but it was also clear: do anything to ensure clients' return consulting business and maintain revenue flow, even if it means padding prices or creating problems for those clients." These kinds of pressures make unethical behavior far more prevalent.

Case Study: Ethical Breakdown in University Governance

The salience of examining ethical misconduct in university governance as a systemic problem becomes clearer by analyzing a recent controversy over a shadow admissions process for high-profile applicants at the University of Illinois. In May 2009, the *Chicago Tribune* revealed that the University of Illinois had long maintained a list of "special interest" applicants applying to its undergraduate program and some graduate programs. Unknown to most faculty, administrators, staff, and students (not to mention the general public), the list, known as "Category I" for undergraduate admissions, featured applicants with connections to prominent donors, public officials, and university trustees and senior administrators.

Although the list was created and sustained to prevent prominent applicants from "slipping through the cracks" of the formal admissions process, it eventually evolved into a shadow admissions process that granted "special interest" applicants preferential treatment (State of Illinois Admissions Review Commission 2009: 14). The Admissions Review Commission—the investigative panel on the controversy established by Illinois governor Pat Quinn—revealed that, between 2005 and 2009, the Category I list included about 800 undergraduate students (State of Illinois Admissions Review Commission 2009: 14). Although applicants on this list tended to report lower standardized test scores and class ranks than their unconnected peers—class ranks, for example, of seventy-sixth percentile and eighty-eighth percentile respectively—Category I applicants enjoyed a higher acceptance rate (77 percent) than unconnected applicants (69 percent) applying through the normal process (State of Illinois Admissions Review Commission 2009: 14).

The averages, however, obscure the essence of the shadow admissions process. Between 2005 and 2009, thirty-three "presumptive denial" admissions decisions, or applicants receiving the lowest rating, from the Category I list were reversed to admittances because of their personal connections (State of Illinois Admissions Review Commission 2009: 15). The Commission found similar examples in some of the university's graduate schools, notably in the College of Law. The Commission, for example, found that the law school admitted twenty-four unqualified students it would have rejected had it not been for the applicants' "special interest" status (State of Illinois Admissions Review Commission 2009).

A striking feature of the shadow admissions process was the number of senior university leaders throughout the governance structure who knew about the process and did nothing to mitigate its influence—or even worse, leveraged and perpetuated the unethical practices. The Commission, for example, found that approximately half of all Category I applicants were referred by public officials, such as state legislators, to staff in the university's Governmental Relations Office, while approximately 20 percent of Category I inquiries were each generated from university trustees or senior administrators (State of Illinois Admissions Review Commission 2009: 14). The former dean of the College of Law, Heidi Hurd, testified to the Commission that, upon arriving as dean in October 2002, she learned of a "well-oiled, self-described 'system' for dealing with 'special interest applicants' or 'special admits'" with connections to elected officials, donors, and trustees (State of Illinois Admissions Review Commission 2009: 26). To the dismay of the Commission, the culprits of this unethical process were not several ambitious admissions officers or rogue trustees, but the preponderance of the university's senior leadership and governance structure—most trustees (including numerous chairs), the Urbana-Champaign campus' chancellor, deans of colleges, other administrators, and the university's president.

Although the Commission and media reports suggest that the list had a long history—Chancellor Richard Herman testified to the Commission that the university had been tracking high-profile applicants for decades and one state representative claimed to have learned about the process after winning election in 1993—the university formalized the process after an applicant with ties to former Illinois governor Jim Thompson was rejected by the formal admissions process in 2002 (Cohen & Malone 2009; Cohen & St. Clair 2009). In recent years, the shadow process had come to resemble a strategic ad hoc working group: Chancellor Herman, who retained final authority over special admits, convened meetings to discuss high-profile applicants on several occasions during admissions season; these meetings included his secretary, senior staff from the Governmental Relations Office, the Associate Provost for Enrollment Management, and other campus administrators.

Understanding the Ethical Breakdown at the University of Illinois

Individual and Organization Levels

The case study underscores that, at the individual and organizational levels of the system, leaders play a critical role in initiating, proliferating, institutionalizing, and socializing unethical behavior. With respect to the Category I process, senior leaders at the University of Illinois clearly failed to establish and uphold high ethical standards. Instead, trustees and administrators sent clear signals condoning, if not encouraging, the shadow admissions process.

The Commission concluded that Richard Herman, then serving as chancellor of the Urbana-Champaign campus and overseer of undergraduate admissions, asserted "unethical" influence over the shadow admissions process. One Commissioner argued that "If Chancellor Herman had said, 'No. This isn't going to happen,' there would have been nothing to write about. There would be no issue here" (Cohen 2009a). Herman had assumed the role of buffer between those making admissions requests—trustees and state legislators—and academic and administrative colleagues such as deans and admissions directors.

The Commission revealed email exchanges in which Chancellor Herman used his authority over campus admissions to direct or pressure admissions staff to reverse admissions decisions on numerous occasions. On one occasion, for example, although Keith Marshall, the Associate Provost for Enrollment Management, told Herman that a Category I undergraduate applicant was "not competitive," Herman responded "Think we need to get this one done" as a not so subtle suggestion to admit an unqualified high-profile applicant (State of Illinois Admissions Review Commission 2009: 20–1). Chancellor Herman sent clear explicit and implicit signals to trustees and other administrators that pulling strings for high-profile applicants was an appropriate practice and in the university's best interest.

The failure of ethical leadership extended beyond Chancellor Herman. The Commission, for example, revealed that some of the most egregious examples of preferential treatment involved admissions decisions in the College of Law. After assuming her position in 2002, Dean Heidi Hurd began negotiating resources for the law school in exchange for admitting less-than-qualified "special interest" applicants. The Commission concluded that "from the beginning, Hurd made clear that she would accept SI [special interest] applicants from Herman, but only for a price" (State of Illinois Admissions Review Commission 2009: 29). Dean Hurd, for example, negotiated three additional full annual scholarships for the law school in exchange for admitting unqualified special interest applicants (State of Illinois Admissions Review Commission 2009: 30). On a different occasion, Chancellor Herman and Dean Hurd negotiated five state government jobs for law school graduates in exchange for admitting an unqualified applicant sponsored by the governor's office. In an email exchange between Hurd and Herman about negotiations with the governor's office, Hurd writes "FYI: The deal is supposed to be that WE get to pick the students—and they are supposed to be bottom-of-the-class students who face a hell of time passing the Bar and otherwise getting jobs!" (Kass 2009).

The university's president also missed opportunities to question—or stop—the shadow admissions process. In testimony to the Commission, President Joseph White explained that he was "very familiar with" the process and justified maintaining special applicant lists "in order to respond courteously" to individuals with connections to the university (State of Illinois Admissions Review Commission 2009: 22). The Commission's investigation concluded that White "was not regularly included in internal correspondences related to Category I" and did not fully appreciate the scope of the process (State of Illinois Admissions Review Commission 2009: 22). During his testimony to the Commission, White also expressed some concerns over the shadow process, particularly its "institutionalized nature" and the fact that presumptive denials were overturned in favor of admittance.

Although President White may not have assumed an active role in the process, the Commission criticized his failure to stem its influence. "At a minimum . . . he [President White] can be faulted for . . . in some measure, not setting the sort of tone or giving the sort of direction to direct subordinates that could have restrained, if not shelved, category I" (State of Illinois Admissions Review Commission 2009: 22). To echo points made earlier in the introduction to this volume, President White, Chancellor Herman, and other administrators missed important opportunities to establish and cultivate an ethical culture: "speak out for transparency," "make ethics a strategic priority," and "ardently encourage ethicality and discourage misconduct."[1] Although White did not assume an active role in proliferating the shadow admissions process, his choice to not question or criticize the practice sent an implicit, but clear signal that offering high-profile applicants preferential treatment was not inconsistent with the university's ethical values.

In addition to administrators, trustees were among the most active participants in the shadow admissions process. The Commission found that trustees not only requested and received status inquiries relating to specific applicants—a practice actually sanctioned in the university's trustee orientation materials in order "to be certain that proper consideration was given" to applications—but also advocated for the admission of applicants or interfered with admissions decisions (State of Illinois Admissions Review Commission 2009: 23). Commission testimony and email transcripts, for example, revealed that, in 2006, Larry Eppley, Chairperson of the Board of Trustees, pressured Chancellor Herman to direct the law school to admit an applicant whose qualifications were "well below" the school's GPA and Law School Admissions Test (LSAT) twenty-fifth percentile indicators at the behest of then governor Rod Blagojevich. The participation of trustees in the shadow admissions process highlights two threats to independence illustrated by Bastedo (2009): political loyalties and personal agendas.

The Commission concluded that almost *all* trustees sought to influence admissions decisions in some way. In the summer of 2009, seven of nine university trustees resigned their positions because of their participation in the Category I admissions process (Cohen 2009b). In a statement released after his resignation in August 2009, Niranjan Shah, Chairperson of the Board of Trustees, stated that, "When I became a Trustee . . . many of the stakeholders in the University of Illinois system . . . Trustees, university administrators and staff, legislators . . . operated under a different set of rules and norms that seemed appropriate at the time" (Malone 2009). Instead of criticizing the shadow admissions process as unethical—and a potential scandal that could undermine the public's trust in the university—trustees ignored their fiduciary duties in favor of rewarding their political and personal allies.

In addition to illustrating the instrumental role of leaders, an examination of the shadow admissions process highlights other elements of the book's systemic framework and profiled process perspectives on organizational misconduct. First, the incremental institutionalization of the shadow admissions process blurred discrete decision points that might have prompted administrators, or even trustees, to raise concerns. Instead of asking whether the process made ethical sense, administrators fell into a pattern of accommodating trustees and public officials; and instead of considering whether their participation in the process reflected their fiduciary responsibilities, new trustees followed the unethical practices of their predecessors to benefit political and personal allies. In a letter to Illinois governor Pat Quinn, the University of Illinois Senate characterized the process as evolving from "small compromises" into "patterns of conduct" (Wood 2009). The public statements of Chancellor Herman also illustrate the power of rationalizing unethical practices as representing the best interests of the organization. Several months into the scandal, Herman seemed to rationalize his actions by saying he "was serving the greater good" of the university by not alienating powerful stakeholders wanting favors, but admitted that the process "went off course" despite its "good intensions" (Cohen 2009b).

In addition, the case highlights how newcomers can be socialized into unethical organizational environments. Legislators, for example, reported learning of the shadow admissions process from colleagues after winning election and entering the legislature; as with trustees and administrators, governors and legislators seemed to believe that the shadow admissions process was simply an extension of their relationships with the university. In addition, the testimony of Dean Hurd of the College of Law highlights how the socialization process consists of co-optation and compromise; once she recognized the scope and scale of the shadow admissions process, Hurd began negotiating rewards and incentives on behalf of the law school. This example illustrates how administrators can actively participate in unethical behavior, yet rationalize such actions as attempts to benefit the organization; although Hurd recognized that the shadow admissions process was potentially detrimental to the law school's ranking by lowering its admissions profile, she justified her participation in the scheme by appropriating resources from the chancellor's office and public officials (State of Illinois Admissions Review Commission 2009: 25).

The case also illustrates how the institutionalization of misconduct can create and sustain an interdependent system of unethical behavior. The shadow admissions process engaged numerous stakeholders, including trustees and administrators, prominent alumni and donors, and political officials such as governors and state legislators. In a letter to Illinois governor Pat Quinn, the University of Illinois Senate stated that, "For us, this scandal reveals the features of a web of moral responsibility, with each party undertaking actions that pressured and impinged upon the options of others" (Wood 2009). The escalation of the shadow admissions process in recent years created a momentum that made it difficult for any group of stakeholders to stem its institutionalization: "over time, the perception that 'this is just how things work' became self-fulfilling and corrupting" (Wood 2009: 25).

Education System and Society Levels

The controversy over the shadow admissions process at the University of Illinois represents a regrettable, but not necessarily novel, ethical dilemma in which administrators field and accommodate requests from the public officials who control constrained financial resources and the trustees who serve as their bosses, as well as trustees obliging the requests of their political and personal allies. This example illustrates the inadequacy of describing unethical governance practices in terms of individual failings; the shadow admissions process represented an extension of the relationships among state public officials and the university's trustees and senior leadership. Instead, the profiled systems framework helps describe how a practice such as the shadow admissions process can infiltrate—and ultimately threaten—the governance structure of a prominent and well-respected research university.

Yet the University of Illinois example illustrates more than how unethical practices can proliferate throughout the governance structures of colleges and universities. It also begins to illustrate *why* governance structures confront ethical threats by paying greater attention to how environmental factors create numerous ethical hazards for colleges and universities. Once the admissions controversy landed the University of Illinois on the front page of the *Chicago Tribune*, Chancellor Herman rhetorically asked, "Do you think that if Barack Obama called me up and said 'My nephew lives in Illinois and is applying,'—I mean, this is the president of the United States calling me—what am I supposed to do?" (St. Clair, Cohen, & Becker 2009). Apart from its hyperbole, Herman's statement underscores a tension facing administrators, trustees, and faculty across the nation: the resource constraints of colleges and universities, as well as increasing calls for university leaders to be "entrepreneurial," present opportunities for university representatives such as presidents, deans, and trustees to pursue unethical behavior that can be rationalized as serving the best interests of their institutions (see chapter 7).

In chapter 3, Bertram Gallant and Kalichman specifically identify the increased competition for scarce public resources as a critical factor influencing the ethical reasoning of individuals in the academy. In a similar vein, increased insecurity concerning resource sources is a central theme of "academic capitalism": administrators and faculty are trying to establish and leverage new external revenue sources by pursuing "entrepreneurial" behaviors in response to declining sources of revenues from traditional sources such as governmental appropriations (Slaughter & Leslie 1997; Slaughter & Rhoades 2004). An important implication of academic capitalism is that that the new entrepreneurial behaviors of administrators and faculty constitute distractions that may lead colleges and universities to align their interests with the agendas of external organizations in exchange for new resources: "the potential costs associated with market alignment are the depletion of academic freedoms and the marginalization of scholarly activities that are not highly valued in the private marketplace" (Mars & Metcalfe 2009: 40).

Within this emerging entrepreneurial context, Slaughter and Leslie (1997: 210) discuss the practical implications of academic capitalism on college and university administrators:

> the concept of academic capitalism may help administrators, who attempt to enhance faculty productivity, assist faculty to tap external resources and develop their own market schemes, and begin to think broadly about how to deploy institutional resources in the changed environment of higher education.

In addition to seeking new external revenue sources through entrepreneurial approaches such as commercializing university research, college and university leaders may also be broadening their conceptualization of "deployable resources" in order to garner resources from conventional sources such as state governments. Within this context, the University of Illinois shadow admissions process can be interpreted as administrators deploying an institutional "asset" or "resource"—admissions slots—in order to garner favor with governors and legislators controlling state appropriations and with the trustees evaluating their performance. Other potential examples of this unexamined extension of academic capitalism include recent cases in Florida and Virginia of current and former legislators receiving positions at colleges and universities after using their political influence to help establish or secure state funding for institutions (Bousquet 2008; Liberto, Klas, & Bousquet 2008; Sizemore 2009a,b; Walker & Sizemore 2009; Zaragoza 2008a,b).

The increased embeddedness of trustees and presidents in economic, political, and social networks also poses potential conflicts of interest. Bastedo (2009), for example, illustrated that conflicts of interest can undermine trustee independence: trustees might violate their fiduciary responsibilities to accommodate external interests, yet convince themselves that accommodating these interests also represents the best interests of their institutions. He suggests that external conflicts will become more prevalent as colleges and universities assume more prominent roles in social and economic development (Bastedo 2009). Senior administrators, especially presidents, might also increasingly encounter conflicts of interest because of their boundary-spanning role across economic, political, and social networks such as participating on corporate boards (June 2007).

Establishing Ethical Governance Practices: Recommendations for Colleges and Universities

Within a complex environment of numerous potential ethical hazards, how should college and university trustees and administrators create and sustain ethical governance practices? Two common solutions—ethical instruction and governance reform—offer some guidance. Ethical instruction entails educating individuals about ethical standards, specifically helping individuals to better distinguish between "right" and "wrong" behaviors (Palmer 2008). This pre-scription, however, reinforces notions that misconduct reflects the behavior of a few "bad apples" and envisions the ethical challenge as reforming perpetrators before they commit wrongdoing. Governance reform entails devising more stringent rules for defining ethical behavior and leveling harsher punishments to those guilty of ethical transgressions (Palmer 2008). Common examples of governance reform include establishing stricter codes of conduct, developing integrity criteria for performance reviews, and creating whistleblower hotlines. The profiled AGB and ACE recommendations, for example, include elements of both ethical instruction and governance reform.

Although these recommendations are useful, they reflect an incomplete conceptualization of misconduct as individual indiscretions rather than organizational failings. Structural changes such as adopting ethics codes and appointing administrators as "ethics officers" might deter some unethical behavior, but such reforms can easily become decoupled from the everyday reality of administrators, faculty, trustees, and staff. Ashforth and colleagues (2008: 674), for example, contend that organizations can mindlessly adopt a "check-off" approach to many ethical solutions: "Do we have a code and do we tell everyone about it? Check. Do we provide regular training? Check. Do we have a hotline? Check. And so on."

Along with attending to the "letter" of reforms, we advise college and university leaders—particularly trustees, presidents, chancellors, provosts, and deans—to actively revisit and discuss the "spirit" of ethical instruction and governance reforms, notably values such as integrity, accountability, and transparency. Leaders potentially undermine ethical reforms by framing the challenge as following rules rather than establishing ethical cultures. Higher education organizations such as ACE and AGB can assume constructive roles not only in establishing a lowest common ethical "denominator"—for example, the "must-have" elements of conflict of interest policies—but also by encouraging trustees and administrators to not settle for "industry" mindsets and instead develop ethical standards and conflict of interest policies that best reflect their institutions' economic, political, and social environments.

In addition, we offer policy prescriptions for creating and sustaining ethical governance practices beyond ethical instruction and governance reform. Instead of only focusing on procedural remedies to unethical behavior, we assert that increased consideration of (1) the relationship between an institution's environment and potential ethical hazards and (2) the organizational processes potentially facilitating unethical behavior offers rich opportunities for under-standing and promoting ethical governance practices. We echo Bertram Gallant and Kalichman's call for fostering "institutional integrity" by heeding greater awareness of the environmental factors that may unavoidably create unethical threats to governance practices. As with Weick and Sutcliffe's (2000: 33–4) vision of "collective mindfulness" for promoting "high reliability organizations," trustees and administrators should adopt a vigilant preoccupation with failure in order to diagnose signals of possible ethical vulnerabilities across institutions. With trustees, for example, a preoccupation with failure would entail working with administrators to investigate and understand localized ethical indiscretions in hopes of mitigating pervasive ethical missteps that could proliferate across the institution and undermine the public's trust in the institution.

Ethical audits could be a useful resource for trustees and administrators wanting to create and sustain awareness of integrity at their colleges and universities. We advise colleges and universities to conduct periodic ethical audits of their governance practices and establish conflict of interest policies. These prescriptions, however, should reflect candid examinations of the full range of ethical hazards confronting institutions and become regular discussions among internal stakeholders such as trustees and presidents and among external stakeholders such as elected officials and business partners. In other words, the strategic discussion of promoting ethical governance practices does not culminate with the adoption of reforms such as conflict of interest policies, but instead begins a continual self-evaluation of whether individuals are meeting the institution's ethical expectations.

Candid discussions of ethical standards among trustees, administrators, and faculty encourage an ongoing awareness of the many ethical hazards confronting colleges and universities. Regular discussions among trustees and administrators about conflicts of interest—in and out of board meetings—would help to ensure that ethical guidelines are "not just window dressing" and to ascertain the effectiveness of such policies (Ashforth, et al. 2008: 674). In the Appendix, we offer sample questions that governing boards can reference when planning or conducting an ethical audit of their institutions, specifically highlighting questions for discussing the fiduciary responsibilities of trustees, formulating conflict of interest policies, and implementing reforms.

Although reversing institutionalized and socialized unethical behaviors poses daunting challenges for colleges and universities, some of the same organizational processes fostering unethical behavior can also be used to encourage more ethical cultures. Administrators can reinforce institutional ethics during recruiting, hiring, orientation, and training practices. The interview and selection process for senior administrators or trustees, for example, could include role-based behavioral simulations in which individuals navigate ethical dilemmas common to the position; the exercise would help to emphasize the institution's commitment to ethical behavior among senior leaders and establish awareness that ethical dilemmas are not aberrations but realities of the positions. In addition, a candid acknowledgement of ethical threats to governance practices might encourage more realistic ethical training programs; trustees, for example, could complete behavioral-based simulations in which governors or legislators request favors in exchange for future personal favors or resources for the institution.

Higher education organizations can also serve an important role in denouncing unethical practices once revealed at colleges and universities. Ashforth and

Anand (2003: 38) argue that external shocks such as negative media exposure represent one of the few actions capable of reversing embedded unethical and corrupt behavior: "significant negative exposure creates a socially undesirable image, often galvanizing change." The University of Illinois case example illustrated that, as a negative image emerges from multiple audiences, leaders such as trustees and administrators begin to reinterpret situations and question the appropriateness of taken-for-granted unethical actions. Higher education organizations could exert greater symbolic leadership by condemning exposed acts of unethical behavior, encouraging thorough investigations of such episodes, and raising awareness of the environmental forces that create ethical hazards for colleges and universities among external audiences such as business leaders, as well as federal and state officials and policy makers.

The potential for ethical transgressions that could undermine the public's trust in American colleges and universities is likely to increase in the coming decade. Our analysis and commentary should not be interpreted as an excuse to exempt individuals for unethical behavior; trustees, administrators, faculty, staff, and students who fail to uphold ethical standards should not go unpunished by their institutions. Yet we want to underscore that unethical behavior undermines governance structures for complex reasons beyond "poor" personal judgment. In hopes of mitigating "bad apples" from rotting into "bad barrels," trustees and administrators need to acknowledge the environmental and organizational forces that encourage and diffuse unethical behavior in institutional governance.

Appendix: Guiding Questions for Ethical Audit[2]

Revisiting the Fiduciary Responsibilities of Trustees

- How does the board define the fiduciary responsibility of each trustee? How does the board define its collective fiduciary responsibility?
- How does the board articulate these responsibilities and values in discussions and interactions with other internal and external institutional stakeholders, including the general public?
- How explicitly does the board define its fiduciary responsibilities in formal policy documents?
- How explicitly does the board discuss its fiduciary responsibilities during board meetings?
- How does the board evaluate its meeting of fiduciary responsibilities and ethical standards? Who conducts this evaluation? Does the board use independent consultation for this evaluation?
- What training does the board offer to both incoming and sitting trustees concerning ethical expectations and responsibilities? Who conducts this training? Does the institution reference best practices at other institutions?
- How does the board engage other members of the campus community to

oversee that actions across the institution reflect the board's commitment to ethical standards and its fiduciary responsibilities?

- How does the board articulate its fiduciary and ethical values in the recruitment (and selection, if appropriate) of prospective trustees?
- How does the board manage ethical inquiries of trustees? What principles and values define the processes for ethics investigations? What parties are involved in these investigations?
- Do board policies and practices reflect the standards of open meeting and open records laws?

Formulating Conflict of Interest Policies

- Under what circumstances, if any, is it appropriate for a trustee, administrator, or faculty member to accept any of the following from external partners such as public officials or public agencies, as well as prospective or current business partners:
  - personal gifts;
  - expenses-paid travel;
  - honoraria (e.g., speaking fees);
  - employment;
  - consulting income;
  - stock;
  - stock or equity options;
  - staff resources.
- Should the procedures and standards for review of conflicts of interest differ by institutional role? Should a trustee's conflict, for example, be assessed differently than the conflict for a dean or a faculty researcher?
- In what circumstances, if any, should conflict of interest policies allow for trustees, administrators, or faculty to exercise their discretion in waiving institutional rules? What procedures should apply to exercise such discretion?
- Under what circumstances should conflict of interest policies allow individuals discretion to decide what conflicts need to be disclosed to the institution?
- Should conflict of interest policies cover *all* trustees, administrators, faculty, and staff? Should conflict of interest policies cover other members of the institutional community such as volunteers or students who might teach, research, and act as agents of the institution?
- How should conflict of interest policies treat transactions and self-interests involving the family members of trustees, administrators, faculty, and staff?
- When a trustee, administrator, or faculty member has a conflict of interest in an institutional decision or action, should these individuals retain the right to participate in discussions or considerations of such decisions?

- How periodically should trustees, administrators, faculty, and staff be required to disclose conflicts of interest? Should disclosures, for example, occur annually for all community members?
- Should conflict of interest policies categorically prohibit some types of conflicts?
- Does the institution provide sufficient notice and training to trustees, administrators, faculty, and staff to ensure that conflict disclosures are made and updated as circumstances change?
- Does conflict of interest training address both ethical and legal compliance?
- How does the board oversee formally affiliated groups of the institution such as foundations or alumni and athletic associations? Does the board discuss potential conflicts of interest for trustees who provide oversight of these affiliated groups?
- Should conflict of interest policies address conflicts such as nepotism that may be addressed in other institutional policies? Should the board and senior administrators integrate all policies concerning ethical conflicts of interest?
- Has the institution conducted a review of potential institutional conflicts of interest? What criteria should guide this review? What institutional members should participate in the review, and who should lead the process?

Implementing Ethics and Governance Reforms

- Does the institution offer ethics training to administrators, faculty, and staff? Is such ethical training required of community members? If so, how regularly does training occur and for whom? What role do trustees assume in ensuring that ethics training reflects the values of the institution?
- What resources and staff does the institution devote to promote and ensure compliance with its conflict of interest policy? Does the institution, for example, check whether all individuals covered by the policy make their required disclosures?
- How does the institution manage violations of the conflict of interest policy? What procedures exist for enforcing violations?
- Does the institution have an anonymous "whistleblower" hotline for community members to contact when identifying violations in its ethical standards or conflict of interest policy? What institutional human and financial resources support such practices?
- What role does the board of trustees assume in overseeing institutional management of ethical standards and conflict of interest policies?
- Has the institution appointed a formal "ethics officer?" If so, how is this administrator situated within the institution's governance structure? Does the ethics officer report to the board of trustees or an administrator? How

does the institution evaluate the performance of the ethics officer? What are the selection criteria for the ethics officer?

Notes

1. The scandal over the shadow admissions process ultimately prompted the resignation of President White and Chancellor Herman in fall 2009.
2. Authors referenced Leslie and MacTaggart (2008) and the American Council on Education (2008) when drafting the profiled questions.

References

American Council on Education. (2008) *Working Paper on Conflict of Interest (for review and comment)*, Washington, DC: Author.
Ashforth, B.E. and Anand, V. (2003) 'The normalization of corruption in organizations', *Research in Organizational Behavior*, 25: 1–52.
Ashforth, B.E., Gioia, D.A., Robinson, S.L., and Trevino, L.K. (2008) 'Re-viewing organizational corruption', *Academy of Management Review*, 33: 670–84.
Association of Governing Boards of Universities and Colleges (AGB). (2006) *The Leadership Imperative*, Washington, DC: Author.
—— (2009) *AGB Board of Directors' Statement of Conflict of Interest*, Washington, DC: Author.
Bastedo, M.N. (2009) 'Conflicts, commitments, and cliques in the university: Moral seduction as a threat to trustee independence', *American Educational Research Journal*, 46: 354–86.
Bousquet, S. (2008) 'Legislator gives up third state paycheck', *St. Petersburg Times* (FL), 25 March, p. 1A.
Brief, A.P., Bertram, R.T., and Dukerich, J.M. (2001) 'Collective corruption in the corporate world: Toward a process model', in M.E. Turner (ed.) *Groups at Work: Advances in Theory and Research*, Hillsdale, NJ: Lawrence Erlbaum & Associates.
Cohen, J.S. (2009a) 'Chancellor "sorry" but staying', *Chicago Tribune*, 12 August, p. 10.
—— (2009b) 'U. of I. chiefs deflect blame', *Chicago Tribune*, 1 September, p. 6.
Cohen, J.S. and Malone, T. (2009) 'How U. of I. scheme began', *Chicago Tribune*, 30 June, p. 1.
Cohen, J.S. and St. Clair, S. (2009) 'Ex-U. of I. leaders blast trustees', *Chicago Tribune*, 13 July, p. 1.
June, A.W. (2007) 'Why presidents are paid so much more than professors', *The Chronicle of Higher Education*, 16 November, p. 12.
Kass, J. (2009) 'Admission-jobs swap has old-school stink', *Chicago Tribune*, 26 June, p. 2.
Leslie, D. and MacTaggart, T. (2008) *The New Ethics of Trusteeship: How Public College and University Trustees Can Meet Higher Public Expectations*, Washington, DC: Association of Governing Boards.
Liberto, J., Klas, M.E., and Bousquet, S. (2008) 'House chief's job not unique', *St. Petersburg Times* (FL), 22 December, p. 1A.
Malone, T. (2009) 'Scandal claims 2nd at U. of I', *Chicago Tribune*, 4 August, p. 1.
Mars, M.M. and Metcalfe, A.S. (2009) *The Entrepreneurial Domains of American Higher Education*, San Francisco, CA: Jossey-Bass.
Palmer, D. (2008) 'Extending the process model of collective corruption', *Research in Organizational Behavior*, 28: 107–35.
St. Clair, S., Cohen, J.S., and Becker, R. (2009) 'The clout route', *Chicago Tribune*, 31 May, p. 1.
Sizemore, B. (2009a) 'A logical hire or a conflict of interest?', *The Virginian-Pilot*, 30 July, p. A10.
—— (2009b) 'ODU dumps Hamilton deal', *The Virginian-Pilot*, 21 August, p. A8.
Slaughter, S. and Leslie, L.L. (1997) *Academic Capitalism: Politics, Policies, and the Entrepreneurial University*, Baltimore, MD: Johns Hopkins University Press.
Slaughter, S. and Rhoades, G. (2004) *Academic Capitalism and the New Economy: Markets, State, and Higher Education*, Baltimore, MD: Johns Hopkins University Press.
State of Illinois Admissions Review Commission (ARC). (2009, August 6). *Report and Recommendations*, Springfield, IL: Author.
Walker, J. and Sizemore, B. (2009) 'As criticism mounts, Hamilton rejects plea to resign his seat', *The Virginian-Pilot*, 24 August, p. B1.

Weick, K. and Sutcliffe, K. (2000) 'High reliability: The power of mindlessness', *Leader to Leader*, Summer: 33–38.

Wood, P. (2009) 'Senate to vote on whether UI chancellor and president should leave', *The News-Gazette* (Champaign, IL), 27 August, p. 1.

Yeager, P.C. (1986) 'Analyzing illegal corporate behavior: Progress and prospects', in J.E. Post (ed.) *Research in Corporate Social Performance and Policy*, Greenwich, CT: JAI Press.

Zaragoza, L. (2008a) 'Senator runs center she helped fund', *Orlando Sentinel* (FL), 22 March, p. A1.

—— (2008b) 'Lawmaker's book deal draws critics', *Orlando Sentinel* (FL), 7 April, p. A1.

III

Empowering Change: Creating the Ethical Academy

9

Enhancing Individual Responsibility in Higher Education

Embracing Ethical Theory in Professional Decision-Making Frameworks

LESTER F. GOODCHILD

How should we resolve ethical problems on college and university campuses? By resolving difficulties professionally with students, among faculty, or with administrators across departmental and collegiate units, campus change for the good can occur. What type of professional decision-making framework would enable such conflicting groups and individuals to meet their ethical obligations and responsibilities? What is the structure of these frameworks? How does traditional applied ethical theory, used in such frameworks, assist us in resolving these conflicts? This approach involves using applied philosophy in a deliberative fashion, as has been used in other professions, such as medicine, business, or law, for the past forty years. Addressing these types of ethical concerns, as they relate to the emerging field of academic ethics (May 1990; Moore 2008; Shils 1983), comprises the rationale for this chapter. To begin, the meaning of ethics is often elusive.

The General Meaning of Ethics

Generally, ethics or morality concerns the beliefs about right or wrong human conduct. Ethicists explore various ideas about how to define and determine which actions or decisions are right or wrong. The Greeks began such study with a focus on the general patterns or ways of life in their community. They perceived good behavior as that which promoted harmonious life within the city, *polis* (MacIntyre 1966). In this sense, whenever anything was done in the city, it had implications for the good of all. Similarly, whatever is done on campus may affect its internal constituencies of administrators, faculty, students, staff, or unionized employees, and even its external constituencies. According to the *Oxford English Dictionary*, the Greek etymology of "ethics" literally means "to do"—*ethikos*; importantly then every act has an ethical dimension. Every time we do something by ourselves or with others, we are confronted with the basic provocative question of: "What 'ought' I to do?"

Formally then, ethics involves the use of reason to support or justify what particular decisions or actions are chosen in response as being good or right as opposed to being bad or wrong. Judith Boss in her book, *Ethics for Life* (2008: 8), pointed to the critical nature of this discourse: "moral norms and guidelines need to be grounded in theoretical ethics; otherwise, morality becomes arbitrary." This insight points to the importance and value of bringing ethical theory and related principles to applied moral problems, and in our case to higher education. The need for an applied ethic is particularly acute when our colleges and universities are faced with economic difficulties, such as the following:

- students' difficulty in paying for the high cost of tuition, fees, and books;
- the reduction of salary among some professors and adjunct faculty;
- the truthfulness of institutional marketing when advertising to students about degree and credential programs;
- the pressure on students to cheat for grades to secure graduation and jobs;
- the increasing incidence of discriminatory language and actions among groups;
- the abusive actions among students, including date rape; or
- providing adequate numbers of faculty and staff on college and university campuses to serve current student educational needs for completing degrees in a timely fashion.

What ethical theories should be considered then in addressing these types of academic ethics problems?

Using Ethical Theories to Enhance Ethical Decision Making

In this section, I offer a concise overview of four traditional foundational sources of ethical and moral theories that can be used in decision-making frameworks (Albert, Denise, & Peterfreund 1975; Beauchamp 2001; Goodchild 1986: 491–2).[1] They represent major theories of historic moral discourse: (1) deontology, following Kantian ethics; (2) utilitarianism, following Bentham's and Mills's consequentialist ethics; (3) virtue ethics, following recent ideas of Alasdair MacIntyre (1981, 1984) about virtuous behavior; and (4) religious/ theological ethics, following some of the ideas of Philip L. Quinn (1978), James Gustafson (1981), and Stanley Hauerwas (1994). For example, does the chosen course of action follow an institutional promise, rule, or policy (a deontological way)? Or does it relate to the greatest good for the greatest number of students, faculty, or members of an external community (a utilitarian way)? Or does it relate to being honest in one's dealings with colleagues and superiors (a virtue way)? Or, finally, does it relate to following a religious ethical principle in dealing with others, such as prohibitions against stealing (a religious/theological way)?

In the section following this overview, I explore eight ethical decision-making frameworks that ethicists, professional ethicists, or higher education scholars have used to suggest how individuals can assume greater ethical responsibility (which is, as you may recall from chapter 3, one of the three characteristics of an ethical academy). Such frameworks enable campus actors to reflect more completely on the ethical theoretical dimensions of problems and resolutions, providing greater certainty that the proposed action is a moral response. In this way, campus individuals are empowered to act in ethically responsible ways.

Deontology

Deontology centers on Immanuel Kant's principle that the individual has an absolute duty to follow rules, norms, or maxims (Albert, et al. 1975; Beauchamp 2001). This Prussian philosopher maintained that "moral duties were absolute" (Boss 2008: 312). His moral ideas focused on the Greek term, *deon*, namely "duty." The individual is duty-bound to obey a priori promises, norms, rules, or maxims without regard to their consequences (see Kant 1785, 1969). Kant's idea of duty is termed a "categorical imperative" because it requires an absolute moral response to rules and norms. In using such an idea to create rules, norms, or maxims, Kant proclaimed that one should "act only on that maxim through which you can at the same time will that it should become a universal law" (as cited by Boss 2008: 318). Practically, then, one of the first considerations in ethically resolving a campus dilemma is to follow the policy or rule, for example concerning faculty research norms, student plagiarism, or campus drinking of alcohol. Conversely, creating policies or rules requires us to consider how this would affect all persons everywhere on campus.

Utilitarianism

On the other hand, utilitarianism proposed that moral choices are determined by their effects or consequences (Albert, et al. 1975; Beauchamp 2001). Jeremy Bentham, an English jurist, philosopher, and social reformer, believed democracy would eventually aid the poor and exploited workers in industrial England. His famous book, *Principles of Morals and Legislation* (1789, 1907), aimed to gain citizens greater happiness in their communities (Boss 2008: 276–9). Bentham's moral principle was to focus on which action produced the greatest good for the greatest number of people. He emphasized that *right* actions produce pleasure or happiness for others. This applied philosophy was revised by John Stuart Mill who argued that some pleasures were qualitatively different and therefore of more worth in determining the appropriate moral choice (Boss 2008: 286–7). Practically, ethically resolving campus dilemmas requires an understanding of the consequences of proposed decisions, rules, or policies. For example, concerning faculty raises, student residential requirements, or guidelines for fraternity or sorority parties, what policies would achieve the greatest good for the greatest number of people on campus?

Virtue Ethics

The first two theories guide individuals in making moral decisions, whereas virtue ethics calls for individuals to become ultimately virtuous persons so that they embrace the "right action" as part of their personas. They develop and adopt good habits—a good trait or behavior that benefits others is seen as a moral virtue (Albert, et al. 1975; Boss 2008: 400–1). The virtues of honesty, integrity, compassion, and striving for excellence easily come to mind (Beauchamp 1982: 212–3). The Greeks again understood this idea and identified it as *arête*—seeking excellence and valor for the city state. Persons who constantly perform good actions can be seen as having virtuous habits. Such habituation comes from a consistent series of decisions that reinforce this behavior. Thus virtue ethics complements other ethical theories in that it represents an embodiment of these moral principles into the formation of a virtuous person. The outcome of such ethical behavior is happiness or well-being, reflecting again the Greek idea of *eudaimonia* (Beauchamp 1982: 215; Boss 2008: 403–4).

In this manner, resolving ethical dilemmas by being virtuous, say by being honest, in situations results in probable reconciliation, thereby producing good will and harmony among individuals and groups. Tom Beauchamp (1982) calls our attention to Aristotle's classic, *Nicomachean Ethics* (1985), as the foundational work in exploring virtue in moral discourse (Hutchinson 1995). The reintroduction of virtue ethics into contemporary moral discourse occurred with the extraordinarily popular Alasdair MacIntyre's *After Virtue* (1981, 1984); his subsequent publications (MacIntyre 1988, 1990) brought virtue ethics to the center of contemporary applied ethical philosophy. With its publication of the *The Fundamental Values of Academic Integrity* in 1999, the Center for Academic Integrity attempted to call attention to the role that virtue ethics plays in resolving student cheating on campus.[2] Practically, being compassionate with or caring for one's colleagues in understanding their situation and struggles, when problematic situations arise, also points to how collaboration can produce an ethical climate on college and university campuses (Noddings 1984; Roper & Longerbeam 2002). (This idea that collaborative, rather than competitive, environments can help create the ethical academy is explored further in the next chapter.)

Theological Ethics

Religion provides another foundational source of making ethical decisions; its many faith traditions offer individuals direction about decisions, actions, and behaviors. One of the major theological ethical theories is divine commands. Philosophers and theologians, again since the time of Plato's *Euthyphro*, reflected on the directives of gods and their implications for human action (Boss 2008: 150). Perhaps more than other theories, the idea of universality is particularly striking here, given such divine laws or principles as the Jewish Ten Commandments, the Christian approach of forgiveness, the Islamic ethical principle of *zakat* (which involves giving to enhance the good of the community) from the Quran, or the Buddhist principle of seeking perfection or wisdom in morality. Prohibitions against killing and stealing clearly point to ethical demands. Augustine's idea of love also reflects similar calls for moral behavior (Goodchild 1986: 494–5). Moving beyond ethical theories, theological ethics, similar to virtue ethics, seeks to shape and form the dispositions of individuals. These habitual actions point to the individual's spiritual character within a religious or philosophical community.

Justification comes from attesting these theological commands or virtues. Philip Quinn's *Divine Commands and Moral Requirements* (1978) posited such moral judgments as having religious universalizable claims on behaviors (as cited by Boss 2008: 152–5). James Gustafson in his *Ethics from a Theocentric Perspective: Theology and Ethics* (1981) sought to discern God's activity in the world through the spiritual behavior of persons to love others. Stanley Hauerwas's *Character and the Christian Life: A Study in Theological Ethics* (1994) explored the individual's role as an agent of religious character. Practically, resolving ethical problems on campus through endorsing or respecting various religious moral theories can be seen as prohibitions again stealing or proactively offering forgiveness to our sometimes less than friendly colleagues. At stake here since the time of the Greeks is the openness to a higher being or power influencing moral behavior among people.

The four foundational sources of ethical theory just reviewed point to rationales and justifications for ethical stances in problematic moral situations. Moreover, ethical decision-making frameworks based on these theories provide specific guides for action.

Going Beyond Codes of Ethics to Comprehensive Ethical Frameworks

This section discusses professional decision-making frameworks for making ethical decisions. Usually higher education scholars point to professional codes of ethics as the first moral response in a situation. These codes [e.g., the National Association Student Personnel Administrators' (NASPA) Standards of Professional Practice (2010)[3]] typically offer deontologically crafted guidelines, such as NASPA's principle that "members execute professional responsibilities with fairness and impartiality and show equal consideration to individuals regardless of status or position." However, campus problems are usually more complex and require a more extensive analytical approach than is typically offered by professional ethical guidelines.

Eight frameworks are explored here, organized by their theoretical complexity (use of a broad spectrum of traditional ethical theories) and by their disciplinary or field approaches. In the first grouping, basic applied frameworks, the two presented frameworks reflect some general applied ethics approaches used in undergraduate or professional courses. The next grouping, applied deontological frameworks, explores the development of educational ethics and the use of basic applied deontological approaches in resolving ethical problems in college and university life during the 1980s and 1990s. The last group, complex foundational applied frameworks, reflects the greatest complexity by using the full span of ethical theories to structure complex foundational decision-making frameworks. Since Henry Sidgwick's famous book, *Methods of Ethics*, in 1891, philosophical scholars have tried to bring both Kantian and Benthamian approaches to justify moral decisions. Some of these frameworks do this and more.

After analyzing these three groupings of frameworks, four integral elements are proposed as essential for developing a more complex ethical decision-making framework for the professions, especially in our case of academic ethics. Determining the quintessential requirements for an ethical framework will assist students, faculty, staff, and administrators in making better professional decisions.

Basic Applied Ethical Frameworks

In comparing eight different frameworks for making an ethical decision, I start with those more general in scope, such as one relating to various life issues, and then focus on those more related to professional practice and ethics (e.g., medicine, business, or law). Here we can learn how mainline ethicists and professional ethicists treat the structure of ethical frameworks. Their efforts offer a beginning conceptual structure to enhance our professional decision making in academic ethics on our college and university campuses. Two basic frameworks outline this approach.

Boss (1998, 2001, 2004, 2008)

Judith Boss's *Ethics for Life* is an excellent overview of traditional ethics (namely, utilitarianism, deontology, rights ethics, and virtue ethics). This course text offers a basic applied framework for making ethical decisions. Boss's (2008: 69–71) approach is rather circumscribed, but points to the basic areas that need to be treated in a framework as described in her "Five Steps for Resolving a Moral Dilemma:"

1. Describe the facts,
2. List relevant moral principles and sentiments [noted were a few deontological maxims there],
3. List possible courses of action,

4. Devise a plan of action, and
5. Carry out the plan of action.

Her treatment emphasizes the basic practical approach to making ethical decisions from gathering all the facts to carrying out the decision. Strangely for a book that focuses on describing at length major traditional ethical theories, she does not integrate them explicitly into the proposed steps for making a moral decision. Other authors have advanced this approach.

Johnson and Ridley (2008)
A more sophisticated basic approach is taken by W. Brad Johnson and Charles R. Ridley in their book, *The Elements of Ethics for Professionals* (2008). They come from significant ethical backgrounds, including Johnson being a professor in the Department of Leadership, Ethics, and Law at the United States Naval Academy and having been the former chair of the Ethics Committee for the American Psychological Association. On the other hand, Charles Ridley is a professor of Counseling Psychology at Texas A & M University. Their approach incorporates professional codes and attends to the integral part that collaboration with colleagues can play in resolving ethical dilemmas. These insights enhance the efficacy of ethical resolutions in their ten-step method (Johnson & Ridley 2008: 202–3):

- Define the situation clearly.
- Determine who will be impacted by the decision.
- Refer to your profession's code of ethics.
- Refer to relevant laws/regulations and professional guidelines.
- Reflect honestly on personal feelings and competence.
- Consult with trusted colleagues.
- Formulate alternative courses of action.
- Consider the possible outcomes for all parties.
- Consult with colleagues and ethics committees.
- Make a decision and monitor the outcome.

This comprehensive basic approach fully addresses the practical aspects of making a decision and implementing it. However, although importantly noting professional codes and related laws, the framework lacks any inclusion of traditional sources of applied ethics or virtues. This shortcoming is addressed by the applied deontological frameworks described next.

Applied Deontological Ethical Frameworks

During the 1990s, higher education professionals had already seen thirty years of periodic treatments on the ethical failings of those in the profession, the most notorious having been Charles J. Sykes's (1988) book, *ProfScam: Professors and the Demise of Higher Education*. In part, these charges of unethical behavior brought other scholarly members of the academy to address these issues in a more positive cast. A series of books sought to identify ethical problems in all parts of college and university life and begin a serious effort to rectify their practice (see chapter 1). The books that used applied deontological ethical frameworks sought to remind colleagues of their professional ethical duties, suggesting the "oughts" and "shoulds" of their professional behaviors. Three approaches to an applied deontological ethical framework in academic ethics are explored next.

Reynolds and Smith (1990)
In 1990, Professor William May from the University of Southern California published the most comprehensive academic ethics book to date, *Ethics and Higher Education*. This work brought together administrators and faculty from across the nation to look at ethical principles, institutional activities, and current problems. One of its opening chapters allowed Professor of Religious Studies Charles Reynolds from the University of Tennessee and David Smith, former executive director of the Society for Values in Higher Education and director of the Leadership, Ethics, and Values Program at North Central College, to offer some guiding ethical principles and to propose steps in an ethical decision-making framework. The Reynolds and Smith framework represents an early attempt to formulate an applied ethics for professional decision making in the developing field of academic ethics.

The guiding academic principles of responsibility, classically deontological in form, offered by Reynolds and Smith (1990: 37–8) include personal principles (e.g., "demonstrate a respect for each person as an individual"), professional principles (e.g., "conduct their professional activities in ways that uphold or surpass the ideals of virtue and competence"), systemic principles (e.g., "be fair, keep agreements and promises, operate within the framework of the law, and extend due process to all persons"), public principles (e.g., "interpret academic values to their constituencies"), and political principles (e.g., "help develop fair and compassionate means of resolving conflict between persons, groups, and nations"). These more practical and pragmatic principles are presented by Reynolds and Smith (1990: 37–8) as a nascent "professional code of ethics for higher education."

These explicit theoretical principles underline Reynolds and Smith's ethical decision-making framework, the inspiration for which came from the famous American Protestant theologian Richard Niebuhr's (1963) "discerning judgment." There are five steps in Reynolds and Smith's (1990: 45–7) framework:

1. Define the concrete ethical issues . . .
2. Review imaginatively the alternatives for resolving the issue . . .
3. Consider carefully each alternative in relation to the academic principles of responsibility [see above] . . .
4. Review imaginatively your preferred resolution of the issue by

checking the proposed solution with your intuitive moral judgment . . .
5. Act on your best deliberative judgment . . .

This five-step framework combines the element of gathering facts and a theoretical section (i.e., deontological principles) with a practical structure for solving
campus ethical problems.

Wilcox and Ebbs (1992)

Two years later in an *ASHE-ERIC Higher Education Report*, John Wilcox and
Susan Ebbs proposed an ethical framework in their monograph, *The Leadership
Compass: Values and Ethics in Higher Education* (1992). As the founding director
for the Center for Professional Ethics at Manhattan College and an associate
vice-president and the dean of Student Life at St. John's University in New York,
respectively, Wilcox and Ebbs focus their coverage on ethical issues relating to
campus leaders, faculty, students, and the entire learning community.

Their ethical decision-making framework is based on the premise that
essentially deontological principles should be integrated into the ethical decisions made in every aspect of campus life. Their main inspiration came from
the University of Denver Counseling Psychology Professor Karen Kitchener's
(1985) chapter "Ethical Principles and Ethical Decisions in Student Affairs," which
explores various principles for ethical action. They also considered Reynolds
and Smith's (1990) code of professional ethics and Kitchener's (1985) two-level
cognitive moral model. In their framework, Wilcox and Ebbs (1992: 39–40)
employ five principles:

1. Respecting autonomy . . .
2. Doing no harm . . .
3. Benefitting others . . .
4. Being just . . .
5. Being faithful . . .

These principles are to be used to review actions proposed to resolve a dilemma,
and "overturned only by stronger ethical obligations, related to doing the least
amount of avoidable harm" (Wilcox & Ebbs 1992: 40). Ethical dilemma resolution
is further tied to identifying "the moral dimension in the situation" and allowing
the political aspects of the problem to be recognized (Wilcox & Ebbs 1992: 40).
In short, their guideline suggests that a careful analysis of the situation and the
development of a proposed response, which should be reviewed according to
these five deontologically framed principles, would result in ethical decision
making.

One of the more insightful comments that these authors make is that professional codes of ethics are "insufficient." Wilcox and Ebbs believe that such codes

are unhelpful in complicated situations because they lack context (a knowledge or understanding of case details) and often provide conflicting advice on what action to pursue. This key insight pointed to the need for a broader framework than just a professional code of ethics (Wilcox & Ebbs 1992: 39).

Strike and Moss (1997)

Addressing directly ethical issues for student affairs, University of Syracuse Education Professor Kenneth A. Strike and Cornell University Pam Moss's book, *Ethics and College Student Life* (1997), bridges the ethical frameworks approach in the general academic ethics treatments from the early 1990s to the next decade. Their general framework for ethical decision making follows the typical pattern of deontological principles up to that time, yet they expand their scope to include other classical applied ethical theories and direct application of virtue ethics. In this sense, they embrace a nascent approach sympathetic to my own foundational normative method (Goodchild 1986, 1992) by including other applied ethical theories within their guidelines. Thus, Strike and Moss (1997: 4–7) offer five principles, yet broaden considerably their scope:

1. Benefit maximization [i.e., consequences associated with utilitarianism;] ...
2. Equal respect for persons and consistency [i.e., rules associated with deontology;] ...
3. Relationship [e.g., caring, respect, and love associated with personal virtue;] ...
4. Community [e.g., well-ordered communities associated with communal virtues;] ... [and] ...
5. Character growth [e.g., developing as a virtuous person.]

The above cluster of deontological statements is linked to the broader explanation of different traditional theories and virtues. In other words, the authors extend their analysis to other traditional ethical theories and historic personal and communal virtues, as particularly espoused by Aristotle and later by Alaisdair MacIntyre in his *After Virtue* (1984). Strike and Moss accompany their ethical principles with a three-page discussion in which they explore the classical virtue ethics and traditional ethical theories in an abbreviated fashion.

This early effort to bridge what up to that time had been a basic deontological approach with other foundational theories demonstrates nonetheless a rather circumscribed analysis. As only these short paragraph-long commentaries are provided, the reader would have to explore elsewhere if interested. In the rest of the case book, the deontological statements are explored in relation to various problems on campus. For example, in the chapter, "On Getting a Life," the authors look at forming an identity, choosing a career, and dealing with divorce.

In particular, Strike and Moss address benefit maximization, relationships, and character growth in responding to the case.

Such an approach is really a nascent attempt to extend beyond the Kitchener (1985) approach of using deontological maxims, such as "Do no harm," as a basic guide to decision making. Here our authors, without much formal philosophical or applied ethical exposition, broach the link to using traditional ethical theories in academic ethics in a pragmatic way. This approach signaled a shift in educational approaches, which had greater success during the next decade.

Complex Foundational Applied Ethical Frameworks

The next three ethical frameworks were advanced with the addition of the traditional ethical theories, virtue theory, and religious ethics into decision-making considerations. Strike and Moss (1997) introduced this approach in academic ethics, yet, as in most initial efforts, the nascent inclusion was not fully integrated into the framework or explored with any conceptual depth. Other efforts before and since have maximized this (what I have called) foundational approach by being more explicit in decision-making steps and more explanatory in the framework. These models are thus foundational, for they integrate these traditional philosophical and religious theories fully into their frameworks. I discuss these three frameworks next.

Goodchild (1986)

For eight years at DePaul University in Chicago, I taught a business ethics course while completing my doctoral work in higher education at the University of Chicago. The School of Commerce there organized a regional symposium on teaching business ethics. From that conference, we edited one issue of the *Journal of Business Ethics*. My article, "Toward a Foundational Normative Method in Business Ethics" (1986: 492–6), proposed the more complex approach described earlier and then suggested a five-step method for making moral decisions. This passionate interest in assisting others led to the creation of an ethical framework for making professional decisions while I was a senior partner in the Carl M. Williams Ethics Institute at the University of Denver. There I taught an academic ethics course to master's and doctoral students in the Higher Education Program and, over this ten-year period, created, with the assistance of those students, a 3,000-case *The Chronicle of Higher Education* database of ethical problems in the academy (Goodchild 1992). Similarly, now at the Santa Clara University, as scholar in its Markkula Center for Applied Ethics, I continue to teach an academic ethics course to our master's students in higher education and co-teach an educational ethics course to our graduate students in K–12 teacher education and principal preparation programs.

The complex foundational applied ethics framework that I created in 1986 brought together four major groups of ethical theory and religious moral theory (namely, deontology, utilitarianism, religious ethics, and theological virtue) so that practitioners could employ the different conceptual dimensions to gain the greatest justification for their decisions. This foundational normative method as a decision-making framework comprises five stages (Goodchild 1986: 496):

1. Is the contemplated decision or action right or wrong according to universal maxims or norms within the context of the community, nation, or international scene?
2. Does the contemplated decision or action lead to good or bad consequences for an individual, a group, or the community?
3. Does the contemplated decision or action endorse or violate the individual or community's notion of divine commands or religious laws thereby representing holy or evil (sinful) action?
4. Does the contemplated decision or action endorse or violate certain theological virtues thereby representing virtuous or vicious action? . . .
5. Will the proposed decision or action benefit or harm the physical or psychological well-being of those persons affected by their decision or action?

What I maintained in this article was the necessity of embracing a complex ethical framework that requires both a philosophical and a theological enterprise if it is to be successful in a more global society. Acknowledging and respecting both individual's and group's religious perspectives reflected an important addition to the typical rational considerations. The next, more complex, frameworks furthered this type of broad scope.

Markkula Center for Applied Ethics (2009)
The Markkula Center for Applied Ethics at Santa Clara University, one of the largest of its kind in the country, explores ethical issues in business, government, medicine, and character education. In 2007, this Center's scholars created a framework for making ethical decisions, "A Framework for Thinking Ethically," and in 2009, they updated that framework. The original leading author was Manuel Velasquez, author of the well-known business ethics book, *Business Ethics: Concepts and Cases* (2005). Additional contributors to the framework included Kirk O. Hanson (the Center's current executive director and the John Courtney Murray, S.J. University Professor in Social Ethics), Claire Andre (a former director of the Center), and five other Santa Clara faculty members (Thomas Shanks, Michael J. Meyer, Margaret R. McLean, David DeCosse, and Dennis Moberg). Together, they composed an ethical decision-making framework that is also complex in its effort to include broad philosophical and human rights perspectives. The 2009 version of this framework has ten steps subsumed under five main tasks (Markkula Center for Applied Ethics 2009):

Recognize an Ethical Issue
1. Could this decision or situation be damaging to someone or to some group? Does this decision involve a choice between a good and bad alternative, or perhaps two "goods" or between two "bads"?
2. Is this issue about more than what is legal or what is most efficient? If so, how?

Get the Facts
3. What are the relevant facts of this case? What facts are not known? Can I learn more about the situation? Do I know enough to make a decision?
4. What individuals and groups have an important stake in the outcome? Are some concerns more important? Why?
5. What are the options for acting? Have all the relevant persons and groups been consulted? Have I identified creative options?

Evaluate Alternative Actions
6. Evaluate the options by asking the following questions:
   • Which option will produce the most good and do the least harm? (The Utilitarian Approach)
   • Which option best respects the rights of all who have a stake? (The Rights Approach)
   • Which option treats people equally or proportionately? (The Justice Approach)
   • Which option best serves the community as a whole, not just some members (The Common Good Approach)
   • Which option leads me to act as the sort of person I want to be? (The Virtue Approach)

Make a Decision and Test It
7. Considering all these approaches, which option best addresses the situation?
8. If I told someone I respect—or told a television audience—which option I have chosen, what would they say?

Act and Reflect on the Outcome
9. How can my decision be implemented with the greatest care and attention to the concerns of all stakeholders?
10. How did my decision turn out and what have I learned from this specific situation?

What is particularly interesting about this framework is its reflection of broad traditional and emerging philosophical approaches to applied ethics. Its five ethical standards (utilitarianism, rights, fairness or justice ethics, common good, and virtue ethics) focus not only on rationales for decision making but also on embracing virtue ethics. In other words, this framework reflects a concern for developing persons of virtue with moral dispositions, which can lead to the formation of ethical habits. Another important feature of this framework centers on its effectiveness in implementation and concern for learning from experience. Again, its complexity reflects one of the highest levels of scope and justification as an ethical decision-making framework in our considerations here.

Goodchild (2010)

In teaching academic ethics and educational ethics at Santa Clara University, my colleague Steve Johnson and I have encouraged our students to review these various ethical frameworks (e.g., Boss 2008; Goodchild 1986; Johnson & Ridley 2008) as a way of understanding different ethical frameworks. As part of our courses, they individually develop a personal ethical framework and, after sharing it with their discussion group, they together create one for the entire group. These frameworks usually demonstrate a serious consideration of the ethical theories and religious theories presented in the course. Their contributions and my own reflections have led me to recast my foundational normative method framework in the following way, "Creating a Moral Method for Academic Ethics" (2010). This nine-step framework with three major tasks incorporates (1) greater attention to the problem or case itself; (2) inclusion of professional codes of ethics; (3) greater clarity concerning the various ethical and religious theories; and (4) a new focus on its implementation and reflections on its outcome.

Analyzing the Ethical Problem and Case

1. Carefully analyze the proposed problem and case and identify a solution.
2. Review the legal aspects of the problem and solution as well as consider the appropriate professional code of ethics.

Using the Foundation Ethical Theories

3. Does the proposed resolution follow or violate any principles or rules? (The deontological question)
4. What are the consequences of the proposed resolution? (Does it result in the greatest good for the greatest number of people—the utilitarian/consequentialist question)
5. Does the proposed resolution follow or violate any virtues or values? (The virtue ethics question)
6. Does the proposed resolution follow or violate any religious ethics rules or norms? (The religious ethics question)
7. Most importantly, does the proposed resolution uphold the major

deontological principle of all ethical decision making ("Do no harm")?

Implementing the Proposed Solution
  8. Discuss proposed solution with all affected persons and parties.
  9. Implement decision and monitor its outcome.

This foundational approach comprises a normative decision-making framework for making professional ethical decisions that embrace philosophical ethics, virtue theory, and theological/religious ethics. In this way, decision making can be justified from deep applied ethical and religious ideas. As the goal of professional decision making remains to insure that no harm is done and that the maximization of good occurs, the broader foundation scope propels our decision making to the highest possible cognitive level.

Four Elements for Applied Ethical Decision-Making Frameworks

In reviewing these eight frameworks, there are some general themes that constitute the critical components necessary for a fully integrated approach anchored to the historic foundations of applied ethics. In other words, as academic ethics seeks to move into the mainstream of applied professional ethics, along with medical, business, and legal ethics, it needs a sophisticated decision-making framework that offers a solid guide to taking a moral position, implementing a moral decision, and being able to fully justify this suggested resolution. The four themes are:

  1. Focus on the case—conduct a thorough understanding of the case with detailed analysis of the facts, problem, and parties involved in the situation.
  2. Reflect on laws and professional codes—use appropriate laws and professional codes of ethics to understand all aspects of the problem and case.
  3. Incorporate foundational theories—consider the traditional foundational approach, including the ethical theories, related virtues, and theological/religious ethics, in reviewing the moral dimensions of the problem and case as well as its resolution.
  4. Collaborate and assess—seek to implement the resolution by collaborating with all affected parties and review its outcomes.

For almost 200 years, applied ethicists have employed a complex theoretical approach to resolving ethical dilemmas. We need to understand and appreciate this history, and embrace it, as we create new frameworks for aiding individuals to assume responsibility for acting ethically and resolving ethical problems in the academy.

Conclusion

The field of academic ethics is ostensibly twenty-seven years old, having formally been launched with the publication of Edward Shils's *The Academic Ethics* (1983). This volume, *Creating the Ethical Academy*, offers one of the most comprehensive overviews of the ethical problems and issues in the emerging field of academic ethics since that time. This chapter provides a more formal professional framework for campus actors to resolve their ethical problems than only a set of deontological ideas, for example "Do no harm," or mandates contained in various valuable codes of professional ethics. The complexity of ethical dilemmas on campus requires a comparable approach that enables individuals to take more responsibility in changing our typical campus cultures or climates to create the ethical academy. Using a foundational normative method for resolving moral problems through a professional framework for making ethical decisions empowers campus decision makers when faced with difficult moral problems in college and university life.

Notes

1. This reflection updates my foundational normative method in the *Journal of Business Ethics* (Goodchild 1986). I am reformulating this method's theoretical structure after having taught academic ethics for fourteen years at the University of Denver and Santa Clara University.
2. See http://www.academicintegrity.org (accessed 11 June 2010) for the *Fundamentals* pamphlet.
3. See http://www.naspa.org/about/standards.cfm (accessed 11 June 2010) for more information.

References

Albert, E.M., Denise, T.C., and Peterfreund, S.P. (1975) *Great Traditions in Ethics*, 3rd edn, New York: D. Van Nostrand.
Aristotle (1985) *Nicomachean Ethics*, trans. Terence Irwin, Indianapolis, IN: Hackett Publishing.
Beauchamp, T.L. (1982; 3rd edn 2001) *Philosophical Ethics: An Introduction to Moral Philosophy*, New York: McGraw-Hill.
Bentham, J. (1789, 1907) *An Introduction to the Principles of Morals and Legislation*, London: Clarendon Press.
Boss, J.A. (1998; 2001; 2004; 4th edn 2008) *Ethics for Life: A Text with Readings*, Boston: McGraw-Hill Higher Education.
Center for Academic Integrity. (1999) *The Fundamental Values of Academic Integrity*, Durham, NC: Center for Academic Integrity. Available at http://www.academicintegrity.org/fundamental_values_project/pdf/FVProject.pdf (accessed 5 July 2008).
Goodchild, L.F. (1986) 'Toward a foundational normative method in business ethics', *Journal of Business Ethics*, 5(6): 485–500.
—— (1992) 'Advancing the study of academic ethics: A taxonomy and database for higher education'. Paper presented at the American Educational Research Association annual meeting in Minneapolis, MN, November 1992.
—— (2010) 'Creating a moral method for academic ethics'. Presentation given at Santa Clara University, Santa Clara, CA, March 2010.
Gustafson, J.M. (1981) *Ethics from a Theocentric Perspective: Theology and Ethics*, Chicago: University of Chicago Press.
Hauerwas, S. (1994) *Character and the Christian Life: A Study in Theological Ethics*, Notre Dame, IN: University of Notre Dame Press.
Hutchinson, D.S. (1995) 'Ethics', in J. Barnes (ed.) *The Cambridge Companion to Aristotle*, Cambridge: Cambridge University Press.

Johnson, W.B. and Ridley, C.R. (2008) *The Elements of Ethics for Professionals*, New York: Palgrave Macmillan.

Kant, I. (1785, 1969) *The Foundations of the Metaphysics of Morals*, trans. Lewis White Beck, Indianapolis, IN: Bobbs-Merrill.

Kitchener, K.S. (1985) 'Ethical principles and ethical decisions in student affairs', in H. Canon and R. Brown (eds) *Applied Ethics in Student Services*, San Francisco: Jossey Bass.

MacIntyre, A. (1966) *A Short History of Ethics*, New York: Macmillan.

—— (1981; 2nd edn 1984) *After Virtue*, Notre Dame, IN: University of Notre Dame Press.

—— (1988) *Whose Justice? Which Rationality?*, Notre Dame, IN: University of Notre Dame Press.

—— (1990) *Three Rival Versions of Moral Enquiry: Encyclopaedia, Genealogy, and Tradition*, Notre Dame, IN: University of Notre Dame Press.

Markkula Center for Applied Ethics. (2009) *A Framework for Thinking Ethically*, Santa Clara, CA: Santa Clara University. Available at http://www.scu.edu/ethics/practicing/decision/framework. html (accessed 18 August 2010).

May, W.W. (ed.) (1990) *Ethics and Higher Education*, New York: American Council on Education/ Macmillan Series on Higher Education.

Moore, S.L. (ed.) (2008) *Practical Approaches to Ethics for Colleges and Universities*, San Francisco: Jossey Bass.

National Association Student Personnel Administrators. (2010) 'Standards of professional practice'. Available at http://www.naspa.org/about/standards.cfm (accessed 9 March 2010).

Niebuhr, H.R. (1963) *The Responsible Self: An Essay in Christian Moral Philosophy*, New York: Harper & Row.

Noddings, N. (1984) *Caring: A Feminine Approach to Ethics and Moral Education*, Berkeley, CA: University of California Press.

Quinn, P.L. (1978) *Divine Commands and Moral Requirements*, Oxford, Clarendon Press.

Reynolds, C.H. and Smith, D.C. (1990) 'Academic principles of responsibility', in W.W. May (ed.) *Ethics and Higher Education*, Phoenix, AZ: American Council on Education/Macmillan.

Roper, L. and Longerbeam, S. (2002) 'Modeling community through campus leadership', in W.W. McDonald and Associates, *Creating Campus Community: In Search of Ernest Boyer's Legacy*, San Francisco: Jossey-Bass.

Shils, E. (1983) *The Academic Ethic: The Report of a Study Group of the International Council on the Future of the University*, Chicago: University of Chicago Press.

Sidgwick, H. (1891) *The Methods of Ethics*, London: Macmillan.

Strike, K.A. and Moss, P.A. (1997) *Ethics and College Student Life*, Needham Heights, MA: Allyn and Bacon.

Sykes, C.J. (1988) *ProfScam: Professors and the Demise of Higher Education*, New York: St. Martin's Press.

Velasquez, M.G. (2005) *Business Ethics: Concepts and Cases*, 6th edn, Upper Saddle River, NJ: Prentice Hall.

Wilcox, J.R. and Ebbs, S.L. (1992) *The Leadership Compass: Values and Ethics in Higher Education*, ASHE-ERIC Higher Education Reports, No. 1, Washington, DC: George Washington University.

10

Enacting Transcendental Leadership

Creating and Supporting a More Ethical Campus

ADRIANNA J. KEZAR AND CECILE SAM

As mentioned in previous chapters, in changing the university as a whole—to the "ethical academy"—we must look further to the unifying factors that create the overall culture and philosophy of the institution (Sanders, Hopkins, & Geroy 2003). We see leadership, more specifically "transcendental leadership," as one of the key factors toward creating and supporting an overall ethical campus culture, encompassing all constituents: faculty, staff, students, and administration.

Burns (1978) proposes that one of the main differences between manage-ment and leadership is that leadership is inherently an ethical practice. His concept of "transformational leadership" clearly ties moral and ethical aims to the actions of leaders. As leaders strive for change, they must think about the ethical underpinnings of the direction they are advocating and the culture they are creating through these actions. Over time, researchers and scholars have added to the concept of transformational leadership and describe "transcendental leadership"—in which the leaders must not only examine the ethical ends of the change agenda and their interactions with others, but also build the ethical capacity of others (Cordona 2000; Sanders, et al. 2003). Transcendental leaders support the personal development of people, specifically creating more ethical motivations, ethical behaviors, and ultimately an ethical culture (Cordona 2000). The connection between leaders and an ethical culture requires a thoughtfulness of action on the part of leaders.

The establishment of an ethical culture in an institution is a necessary component in building an ethical academy, and should be foremost in the minds of leaders at the institution. Unfortunately, building an ethical culture has not been heavily researched in academic settings, so we must turn to other disciplines for empirical evidence, such as business and psychology.[1] According to the literature, *the cultivation of an ethical culture—focusing on values, norms, and basic assumptions—trumps lone bureaucratic efforts (a superficial cultural change), such as establishing codes of conduct* (Douglas, Davidson, & Schwartz 2001; Kelley, Agle, & DeMott 2005; Trevino, Weaver, & Reynolds 2006; Udas, Fuerst, & Paradice 1996). We focus on the leadership practices and organizational levers that consistently have been proven to impact ethical behavior, as shown through multiple research studies. Thus, we begin this chapter by explaining our underlying premise—that maintaining an ethical culture is the most important condition for creating an ethical academy—and then we move on to examine how college administrators, through a transcendental leadership style, can create a culture of ethicality by fostering their own leadership, building a cadre of transcendental leaders on campus, and using organizational levers for change.

Why Is Culture so Important?

Altering the organizational culture of the institution is the best way to create an ethical organization. Various studies have identified how ethical structures can be in place, such as codes of conduct, but ethical awareness, decision making, and conduct do not necessarily follow (Douglas, et al. 2001; Kelley, et al. 2005; Udas, et al. 1996). A disconnect between ethical structures and ethical behaviors can result if the actual culture of the organization encourages and rewards unscrupulous behavior. Culture is the glue that makes ethical practices stick. Schein (1992) stresses that all three levels of organizational culture—basic assumptions, values and norms, and artifacts and structures (such as codes of conduct or sanctioning programs)—need to be addressed by organizational leaders if they want to change the ethical direction of an institution. Schein cautions that leaders tend to focus on visible artifacts and ignore the values and basic assumptions. In addition, it is important to lead with basic assumptions, norms, and values because, unless those have been addressed, changing artifacts will create confusion and resistance.

Schein (1992) further argues that the behavior of leaders is the primary mechanism for embedding culture—how they react, allocate resources, coach, reward and punish, hire and fire not only establishes the underlying assumptions and values of the organization, but also provides concrete cues to the other members of the institution regarding acceptable behavior and decision making. If ethical artifacts are not supported with the behaviors of leadership, then employees are more likely to ignore the ethical structures in place. Hence, the rest of this chapter describes how leaders can build an ethical culture necessary to elicit consistent ethical behavior from members of an institution.

Transcendental Leadership

Leadership is one of the key components to organizational change and recreating culture, especially in institutions of higher education (Kezar, Carducci, & Contreras-McGavin 2006). When looking for change of an ethical nature, the type of leadership that takes place is of vital importance. We argue that transcendental leadership has the potential to move the institution toward the ethical academy, and the very nature of transcendental leadership fits well into the existing culture of higher education. However, to better understand transcendental leadership, we must first understand this form of leadership in relation to both transactional and transformational leadership styles.

Both transactional and transformative leadership styles place an emphasis on what followers are able to produce in an organization. Transactional leadership focuses on formalized and established roles that occur within a traditional hierarchy (Cordona 2000; Sanders, et al. 2003). In many ways, this leadership is "transactional" because there is an economic exchange between leader and the follower. Transactional leaders influence others through setting goals, establishing and communicating preferred outcomes, and controlling rewards and punishments (Dvir, Eden, Avolio, & Shamir 2002). Transformational leadership incorporates some elements of transactional leadership, but expands beyond a simple exchange of work for reward (Dvir, et al. 2002). Rather, transformational leaders in many ways inspire followers and convince them to align their goals with the goals of the organization. This shift is achieved through intrinsic rewards, open communication, and providing the support necessary for followers to have the confidence to not only achieve set goals, but also to want to go beyond the expected requirements of the position (Bass & Avolio 1994). In an "ends–means" distinction, both leadership styles lean more in the direction of the individual as a means to achieving the goals of the organization. Relying on external rewards, job descriptions, goal orientations, persuasion and inspiration, though positive in their own right, does not necessarily entail the empowerment of the individual person when left to her own devices. These styles may work well in the hierarchical structures found in many organizations, where roles and chains of command are clearly defined. However, organizational structures that require more autonomy—such as loosely coupled networks, like colleges and universities—may rely more on the individual to make decisions without the usual oversight found in other environments. For example, faculty teach and students conduct their academic work largely "in private," that is, without anyone overseeing every step of their work. Transcendental leadership fits well into this type of structure. Rather than emphasizing the outcomes of individuals, transcendental leadership sees individuals as "ends"—developing them to be better people and exemplars in their own right (Cardona 2000).

Transcendental leadership emphasizes a spiritual component with three dimensions: consciousness, moral character, and faith (Sanders, et al. 2003). Consciousness is developed meaning-making; moral character is defined as the latter stages of Kohlberg's moral development model—universal principles of morality; and, finally, faith is defined as not necessarily an issue of religion, but a way of making sense of one's existence (Fowler 1981 as cited by Sanders, et al. 2003). Although still incorporating many of the aspects of both transactional and transformational leadership, transcendental leadership aims to develop individuals as transcendental leaders rather than maintaining them as followers (Fry 2003; Korac-Kakabadse, Kouzmin, & Kakabadse 2002). More than inspiration and persuasion, transcendental leadership looks to changing the very value structures and beliefs of the individual through empowerment and example.

Transcendental leadership is ultimately a style of leadership that bases itself on service, community building, and collaboration (Cordona 2000; Fry 2003)—aspects that are important in institutions of higher education. Rather than relying on hierarchical organizational structures to establish legitimacy and maintain influence, transcendental leaders rely on a sense of unity and care for others to work toward mutual goals (Fry 2003). Thus, faculty, staff, administrators, and students throughout the institution can be transcendental leaders who are all contributing to the shaping of the ethical academy.

Leaders Shaping Ethical Cultures

Being a moral exemplar has numerous effects that radiate beyond the individual leader. Over the past thirty years, studies in business consistently demonstrate that "significant others" (usually leaders or direct supervisors) have an influence on ethical decision making—positive and negative (Neubert, Carlson, Kacmar, Roberts, & Chonko 2009; O'Fallon & Butterfield 2005; Zabid & Alsagoff 1993). This influence was explored throughout Part II of this volume as we saw how teachers can affect the ethical conduct of students, organizational leaders can affect the conduct of staff, and coaches can affect the conduct of athletes. Although one's immediate supervisor may have the greatest influence on ethical behavior (Zabid & Alsagoff 1993) because of the frequency and level of interaction (Trevino, et al. 2006), studies on exemplary ethical organizational cultures demonstrate that peers and senior executives are also critical to the creation of a culture of ethics (Bowen 2004). It is through the commitment of resources, "personal actions and interpersonal relationships, and the promotion of [ethical] conduct . . . through two-way communication, reinforcement and decision-making" (Trevino, et al. 2006: 967) that moral exemplars can establish social norms, convey organizations' values, increase job satisfaction, and develop the moral reasoning of others.

First, the behavior of leaders establishes the behaviors that are acceptable or unacceptable in an organization—the social norms. Those in positions of formal or legitimate authority have this power to shape organizational or social norms. When people look toward others for behavioral cues, they often turn to those with more authority (Pearce, Kramer, & Robbins 1997; Sims & Brinkmann 2003). If others observe the supervisor (the instructor in the case of students) acting unethically, the implication is that such behavior is rewarded and valued (Sims & Brinkmann 2003). However, if the supervisor acts ethically and upholds ethical standards for others, then organizational members are much more likely to act ethically as well. Not only do "salient authority figures ... have the power to gain [organizational members'] attention and to hold them accountable to ethical standards" but "ethical leaders" are able to influence behavior through "social exchange and norms of reciprocity" (Trevino, et al. 2006: 967). Those in positions of formal authority also then have an impact on the ways that followers understand the reigning values and goals of the organization (White & Lean 2008). Numerous studies on ethical failures in the workplace find that employees often gauge what is more important in the organization by the reward and punishment structures (Sims & Brinkmann 2003; Trevino, et al. 2006). If unethical behavior is rewarded and ethical behavior ignored or even punished, organizational members learn what the organization truly values, rather than what the organization may say it values. For example, when institutions place heavy emphasis on the number of articles published in order to obtain tenure, the message sent to researchers is that quantity matters more than quality (Anderson, Ronning, De Vries, & Martinson 2007). As a result, many researchers admit to publishing findings prematurely or publishing those findings not yet able to be repeated (for more information, see chapter 6 in this volume).

Second, the behaviors and values of ethical leaders also influence employee job satisfaction and organizational commitment (Brown & Trevino 2006; May, Gilson, & Harter 2004). For example, organizational leaders who use ethical reasoning in decision making positively shape the attitudes of the organizational members toward work resulting in greater job satisfaction, organizational commitment, and retention (Schminke, Ambrose, & Neubaum 2005). The literature suggests that this effect is a result of norms of reciprocity—ethical leaders are more dedicated to others, and commitment *to* others often elicits commitment *from* others.

Finally, the literature demonstrates that ethical role modeling affects individual moral reasoning, development, and conduct. For example, Trevino and colleagues (2006) found that business leaders with strong moral development scores are more likely to have ethical employees than those business leaders who score lower on moral development tests. Zhu (2008) found that ethical leadership actually developed senses of moral identity and development. Zhu ascribes this trend to the idea that ethical leaders are more likely to respect autonomy, be inclusive in decision making, and encourage full engagement at work, leading to a sense of empowerment and strengthened moral identity. In higher education, ethical role modeling can occur in all types of interactions, such as between faculty and students (either in the classroom or in the advisement capacity), students and students (e.g., in student government or student organizations), or faculty and administrators (e.g., in shared governance).

Ultimately, transcendental leadership looks to develop the individual as an ethically autonomous person who will also become a moral exemplar. Personal factors and attributes are complex to shape, but leaders and organizational culture can influence them. Zhu (2008: 63) found that ethical leadership shapes followers' sense of moral identity—"the convergence of moral ideas with one's personal identity"—and those people with a high sense of moral identity tend to behave in ethically consistent ways. Functioning in an ethical culture with appropriate role models can have a significant impact on the moral identity of an individual. The moral development of the individual goes beyond the organization to other facets of the individual's life. This development of a moral exemplar means that leaders can be found throughout the organization, and each type of leader (peers, immediate supervisors, senior administrators) has an impact on the organizational culture.

Most studies emphasize formal leadership positions, such as supervisors and managers, because they are often considered most influential because of their greater authority (White & Lean 2008). However, transcendental leadership is not limited to positions of formal authority. Transcendental leadership can be cultivated at all levels of an organization, including amongst peers. Again, people have frequent contact and intense interactions with not only immediate supervisors, but also peers. Being a moral exemplar amongst peers can also have positive effects on members of an organization; likewise unethical peers can have negative effects (Ferrell & Gresham 1985; Zey-Ferrell & Ferrell 1982).

The findings about peers are intriguing because higher education operates much less hierarchically than businesses, with characteristics such as shared governance; a complex system of authority between trustees, administrators, and faculty; professional autonomy; academic freedom; and multi-faceted and ambiguous goals. Many of these characteristics have been described as a professional bureaucracy, with a decentralized system reliant on the expertise and autonomy of the individual. Thus, faculty, students, and staff are often more likely to consider peers to be influential in their behavior, a higher education factor that constrains the ability of top-down leaders to create change, make decisions, and influence the organization (Birnbaum 1988; Kezar & Eckel 2002).

Especially with students, peers have a particularly strong influence on individual behavior and establishing ethical norms (McCabe, Trevino, & Butterfield 2001). Peer influence is often a key factor in the culture created amongst students themselves and how they interact with the academic culture. To know that peers can have a significant influence on ethical behavior reinforces the idea that leaders at all levels of the organization can be influential. In higher education—where power and influence are distributed through deans, department chairs, key faculty leaders, different staff subdivisions, student government, student clubs, or Greek associations—the knowledge that most direct supervisors and peers influence behavior is important for intervention strategies. In other words, it will not be enough for college presidents to declare their support for an ethical campus environment. This message will need to be reinforced by leaders throughout different units and divisions.

Key Organizational Levers

In the early part of this chapter we spoke directly about the role that transcendental leaders play in creating a culture supportive of ethical behavior. In this section we highlight four key organizational levers and aspects of the infrastructure that empirical research has shown to enhance ethical culture: training, a climate of co-operation, open communication, and a formalized code of ethics. All of these levers are mechanisms that help socialize members to the ethical commitments of the institution. These organizational levers can be more effective when combined with the individual and personal efforts of the transcendental leader.

Ethical Training

Training is the formal, professional development efforts by the organization to help people understand ethical decision making and the ethical commitments and values of the organization. Formal training is one method used to socialize members into the ethical culture. Most studies demonstrate that training tends to be more successful when it is longer term (all-day workshops or ongoing sessions over several weeks) and integrated into day-to-day routines rather than delivered through a short workshop or online class (King & Mayhew 2002). For example, ethics seminars can be integrated into monthly and weekly management meetings and regular organizational seminars and conferences (Bowen 2004). Incorporating ethics training through residential programs or student affairs would be a way to integrate ethics into the lives of students.

A key to successful ethical training is making the training specifically devoted to ethics, rather than making ethics a subtopic in a larger training program (King & Mayhew 2002). Knouse and Giacalone (1997) propose six components for successful ethics training: (1) provide a background on ethical judgment, philosophies, and heuristics; (2) ground such ideas in practical areas of concern related to the group (the ethical dilemmas of faculty may be different from the dilemmas of administration); (3) provide the established ethical rules of the organization, taking time to explain them; (4) allow for those in training to explore their own ethical tendencies and moral identity; (5) acknowledge the difficulties of ethical behavior and the realities of the situation; and (6) allow for time when trainees can go and apply ideas, and have them return for further reinforcement. Incorporating all six components involves an investment of both time and effort, something that cannot necessarily be achieved in a single, short session or solely through an online component without interaction from others. As for pedagogical strategies, the most effective seem to be "active learning, reflection and faculty–student interaction" (Mayhew & King 2008: 35). Faculty–student interaction entails mentorship and open dialogue. However, even the most favorable strategies do not have as much impact as simply teaching ethical content alone.

Unfortunately, higher education institutions lack a robust training infrastructure. Kelley and colleagues (2005) surveyed higher education institutions and found that only 30 percent of postsecondary institutions offer ethics training (compared with 70 percent of business organizations) and much of this is online. In addition, only 34 percent of postsecondary institutions report offering resources to obtain advice on ethical issues. Business organizations, on the other hand, report having many resources in place to advise employees on ethics and 73 percent have ethics hotlines to report misconduct and ask questions (Kelley, et al. 2005).[2] If there is no training in place or resources to understand codes of conduct or compliance programs, then there are no tools to reinforce appropriate behavior and unethical decisions are likely to be made. Therefore, one of the most important changes that leaders in colleges and universities can make is creating meaningful ethical training programs that are aligned with the effective practices described in the literature—in-depth, case based, with opportunities for discussion and dialogue among participants. Online programs, favored by higher education institutions, do not allow for the type of discussion that is necessary to inculcate ethical values.

Because higher education has so many different subcultures, training programs will also need to be developed with attention to the needs and values of different groups. For example, student training is likely to be more successful if it involves students in the training, is hands-on and experiential, and employs humor and fun. Faculty would likely want a training that is research based, describes the science behind ethical frameworks, and is didactic and dialogic in nature. Staff will appreciate training that deals with the practical problems and dilemmas and which allows them to describe challenges they face. Generic training is unlikely to be successful, and professional training experts who work with members of the different campus subcultures are most likely to create the best training programs. Mayhew and King (2008) also found that students who enrolled willingly into courses with explicit content regarding ethics showed the most gains. This willingness is something that transcendental leaders can foster through example, encouragement, and use of external and internal incentives.

Creating a Climate of Co-operation

Climates of co-operation are important levers used to encourage ethical behavior. Co-operative climates emphasize collegiality, openness, integrity, and trust among members of an organization; whereas competitive environments increase the propensity for unethical behavior (Hunt & Jennings 1997; Robertson & Rymon 2001). Competitive climates can lead to unethical behavior if people feel that they will be punished or lose out on some type of reward if they do not meet an established goal (Trevino, et al. 2006). A competitive environment can also lead to role conflict and a lack of clarity on the organizational goals that are most important (e.g., is it to create a good student affairs program or to generate revenue?). In addition, competitive environments reinforce organizational values of self-interest, while simultaneously reducing a sense of community and trust (Anderson, et al. 2007). For example, in chapter 6 of this volume, we saw that in highly competitive research environments there was a decline in open sharing of information, increases in sabotaging replication studies through omission, careless research, and interference in the peer review process. There was also a degradation of collegial relationships among graduate students, faculty, and professional peers in other institutions.

Leaders are positioned to influence the competitive or co-operative values of the organization by clarifying goals and roles, not creating too much pressure around meeting goals, and being careful about the messages they send related to competition. Ways to encourage a culture of co-operation over competition can begin with the influence of the transcendental leader. The emphasis on community needs over self-interest sets the tone for the rest of the community. With the current economic crisis and external and internal pressures placed upon colleges and universities, how leaders react to crises establishes the value structure (Sims & Brinkmann 2003). Modeling and rewarding behavioral choices made in favor of unity and collaborative endeavors help to foster a more co-operative culture. Hiring and firing practices are also structures that can be examined to determine if competition is the idea most valued. Trust is a key component to fostering a collaborative culture (Hosmer 1995; Wheelan 2005). In organizations with a competition-dominant culture, members often distrust not only leaders, but peers as well (Anderson, et al. 2007; Kulik, O'Fallon, & Salimath 2008; Sims & Brinkmann 2003).

It is unrealistic to argue that a competitive climate can be removed completely from higher education in place of a co-operative one. However, higher education does have a historic culture with systems that support co-operative values and norms (e.g., shared governance) and these could be leveraged to inculcate ethical behavior in the face of competitive pressures. Like training, reinforcing co-operative norms in the face of competitive pressures will require attention to different subcultures and the particular problems that they face. Staff face pressures in admissions (discussions need to be around pressures for enroll-ments and how these impact the diversity), in athletics (pressures for winning teams and branding opportunities), and in student affairs (pressures may stem from subjective decisions involving students). Faculty need to discuss and sort out pressures around research, in particular. Students face competitive pressure around performing in school and balancing work and school. All members should be made aware that, despite competitive pressures, they should look for alternatives or solutions that better support a climate of co-operation than one of competition.

Communication Forums and Open Deliberation

Various studies have identified how communication within the organization is a good predictor of ethical awareness, decision making, and conduct (e.g., Bowen 2004; Trevino, et al. 2006). As we have mentioned several times, open communication and deliberation produces an environment in which people can explore ethical choices and make better ones. A participative communication environment is open to employee input and reduces the hierarchical distance between employees and managers, making relationships less formal. Employees feel free to discuss ethical concepts, that their supervisors are not judging them, and that it will not impact their performance appraisal. In the case of higher education, a participative communication environment is open to input from all organizational members—students, faculty, staff, administration—and in some ways makes institutional leaders (such as presidents and provosts) less remote.

There is also the idea of "voice"—the "option chosen by those who are willing to stand up for ethical principles in the belief that change will result" (Boisjoly 1993: 59). Without some venue for "voice" to openly question and debate ethical issues, the school could easily slip into an institution that falls prey to groupthink, bias, or myopia which works against social justice or the public good. Voice can be fostered through both formal dissent channels and established, trusted, informal dissent channels. These dissent channels are vital to the empowerment of people so that they can feel that they have choices and options toward doing the ethical action (Cooper 2006).

The creation of communication forums is both a challenge and an opportunity in higher education. The shared governance process provides an opportunity for open deliberation and discussion of ethical decisions. In fact, many have suggested that shared governance has been the key infrastructure within postsecondary institutions to foster ethical decision making (Kezar 2004; Tierney 2006). Faculty and students are usually included formally in shared governance through faculty senate and student government bodies, but colleges and universities also include members in committees and ad hoc groups that deliberate various campus issues. Yet a challenge is that only a small number of students, faculty, and staff are involved in governance processes. Most faculty and students, in particular, work autonomously and are not shaped by these processes. Students, like faculty, have few forums where they meet as a whole, and so creating communication venues for diverse sets of students and faculty will be extremely challenging. Although staff do not always have formal governance structures, they do operate much like leaders in business and thus weekly routines (such as meetings) could be leveraged to have regular indications about ethics.

In addition, although these shared governance infrastructures exist, there has not been a conscious effort to connect ethical conversations, ethics training, codes of conduct, and other support systems to these deliberation processes. Leaders can examine the entire system of the campus and connect these emerging ethical infrastructures in order to support each other.

Codes of Conduct and Statements of Ethics

We describe codes of conduct last because, although they are important, they tend to be overemphasized and used in isolation. Studies of higher education demonstrate that codes of conduct are the only ethical infrastructure regularly in place, with 74 percent of the institutions having policies and codes (Kelley, et al. 2005). Research around codes of conduct shows that they often have varying degrees of success (Ford & Richardson 1994; O'Fallon & Butterfield 2005; Stevens 2008). However, upon further analysis of the various codes that exist, the reasons behind a code's effectiveness and ineffectiveness can be tied to various organizational factors. When an organization uses an ethical code to exert control over individuals, it fails to curtail unethical behavior (Stevens 2008). This failure is ascribed to the fact that ethical codes created to control behavior are often placed outside of the organizational structure and climate (Schwartz 2000; Trevino & Weaver 2003). Ethical codes are even more ineffectual when those in leadership positions fail to comply with the very codes they try to establish. To make matters worse, leaders who actively ignore ethical codes promote the idea that unethical behavior is not only acceptable, but the norm.

However, when implemented correctly, ethical codes can strengthen positive organizational culture and influence ethical decision making (Stevens 2008). Instead of requiring compliance, codes of ethics should place more emphasis on integrity—"encouraging shared commitment by employees [organizational members] to responsible self-managed conduct" (Thomas, Schermerhorn, & Dienhart 2004: 63). Codes of ethics have the greatest impact when they are actually embedded in the organizational culture. Grounding a code of ethics in an organizational culture can occur in numerous ways in higher education, some of them in tandem with the organizational levers already discussed in this chapter. The first is through training so that members of the organization are not only aware of the ethical code, but also have time to reflect, question, and further understand what the code entails (Stevens 2008; Weaver, Trevino, & Cochran 1999). The second is through clear and open communication lines, so that concerns and questions about the code as well as possible options for behavior can be discussed (Weeks & Nantel 1992). This element is especially important for staff and students who may not have an available person to discuss ethical issues. Often offices, such as student judicial affairs, respond to infractions rather than open concerns or proactive inquiries. For codes to be successful they must be upheld and any violations of the code appropriately sanctioned, ensuring that the organization gives the message that the ethical code is to be taken seriously (Scalet 2006; Stevens 2008). On all levels, when promoting a code of ethics, there should be clear accountability standards to ensure that there is some sense of order. These standards should "clarify the limits of authority and the lines of accountability" and hold people accountable for their conduct (Cooper 2006: 200). Finally, the key factor in successful implementation falls again to the existence of ethical role models—when exemplars uphold the moral ethical code, their behavior conveys the overall organizational culture and provides a guideline for everyone else to follow (Stevens 2008; Trevino & Weaver 2003; Weaver, et al. 1999).

In a study of an organization with an exemplary ethical culture, Bowen (2004) demonstrates that a statement of ethics, when implemented well, can support an ethical culture by providing a tangible framework that clearly and positively expresses the core values of the organization. As an executive and several employees noted in Bowen's study: "I always return to the central question when facing an ethical dilemma: what would the ethics statement have us do?" (Bowen 2004: 316–17). Thus, for those organizational members who already have a firm moral grounding, this code provides supplemental reassurance, and for those less sure it can provide guidelines for behavior and socialization.

Summary

Institutions of higher education can be prime environments for transcendental leadership to have a great impact on the ethical culture. Higher education institutions harbor some basic assumptions and values that are directed toward ethics. Colleges and universities are reputed to be altruistic institutions, adding to the greater good of society, and espousing various values of social justice, advocacy, and knowledge (Bergquist & Pawlak 2008). The non-profit component makes higher education institutions unique, as the goals and desired outcomes move beyond economic gain (Malloy & Agarwal 2003). Many of these are basic assumptions and values that can work toward an ethical academy, such as valuing equity over competition, or quality over quantity. Transcendental leaders can harness these positive assumptions and values to further change the organizational culture, which in turn supports the organizational levers making them more effective.

Concluding Thoughts

One of the most important messages to take from this chapter is that leaders can make a significant difference in the ethical climate/culture on college campuses. Study after study demonstrates that, more than codes of conduct or training, people respond to the expectations and norms of those around them. We can create organizational levers to support our words and deeds as leaders, but in the end it is the examples of people within the organization that create the ethical academy. Transcendental leadership allows for ethical leaders to emerge from all levels: faculty, administration, staff, and students. These leaders in turn will shape the culture and create more exemplars. Therefore, leadership training on campus that emphasizes ethics can be one of the most powerful ways to shape the ethical climate. Once leaders are in place, creating an ethical infrastructure can support their work, socialization processes, communication forums, codes of conduct, and co-operative climate codes.

Notes

1. Much of the literature upon which we will draw stems from the last forty years of research and writings in the business field because very little research has been conducted on ethics within the academy, particularly examining culture, leadership, or organizational levers or infrastructure. We focus on the leadership practices and organizational levers that, through multiple research studies, have been consistently proven to impact ethical behavior.
2. Although no colleges and universities reported having ethics hotlines in the study by Kelley and colleagues, some campuses may have later implemented them. The University of California is an example of one system that has.

References

Anderson, M.S., Ronning, E.A., De Vries, R., and Martinson, B.C. (2007) 'The perverse effects of competition on scientists' work and relationships', *Science Engineering Ethics*, 13: 437–61.

Bass, B.M. and Avolio, B.J. (1994) *Improving Organizational Effectiveness through Transformational Leadership*, Thousand Oaks, CA: Sage Publications.

Bergquist, W.H. and Pawlak, K. (2008) *Engaging the Six Cultures of the Academy*, San Francisco, CA: Jossey-Bass.

Birnbaum, R. (1988) *How Colleges Work: The Cybernetics of Academic Organization and Leadership*, San Francisco, CA: Jossey-Bass.

Boisjoly, R.M. (1993) 'Personal integrity and accountability', *Accounting Horizons*, 7: 59–69.

Bowen, S.A. (2004) 'Organizational factors encouraging ethical decision making: An exploration into the case of an exemplar', *Journal of Business Ethics*, 52: 311–24.

Brown, M.E. and Trevino, L.K. (2006) 'Socialized charismatic leadership, values congruence, and deviance in work groups', *Journal of Applied Psychology*, 91: 954–62.

Burns, J.M. (1978) *Leadership*, New York: Harper and Row.

Cooper, T.L. (2006) *The Responsible Administrator*, San Francisco, CA: Jossey-Bass.

Cordona, P. (2000) 'Transcendental leadership', *Leadership and Organization Development Journal*, 21: 201–6.

Douglas, P.C., Davidson, R.A., and Schwartz, B.N. (2001) 'The effect of organizational culture and ethical orientation on accountants' ethical judgment', *Journal of Business Ethics*, 34: 101–21.

Dvir, T., Eden, D., Avolio, B., and Shamir, B. (2002) 'Impact of transformational leadership on follower development and performance: A field experiment', *Academy of Management Journal*, 45: 735–44.

Ferrell, O.C. and Gresham, L.G. (1985) 'A contingency framework for understanding ethical decision making in marketing', *Journal of Marketing*, 49: 87–96.

Ford, R.C. and Richardson, W.D. (1994) 'Ethical decision making: A review of the empirical literature', *Journal of Business Ethics*, 13: 205–21.

Fry, L. (2003) 'Toward a theory of spiritual leadership', *Leadership Quarterly*, 14: 693–727.

Hosmer, L.T. (1995) 'Trust: The connecting link between organizational theory and philosophical ethics', *Academy of Management Review*, 20: 379–403.

Hunt, T.G. and Jennings, D.F. (1997) 'Ethics and performance: a simulation analysis of team decision making', *Journal of Business Ethics*, 16: 195–203.

Kelley, P.C., Agle, B.R., and DeMott, J. (2005) 'Mapping our progress: Identifying, categorizing and comparing universities' ethics infrastructure', *Journal of Academic Ethics*, 3: 205–29.

Kezar, A.J. (2004) 'What is more important to effective governance: Relationships, trust, leadership, or structures and formal processes?', *New Directions for Higher Education*, 127: 35–46.

Kezar, A. and Eckel, P. (2002) 'The effect of institutional culture on change strategies in higher education: Universal principles or culturally responsive concepts?', *Journal of Higher Education*, 73:.435–60.

Kezar, A.J., Carducci, R., and Contreras-McGavin, M. (2006) *Rethinking the "L" Word in Higher Education: The Revolution in Research on Leadership*, San Francisco, CA: Jossey-Bass.

King, P. and Mayhew, M. (2002) 'Moral development in higher education: Insights from the defining issues test', *Journal of Moral Education*, 31: 247–70.

Knouse, S.B. and Giacalone, R.A. (1997) 'Six components of successful ethics training', *Business and Society Review*, 98: 10–13.

Korac-Kakabadse, N., Kouzmin, A., and Kakabadse, A. (2002) 'Spirituality and leadership praxis', *Journal of Managerial Psychology*, 17: 165–82.

Kulik, B.W., O'Fallon, M.J., and Salimath, M.S. (2008) Do competitive environments lead to the rise and spread of unethical behavior? Parallels from Enron', *Journal of Business Ethics*, 83: 703–23.

McCabe, D.L., Trevino, L.K., and Butterfield, K.D. (2001) 'Dishonesty in academic environments', *Journal of Higher Education*, 71: 29–40.

Malloy, D.C. and Agarwal, J. (2003) 'Factors influencing ethical climate in a nonprofit organization: An empirical investigation', *International Journal of Nonprofit and Voluntary Sector Marketing*, 8: 224–50.

May, D.R., Gilson, R.L., and Harter, L.M. (2004) 'The psychological conditions of meaningfulness, safety and availability and the engagement of the human spirit at work', *Journal of Occupational and Organizational Psychology*, 77: 11–37.

Mayhew, M. and King, P. (2008) 'How curricular content and pedagogical strategies affect moral reasoning development in college students', *Journal of Moral Education*, 37: 17–40.

Neubert, M.J., Carlson, D.S., Kacmar, M.K., Roberts, J.A. and Chonko, L.B. (2009) 'The virtuous influence of ethical leadership behavior: Evidence from the field', *Journal of Business Ethics*, 90: 157–70.

O'Fallon, M.,J. and Butterfield K.D. (2005) 'The review of the empirical ethical decision making literature: 1996–2003', *Journal of Business Ethics*, 59: 375–413.

Pearce, J.A., Kramer, T.R., and Robbins, K. (1997) 'Effects of managers' entrepreneurial behavior on subordinates', *Journal of Business Venturing*, 12: 147–60.

Robertson, D.C. and Rymon, T. (2001) 'Purchasing agents' deceptive behavior: A randomized response technique study', *Business Ethics Quarterly*, 11: 455–515.

Sanders, J., Hopkins, W.E., and Geroy, G.D. (2003) 'From transactional to transcendental: Towards an integrated theory of leadership', *Journal of Leadership and Organizational Studies*, 9: 21–31.

Scalet, S. (2006) 'Prisoner's dilemmas, cooperative norms, and codes of business ethics', *Journal of Business Ethics*, 65: 309–23.

Schein, E.H. (1992) *Organizational Culture and Leadership*, New York, Jossey-Bass.

Schminke, M., Ambrose, M.L., and Neubaum, D.O. (2005) 'The effect of leader moral development on ethical climate and employee attitudes', *Organizational Behavior and Human Decision Processes*, 97: 135–55.

Schwartz, M. (2000) 'Why ethical codes constitute an unconscionable regression', *Journal of Business Ethics*, 23: 173–84.

Sims, R.R. and Brinkmann, J. (2003) 'Enron ethics (or: Culture matters more than codes)', *Journal of Business Ethics*, 45: 243–56.

Stevens, B. (2008) 'Corporate ethical codes: Effective instruments for influencing behavior', *Journal of Business Ethics*, 78: 601–9.

Thomas, T., Schermerhorn, J.R., and Dienhart, J.W. (2004) 'Strategic leadership of ethical behavior in business', *Academy of Management Executive*, 18: 56–66.

Tierney, W.G. (2006) *Trust and the Public Good: Examining the Cultural Conditions of Academic Work*, New York: Peter Lang Publishers.

Trevino, L.K. and Weaver, G.R. (2003) *Managing Ethics in Business Organizations: Social Scientific Perspectives*, San Jose, CA: Stanford University Press.

Trevino, L.K., Weaver, G.R., and Reynolds, S.J. (2006) 'Behavioral ethics in organizations: A review', *Journal of Management*, 32: 951–90.

Udas, K., Fuerst, W.L., and Paradice, D.B. (1996) 'An investigation of ethical perceptions of public sector professionals', *Journal of Business Ethics*, 15: 721–34.

Weaver, G., Trevino, L.K., and Cochran, P.L. (1999) 'Corporate ethics programs as controls systems: Influences of executive commitment and environmental factors', *Academy of Management Journal*, 42: 41–57.

Weeks, W.A. and Nantel, J. (1992) 'Corporate codes of ethics and sales force behavior: A case study', *Journal of Business Ethics*, 11: 753–60.

Wheelan, S. (2005) *The Handbook of Group Research and Practice*, Thousand Oaks, CA: Sage Publications.

White, D.W. and Lean, E. (2008) 'The impact of perceived leader integrity on subordinates in a work team environment', *Journal of Business Ethics*, 81: 765–78.

Zabid, A.R. and Alsagoff, S.K. (1993) 'Perceived ethical values of Malaysian managers', *Journal of Business Ethics*, 12: 331–7.

Zey-Ferrell, M. and Ferrell, O.C. (1982) 'Role-set configuration and opportunity as predictors of unethical behavior in organizations', *Human Relations*, 35: 587–604.

Zhu, W. (2008) 'The effect of ethical leadership on follower moral identity: The mediating role of psychological empowerment', *Leadership Review*, 8: 62–73.

11
Integrating Ethics Education Across the Education System

PETER A. KELLER

This chapter provides an overview of efforts for building and sustaining ethical knowledge, habits, and cultures across educational settings. It is based on the assumption that ethics education must be intentional and systematic in order to develop graduates who model personal integrity and are prepared to contribute positively to society.

The interest in ethics education is far from new in American culture, although the focus and methodologies have varied across time, sects, and geographic regions. Generally speaking, these variances stem from the ongoing struggle to determine which values should be taught and who should teach them. In the early 1600s, the puritans wanted to retain a connection between schooling and religion but by the late 1700s and early 1800s there came to be a realization that virtue, "defined roughly as the willingness to set aside purely selfish motives and work for the good of the larger society," could be taught despite differences between religions and cultures (McClellan 1999: 13). It was this concept of virtues education that enabled communities to see the increasing role that public schools could play in ethics education, despite the primary role retained by families, particularly mothers. There was also, at last, a recognition that the values often associated with beneficence—acts of kindness or doing good for others—serve as important foundations for ethical behavior (Beauchamp 2008).

The realization that schools can play a role in teaching ethics sustained an emphasis on character education across the eighteenth and nineteenth centuries (Arthur 2008). Dewey's work was particularly influential in establishing this idea and in shaping the methods. He advocated change in the existing authoritarian notions of moral education and emphasized the "social character" of schools as an instrument of moral education. Dewey (1909: 26) wrote that

the introduction of every method that appeals to the child's active powers, to his capacities in construction, production, and creation, marks an

169

opportunity to shift the centre of ethical gravity from an absorption which is selfish to a service which is social.

Dewey (1909: 40) further noted that

what the normal child continuously needs is not so much isolated moral lessons upon the importance of truthfulness and honesty, or the beneficent results that follow from a particular act of patriotism, as the formation of habits of social imagination and conception.

Dewey had the foresight to emphasize the development of "social intelligence" and the importance of a child's capacity to make ethical judgments as essential elements of education.

More recently education has focused on three complementary approaches—academic integrity, character development, and ethics education. There is considerable alignment between the values or virtues emphasized by these approaches even though they differ in their methodologies and foci.

The narrowest of these approaches has been focused on *academic integrity*, which emphasizes responsibility for one's own academic work and avoidance of various forms of academic dishonesty. One of the most articulate explications of this concept can be found within the International Center for Academic Integrity's (ICAI)[1] (1999: 1) *The Fundamental Values of Academic Integrity*, which states that "academic integrity is a commitment, even in the face of adversity, to five fundamental values: honesty, trust, fairness, respect, and responsibility. From these values flow principles of behavior that enable academic communities to translate ideals into action." Though articulated by the ICAI, these values (along with compassion) are shared by people across different cultures and nation-states (Kidder 2006). So although particular religious, social, or ethnic groups may adopt certain normative behaviors that they view as having a moral dimension, it is important to distinguish such social conventions from core moral values, which are more likely to be shared (Nucci 2008).

It is because of these widely shared moral values or principles that there exists the potential for most educational institutions to establish common ground for building programs of ethical education that are in alignment. Although shared values offer a framework for institutions that wish to promote ethical behavior and character development more broadly, the majority of schools and universities utilize them only to reduce academic cheating. This emphasis prevails largely because it is much more challenging to promote ethical decision making and behavior across all areas of responsibility. However, the evidence (e.g., Bertram Gallant 2008) suggests that genuine success in promoting integrity in the academy requires a more extensive focus on ethics that pervades all aspects of an institution's culture. The academy can choose not to engage ethics education directly, but either way, the institutional ethos will shape the quality of its members' moral thought and action.

The impact of an absence of intentional ethics education is a point that deserves more consideration. In the earlier chapter by Braxton, we saw that student and faculty incivilities shape and are shaped by the other. Writing about elementary education, Harmon and Jones (2005: 78) note that "the act of teaching is an inherently moral activity as it communicates the values, beliefs, and attitudes of the teacher." However, the teacher can also communicate the values, beliefs, and attitudes of the school, that is, the ethical values by which all are expected to work and study. From this perspective, it seems essential that educational institutions at all levels recognize their roles in the intentional development of ethical thought and action.

Intentional Ethics Education in Schools

Nucci and Narváez (2008) observe that 80 percent of states have some form of mandate for character education. The modern character education movement, which is closely linked with other efforts to promote moral education and has played an important role in establishing common ground for the reform of elementary and secondary schools, traces its roots to a variety of initiatives (e.g., Association for Moral Education n.d.; Murphy 2002; Rusnak 1998; Shumaker & Heckel 2007). Each in its own way recognizes that the complex relationships between schools, parents and families, religious institutions, and communities must be taken into account in designing education strategies and maintaining support for character education.

One way to do this is through an "integrated approach" in which character education is not a subject of study, but integrated into all subjects through lessons highlighting the values of "responsibility, respect, cooperation, hope, and determination" (Rusnak 1998: 4). Ideally, instructors not only teach the values but also model them in action, resulting in the teaching of associated behaviors that contribute to a positive and supportive school environment. With an integrated approach, there is a synergy between school administrators and board members, teachers, students, parents, and community as they work collaboratively to teach and model the values of character education.

Despite the sensibility of this integrated approach, there is far from universal agreement on the best character education methodologies (Nucci & Narváez 2008). However, there may be some common underlying principles that can be used to intentionally design character or ethics education. The Character Education Partnership, for example, identifies eleven principles that define character education focus, practice, and methodologies (Lickona, Schaps, & Lewis 2007). The focus, for example, should be on core ethical values and values-in-action (including thought, feeling, and behavior) in a way that fosters students' motivation and a caring community. The practice should be the creation of a comprehensive, intentional, and proactive curriculum that provides students with opportunities for moral action. And the methodologies should engage staff, families, and community members through shared leadership, the intentional modeling of the values and behaviors expected of students, and assessment of the character education initiative.

This focus on moral action, not just moral character, reflects a paradigm shift in character education that Davidson, Likona, and Khmelkov (2007, 2008) describe as combining "moral character" and "performance character." Their work is based on an extensive study of character development and student achievement in twenty-four high-performing secondary schools. By their definition,

> performance character consists of all those qualities that enable us to achieve to our highest potential in any performance environment (such as the classroom or workplace). Moral character consists of all those qualities that enable us to be our ethical best in relationships and roles as citizens.
>
> (Davidson, et al. 2007: 32)

The work of Davidson and colleagues suggests that schools focused on character development are more likely to promote a stronger commitment to performance character that will lead to academic success as well as personal and social responsibility.

Sound moral development, ethical decision making, and academic success may also be tied to social–emotional learning (SEL) (Elias 2006). The Collaborative for Academic, Social, and Emotional Learning (CASEL 2009) identifies an essential set of skills for academic and social–emotional learning that includes (1) self-awareness, (2) self-management, (3) social awareness, (4) relationship skills, and (5) responsible decision making. It also clarifies associated behavioral expectations for each school level. For example,

> with regard to *self-awareness*, children in the elementary grades should be able to recognize and accurately label simple emotions such as sadness, anger, and happiness. In middle school, students should be able to analyze factors that trigger their stress reactions. Students in high school are expected to analyze how various expressions of emotion affect other people.
>
> (CASEL 2009: 2)

Subsumed under each of these elements are various aspects of emotional development and maturity, as well as ethical thinking and action. Elias (2006: 7) proposes as a fundamental principle the notion that "effective, lasting academic learning and SEL are built on caring relationships and warm but challenging classroom and school environments." Put differently, the culture and climate of an educational setting in conjunction with goal setting and other aspects of instructional competence play critical roles in building a foundation for sustainable learning, as well as character development and ethical thinking and action.

Elias, Parker, Kash, Weissberg, and O'Brien (2008) offer a comparative analysis of social and emotional learning, moral education, and character education as approaches to the moral or character development of students. They note that "moral education focuses on values and social–emotional learning focuses on the skills and attitudes needed to function in relevant social environments" (Elias, et al. 2008: 248). They make the further distinction that, although moral education has concentrated on moral thinking and knowing, social–emotional learning has focused on problem solving. Despite these differences, Elias and colleagues (2008: 249) note that the two approaches converge in an appreciation of the interplay between "affect, behavior, and cognition" and the role that context plays in character and moral development. In other words, learning and durable ethical development require the emotional engagement of students within a supportive setting.

Such supportive settings may be found in the "schools of integrity" (Mirk 2007) being developed by the Institute for Global Ethics and the National Association of Independent Schools. Schools of integrity are those that emphasize an understanding of ethical principles as well as develop the critical thinking and decision-making skills needed to understand and resolve ethical dilemmas (Institute for Global Ethics 2009). Particularly important in schools of integrity is the development of cultures that support ethical thinking and action by leaders, instructors, and students within settings of trust. Finally, schools of integrity develop "ethical literacy" across all aspects of a school's culture.

The schools of integrity project identifies ten replicable practices: (1) make ethics and values a cross-cutting dimension of school culture; (2) promote critical thinking at every opportunity; (3) build relationships to build trust; (4) promote a culture of open feedback; (5) engage trustees in a focus on trust; (6) establish a tone at the top of the school that is in alignment with the values and that models and promotes professional growth; (7) promote a tolerance for ambiguity; (8) draw from the ranks among the school's faculty and staff to promote responsibility for teaching each other; (9) trust students with authentic input; and (10) make mistakes an opportunity for growth, not punishment (Mirk 2007: 25–6). These practices are aimed at building a strong positive ethos for promoting ethics because they are aimed at establishing collaborative responsibility for thinking and acting ethically.

Summary

What can we conclude from this brief overview of contemporary approaches to moral, character, and ethics education at primary and secondary levels? First, there is evidence of reasonably broad support for character or ethics education, and many schools and school systems have established some form of ethics or character education as a priority. Instructional methodologies vary, but there is a growing convergence on the need for integrated, multi-faceted approaches that are built around the development of age-appropriate critical thinking about moral or ethical dilemmas rather than the establishment of particular sets of rules. In addition, there appears to be significant potential in the integration of the social and emotional learning model, which has generated a considerable amount of empirical evidence to support its programming.

Second, the alignment of character or ethics education with the promotion of academic excellence is an important theme emerging from the work of Davidson and colleagues (2007, 2008). And third, ethics education should not be attempted without simultaneous attention to developing a school culture and climate that will support ethics and character development. This finding strongly suggests the importance of institutional leadership at all levels in determining the success of ethics education and the creation of the ethical academy (see chapter 10 for more on the importance of institutional leadership).

Promoting Ethics in Higher Education

Two decades ago Harvard president Derek Bok (1988) offered his analysis of the failure of higher education to thoughtfully address the development of ethical understanding and behavior in its students. Whether born of an increasing specialization of study, neglect, or fear of criticism from either the political left or right (Rocheleau & Speck 2007), for various reasons there has been a widespread failure among colleges and universities to address the ethical development of students in a systematic manner.

McClellan (1999) observed that a once-flourishing emphasis on moral education within colleges and universities was well into decline by the middle of the twentieth century. He linked the decline during this period to several factors, including a changing curriculum with a need to address expanding knowledge, a new emphasis on science and research, and the development of professional education. As programs of study grew more focused, there was generally less attention given to a core curriculum focused on various aspects of moral education and, at least for a period, more of a focus on ethical relativism.

The tendency toward specialized career, professional, and scientific curricula is seen by many as a barrier to a stronger core or liberal studies curriculum that might support more generalized ethical or character education. In fact, the value of higher education is often assessed by students, families, and legislators on the basis of its capacity to lead to employment, rather than its ability to prepare students for proficiency in any of the essential components of ethical behavior.

Contemporary efforts to promote the development of ethical thinking and behavior among college students might best be described as inconsistent, though some notable new directions are emerging. Pascarella and Terenzini (2005), based on their extensive study of how college affects students, discuss the impact of college on students' use of principled reasoning in judging moral issues. They found that the college experience has "a positive influence on increases in principled moral reasoning" (Pascarella & Terenzini 2005: 347). They note the work of Rest and Narváez (1994) in suggesting that college tends to encourage students to reflect on their moral judgments in ways that have a positive impact. Evidence based on an examination of data across different types of institutions suggests differences between changes in moral reasoning of students attending liberal arts colleges, bible colleges, and universities; students at liberal arts colleges seem most likely to make gains in moral reasoning. Despite Pascarella and Terenzini's (2005) positive findings, the evidence of gains in moral development as a result of college experiences is confounded by a variety of cultural factors on and off the campus that affect students before, during, and subsequent to their college experiences, making it difficult to draw conclusions about how college shapes students' moral development with assurance.

Yet colleges, universities, and related associations are implementing and studying initiatives intended to shape students' moral and ethical development. For example, the Association of American Colleges and Universities (AAC&U) is, through its Liberal Education and America's Promise (LEAP) program, identifying the tools needed to establish a contemporary liberal education (AAC&U n.d.a). The ideal curriculum is designed around seven "principles of excellence," which include "fostering civic, intercultural, and ethical learning" (National Leadership Council for Liberal Education & America's Promise 2007: 26). An important objective of this curricular reform is to "make the essential learning outcomes a framework for the entire educational experience, connecting school, college, work, and life" (National Leadership Council for Liberal Education & America's Promise 2007: 26). This approach recognizes the development of the student as a whole person, which is also foundational for character development and ethics. Moreover, this perspective recognizes the importance of liberal learning as a process that cuts across different types of institutions and academic disciplines.

The AAC&U has more recently introduced their "core commitments" initiative to encourage colleges and universities to engage in cultural, climate, and curricular changes to intentionally focus on students' ethical and moral development. Similar to the principles for character education at the elementary and secondary levels of education, AAC&U emphasizes that the entire campus culture must support ethics education, from the mission to the leadership, curriculum, community involvement, and outcomes assessment. Thus, institutions that join the core commitments initiative are asked to pledge their attention to educating students across five dimensions: (1) striving for excellence, (2) cultivating personal and academic integrity, (3) contributing to a larger community, (4) taking seriously the perspectives of others, and (5) developing competence in ethical and moral reasoning (AAC&U n.d.b).

Much of the supporting evidence for this effort is described within the work of Dey and his associates (2008, 2009) who surveyed 23,000 undergraduates as well as some 9,000 faculty, staff, and administrators across twenty-three institutions to assess campus climates for supporting the development of students' personal and social responsibility. Although the majority of respondents surveyed strongly supported a focus on personal and social responsibility development in college, considerably fewer respondents agreed that such a focus currently exists at their college or university. The work of Dey and his associates suggests that the ethical education pipeline may currently be fractured within higher education.

Similar to the AAC&U initiatives, Pavela (n.d.) proposes that ethical education must be treated as a responsibility that is broad in design and shared by faculty, staff, and students. Pavela describes fifteen principles that he believes would support ethical education in colleges and universities. He begins his discussion of the principles by emphasizing the importance of a "community consensus" about the standards for ethical development at each institution. Among other principles, he advocates the importance of promoting "ethical development through experience, collaboration, conflict, and guided reflection, rather than formal 'instruction' alone" (Principle 5); recruiting "students, administrators, and faculty members who are truth-seeking, and intellectually and ethically alive" (Principle 8); designing "a curriculum that poses challenging ethical questions, and helps students acquire the knowledge and experience to address them" (Principle 9); implementing " 'wellness' and substance abuse programs that include an awareness of responsibilities to self and others" (Principle 14); and encouraging "staff members to develop and use the skills of ethical dialogue" (Principle 15).

The AAC&U core commitments project, as well as compatible principles and processes proposed by Pavela (n.d.), McCabe (2005), McCabe and Pavela (2004), Whitley and Keith-Spiegel (2002), McCabe and Drinan (1999), and others, provide a promising framework as well as a selection of practical tools for colleges and universities that are prepared to engage such initiatives. Some institutions already have made strong commitments to the development of students' personal and social responsibilities,[2] but neither the list of accomplishments nor the literature supporting such efforts is broad or deep at this point. The intentions of such initiatives are laudable and potentially significant, but the challenges associated with building sustainable cultures and climates with the capacity to make the core commitments of ethics and personal and social responsibility a campus reality are substantial. Among them are the changes over time generally toward an institutional focus on more specialized education, the growth of online learning, which adds new dimensions to the culture, the traditional autonomy accorded faculty who often resist supporting ethical or character education, and the lack of leadership prepared to engage diverse constituencies in such initiatives.

Promoting Ethics Within Professional Education

As Schein (2004: 20) observes, professional occupations require "an intense period of education and apprenticeship" and are likely to have "shared learning of attitudes, norms and values that will eventually become taken-for-granted assumptions for the members of those occupations." Within most well-developed professions there are codes of ethics that guide appropriate individual and orga-nizational behaviors. Unfortunately, in some professions, such as teaching, there is no widely accepted national code of ethics and ethics regulation is largely left to the jurisdiction of licensing or certification boards at the state or provincial level.

Ethics codes typically define a set of underlying principles as well as specific standards with which professional members are to comply. The principles are in many respects aspirational and represent a profession's effort to establish a philosophical and professional foundation for ethical decision making and practices. Professionals are typically introduced to behavioral standards as well as processes for resolving ethical conflicts or dilemmas, but there may be substantial inconsistency in ethics training. For example, one professional training program may separate ethics education from the other parts of the curriculum, whereas another may integrate the training across the curriculum and emphasize ethical analysis and problem solving in ways that are more effective than others. Some professions require continuing professional education in ethics across the career life span of individuals in the profession, depending on the state or province in which they are licensed.

Handelsman, Gottlieb, and Knapp (2005) cite several reasons why the promo-tion of ethical behavior in a profession is challenging. First, they note that the rules or regulations within a code may lack specificity or actually be in conflict with one another. They also point out that learning about ethics is often accomplished through observing role models within the discipline, a process fraught with challenges depending on the culture of a particular professional discipline and the clarity of related ethical expectations. Finally, they observe that "ethics is the study of right and wrong but is often taught as the study of wrong. Many ethics courses are devoted to laws, disciplinary codes, and risk management strategies and do not focus on best practices" (Handelsman, et al. 2005: 59). Thus, even in the case of well-developed professions, one cannot take either an understanding of ethical principles or best ethical practices for granted.

As in ethics education at other levels, professions are faced with the challenge of promoting and supporting moral sensitivity, moral judgment, and moral action among their members, as well as sustaining moral motivation in the face of threats or temptations that may exist outside the profession (Rest 1994). If there are clearly defined and well-developed ethical standards, as well as ongoing ethics education and consultation, there is presumably substantial guidance for applying the components of moral action. However, one must also consider various practical matters such as the circumstances under which a profession is practiced, the nature and quality of contact with colleagues who share similar ethical responsibilities, the values of the institutions or organizations in which the profession is practiced, and the role of professional societies in emphasizing ethics as a core part of their mission and activities.

Most professions define educational, consultative, and regulatory or disci-plinary functions for an ethics committee associated with professional societies at the national, state, or, in a few instances, a more regional level. Professional associations and other providers also generally offer continuing ethics education at these levels, and in some instances a state may require that a portion of continuing professional education focus on ethics (Gottlieb, Handelsman, & Knapp 2008). For example, the Ethics Education Task Force of the Association to Advance Collegiate Schools of Business (2004) describes eleven ethics education quality and effectiveness measurements including the purposeful selection of members who practice ethics, integration of business ethics education within the curriculum, implementation of structures for identifying and managing misconduct, and the creation of cultures and climates that support ethics.[3]

The approach by the business profession is in alignment with the work of Handelsman, Gottlieb, and Knapp (2005) who propose an acculturation model for helping psychologists develop their *identities* as ethical professionals. Their focus on the development of "ethical identities" recognizes that the capacity to think and act ethically cannot be externally regulated but must exist at the core of an individual's professional sense of self. Handelsman, Knapp, & Gottlieb (2002) have also introduced the concept of *positive ethics*, which shifts from a traditional emphasis on avoiding punishment to an emphasis on striving to achieve the highest principles of ethical professional practice. Handelsman and colleagues also conceptualize ethics education as a lifelong process that, at least in part, is experiential and has an affective component. They further believe that ethics education should be an engaging, socially supportive, and collaborative developmental process, rather than a threatening, rule-based model that may unintentionally generate anxiety and avoidance of ethical reflection or action.

As in the other parts of the ethical pipeline, there appears to be a considerable amount of variability in ethics education across professions. Some professions, for example business and teaching, provide remarkably little guidance in the form of a widely accepted code of ethics. Other disciplines, for example in certain health sciences, have well-developed codes of ethics that are embedded in cultures of care and respect. In a sense, ethics education may be a somewhat easier accomplishment in the later instances because of a natural alignment with the values held by professions devoted to the care of others.

Beyond the formal codes that promote professional responsibility is the matter of how ethics are taught within professions. As in the other parts of the ethical pipeline, it seems important to recognize that ethical decision making and action require the support of positive ethical cultures that promote the development and maintenance of professional responsibility across all areas, from initial entry and orientation into a profession through continuing education across the career span. Thus, ethical professions require well-developed statements of foundational ethical principles, clear codes for professional conduct, expectations and processes for ethics education across the professional life span, and processes for reviewing and regulating behaviors that clearly violate ethical standards, as well as a recognition that ethical decision making and practice require the continuing support of professional colleagues who aspire to the highest moral standards and provide role models for their students as well as for each other.

The Pipeline for Ethics Education: Shaping it for the Future

This chapter has provided a brief overview of ethics education from the early years of education through professional training. The roots of American culture are closely intertwined with a fairly consistent set of ethical values, but there is inconsistency in the ways educational institutions have implemented efforts to promote students' ethical development across all levels of learning. In fact, there is evidence that we have lost ground over time, particularly in higher education, with efforts to sustain an effective ethical pipeline.

John Dewey and many subsequent scholars and educators have noted the ways in which moral or ethical thinking and related actions occur within powerful cultural contexts that contribute to an individual's capacity to recognize and reflect on the moral dimensions of their lives. Educating for ethics requires an appreciation of the processes of human development as well as an understanding of the complex interaction of the larger culture with the education system and the essential components of moral thinking and action. As many cited in this chapter have inferred, successful ethics education requires an understanding of the interaction of culture, moral sensitivity, and judgment with the development of moral motivation and the character to sustain ethical action on a consistent basis (Rest 1994). If the desired outcome is a society that prioritizes and acts in accord with ethical values, any single part of the pipeline could achieve only limited success in ethics education without the support of the other elements.

The current state of the ethics education pipeline strongly suggests the need for a high-level national, if not a global, commitment to comprehensively integrate ethics education across all levels of the education system. Ethics education is fundamental to establishing educational contexts that support the responsibility and integrity required for success in all types of learning. It also promotes critical thinking and teaches decision-making skills. Without an emphasis on ethics across the educational pipeline, personal and social responsibilities are presumably diminished and other aspects of learning and professional behavior impaired, as evidenced in earlier chapters of this volume.

Promising models at all levels of study, such as those proposed by the Character Education Partnership and AAC&U, should be identified. Because we all gain from acting ethically, public–private partnerships for supporting ethics education should be encouraged. Employers as well as schools and communities will benefit when ethical cultures are established, and shared support for improving the ethical education pipeline becomes an imperative.

Ensuring both the instructional and leadership resources needed to support ethics education is a significant challenge. As noted earlier in this chapter, even the teaching profession itself lacks a nationally recognized code of ethics. Among higher education faculty, academic freedom has often been emphasized to the detriment of efforts to promote personal, professional, and social responsibility (Association of American Colleges and Universities 2006; Rocheleau & Speck 2007). The lack of support for a focus on ethics education in colleges and universities stems not just from a paucity of supportive structures and cultures, but from a lack of confidence among many faculty and teachers that they have the skills or knowledge to "teach" ethics. Yet colleges and universities are rich in professionals and disciplines that have expertise in ethical theory, applied ethics, and the teaching of ethical, personal, and social development. Nonetheless there remains an inconsistency in the ways and extent to which ethics education is integrated into undergraduate, graduate, and professional education.

What, then, is needed to establish a sustainable ethical pipeline across all levels of education? First, there remains within our culture a strong public interest in, as well as support for, educating for character and moral development, especially from a positive rather than a proscriptive or regulatory perspective. When learning ethics is approached merely as learning sets of rules, the process may seem off-putting to students. At its best, the learning of ethics is cultivated from a positive perspective that engages the heart as well as the mind and encourages development of moral sensitivity and analysis, which consequently strengthens the motivation to act ethically.

Second, the promising work that has been done in contemporary primary and secondary schools to promote character or ethics education must be replicated or applied within higher education. Although many college or university students may take various ethics courses in the core curriculum or a professional area, there are varying degrees of emphasis on academic integrity across contexts and a considerable reluctance among all but a minority of institutions to candidly assess the ethical qualities of their curricular and extracurricular programs or to develop broader initiatives that would promote learning-centered cultures of positive ethics and personal and social responsibility.

In the long run, successful efforts to ensure the reliability of an ethics education pipeline across all levels of our education system require a stronger commitment to ensuring students have access to schools and universities that consistently reflect an ethos of integrity and personal and social responsibility. This requires a more ethics-centered leadership for education at institutional, state, and federal levels. Only when we have such alignment will we be able to support the sustained effort needed to build a larger culture that is ethically informed and acts in ways that value personal and social responsibility over self-interest.

Notes

1. Formerly known as the Center for Academic Integrity (CAI).
2. For one organization's interpretation of such colleges and universities, see the John Templeton Foundation's *Guide to Colleges that Encourage Character Development: A Resource for Parents, Students, and Educators* (1999), Philadelphia: Templeton Foundation Press.
3. See the document at http://www.aacsb.edu/resource_centers/ethicsedu/EthicsEdu-in-B-Schools.

pdf (accessed 16 October 2009) for all eleven measurements defined in terms of assessment questions.

References

Arthur, J. (2008) 'Traditional approaches to character education in Britain and America', in L.P. Nucci and D. Narváez (eds) *Handbook of Moral and Character Education*, New York: Routledge.

Association of American Colleges and Universities. (2006) *Academic Freedom and Educational Responsibility*, Washington, DC: Association of American Colleges and Universities. Available at http://www.aacu.org/about/statements/documents/academicFreedom.pdf (accessed 13 February 2010).

—— (n.d.a) *Liberal Education and America's Promise*, Washington, DC: Association of American Colleges and Universities. Available at http://www.aacu.org/leap/vision.cfm (accessed 15 July 2008).

—— (n.d.b) *Core Commitments: Educating Students for Personal and Social Responsibility*, Washington, DC: Association of American Colleges and Universities. Available at http://www.aacu.org/core_commitments/index.cfm (accessed 14 July 2008).

Association to Advance Collegiate Schools of Business. (2004) *Ethics Education in Business Schools*, Tampa, FL: AACSB. Available at http://www.aacsb.edu/resource_centers/ethicsedu/EthicsEdu-in-B-Schools.pdf (accessed 16 October 2009).

Association for Moral Education. (n.d.) *About AME*, Wenham, MA: Association for Moral Education. Available at http://www.amenetwork.org/about.html (accessed 5 December 2009).

Beauchamp, T. (2008) 'The principle of beneficence in applied ethics', *Stanford Encyclopedia of Philosophy*, Fall. Available at http://plato.stanford.edu/entries/principle-beneficence/ (accessed 15 July 2009).

Bertram Gallant, T. (2008) *Academic Integrity in the Twenty-First Century: A Teaching and Learning Imperative*, San Francisco: Jossey-Bass.

Bok, D. (1988) 'Ethics, the university, & society', *Harvard Magazine*, May–June: 39–50.

Center for Academic Integrity. (1999) *The Fundamental Values of Academic Integrity*, Durham, NC: Center for Academic Integrity. Available at http://www.academicintegrity.org/fundamental_values_project/pdf/FVProject.pdf (accessed 5 July 2008).

Collaborative for Academic, Social, and Emotional Learning (CASEL). (2009) *Collaborative for Academic, Social, and Emotional Learning—Past, Present, and Future*, Chicago, IL: Collaborative for Academic, Social, and Emotional Learning. Available at http://casel.org/home.php (accessed 5 December 2009).

Davidson, M., Lickona, T., and Khmelkov, V. (2007) 'Smart and good schools', *Education Week*, 27: 31–40.

—— (2008) 'Smart and good schools: A new paradigm for high school character education', in L.P. Nucci and D. Narváez (eds) *Handbook of Moral and Character Education*, New York: Routledge.

Dewey, J. (1909) *Moral Principles in Education*, Cambridge, MA: Riverside Press.

Dey, E.L. and Associates (2008) *Should Colleges Focus More on Personal and Social Responsibility?*, Washington, DC: Association of American Colleges and Universities. Available at http://www.aacu.org/core_commitments/documents/PSRII_Findings_April2008.pdf (accessed 14 July 2008).

—— (2009) *Civic Responsibility: What is the Campus Climate for Learning?*, Washington, DC: Association of American Colleges and Universities.

Elias, M.J. (2006) 'The connection between academic and social-emotional learning', in M.J. Elias and H. Arnold (eds) *The Educator's Guide to Emotional Intelligence and Academic Achievement*, Thousand Oaks, CA: Corwin Press.

Elias, M.J., Parker, S.J., Kash, V.M., Weissberg, R.P., and O'Brien, M.U. (2008) 'Social and emotional learning, moral education, and character education: A comparative analysis and a view toward convergence', in L.P. Nucci and D. Narváez (eds) *Handbook of Moral and Character Education*, New York: Routledge.

Gottlieb, M.C., Handelsman, M.M., and Knapp, S. (2008) 'Some principles for ethics education: Implementing the acculturation model', *Training and Education in Professional Psychology*, 2: 123–8.

Handelsman, M.M, Gottlieb, M.C., and Knapp, S. (2005) 'Training ethical psychologists: An acculturation model', *Professional Psychology: Research & Practice*, 36: 59–65.

Handelsman, M.M., Knapp, S., and Gottlieb, M.C. (2002) 'Positive ethics', in C.R. Snyder and S.J. Lopez (eds) *Handbook of Positive Psychology*, New York: Oxford University Press.

Harmon, D.A. and Jones, T.S. (2005) *Elementary Education: A Reference Handbook*, Santa Barbara, CA: ABC-CLIO.

Institute for Global Ethics (2009) *Building Decision Skills*, 4th edn, Rockland, ME: Institute for Global Ethics.

Kidder, R.M. (2006) *Moral Courage*, New York: HarperCollins.

Lickona, T., Schaps, E., and Lewis, C. (2007) *CEP's Eleven Principles of Effective Character Education*, Washington, DC: Character Education Partnership. Available at http://www.character.org/uploads/PDFs/Eleven_Principles.pdf (accessed 12 October 2009).

McCabe, D.L. (2005) 'It takes a village: Academic dishonesty and educational opportunity', *Liberal Education*, 91: 26–31.

McCabe, D. and Drinan, P. (1999) 'Toward a culture of academic integrity' *The Chronicle of Higher Education*, 46: B7.

McCabe, D.L. and Pavela, G. (2004) 'Ten principles of academic integrity'. Available at http://www.academicintegrityseminar.com/Teaching/TenPrinciples.html (accessed 14 April 2010).

McClellan, B.E. (1999) *Moral Education in America: Schools and the Shaping of Character from Colonial Times to the Present*, New York: Teachers College Press.

Mirk, P. (2007) *Tell Me What You Really Think: A Report on the Schools of Integrity Project*, Rockland, ME: Institute for Global Ethics. Available at http://www.globalethics.org/resources/Schools-of-Integrity-Report/80/ (accessed 15 July 2009).

Murphy, M.M. (2002) *Character Education in America's Blue Ribbon Schools: Best Practices for Meeting the Challenges*, 2nd edn, Lanham, MD: Scarecrow Press.

National Leadership Council for Liberal Education and America's Promise. (2007) *College Learning for the New Global Century*, Washington, DC: Association of American Colleges and Universities. Available at http://www.aacu.org/leap/documents/GlobalCentury_final.pdf (accessed 13 December 2009).

Nucci, L.P. (2008) 'Social cognitive domain theory and moral education', in L.P. Nucci and D. Narváez (eds) *Handbook of Moral and Character Education*, New York: Routledge.

Nucci, L.P. and Narváez, D. (2008) *Handbook of Moral and Character Education*, New York: Routledge.

Pascarella, E.T. and Terenzini, P.T. (2005) *How College Affects Students: A Third Decade of Research*, San Francisco: Jossey-Bass.

Pavela, G. (n.d) 'Fifteen principles for the design of college ethical development programs'. Available at http://www.academicintegrityseminar.com (accessed 5 June 2009).

Rest, J.R. (1994) 'Background: Theory and research', in J.R. Rest and D. Narváez (eds) *Moral Development in the Professions: Psychology and Applied Ethics*, Hillsdale, NJ: Lawrence Erlbaum Associates.

Rest, J.R. and Narváez, D. (1994) *Moral Development in the Professions: Psychology and Applied Ethics*, Hillsdale, NJ: Lawrence Erlbaum Associates.

Rocheleau, J. and Speck, B.W. (2007) *Rights and Wrongs in the College Classroom: Ethical Issues in Postsecondary Teaching*, Bolton, MA: Anker.

Rusnak, T. (1998) *An Integrated Approach to Character Education*, Thousand Oaks, CA: Corwin Press.

Schein, E.H. (2004) *Organizational Culture and Leadership*, 3rd edn, San Francisco: Jossey-Bass.

Shumaker, D.M. and Heckel, R.V. (2007) *Kids of Character: A Guide to Promoting Moral Development*, Westport, CT: Prager.

Whitley, B.E. Jr. and Keith-Spiegel, P. (2002) *Academic Dishonesty: An Educator's Guide*, Mahwah, NJ: Lawrence Erlbaum Associates.

12

Expanding the Radius of Trust to External Stakeholders

Value Infusions for a More Ethical Academy

PATRICK DRINAN

As we saw in chapter 3, context can support the ethical academy. One of the more important and potentially more significant influences on the ethical academy is the network of external stakeholders represented by a range of actors primarily including government, accreditation agencies, foundations, and a variety of non-accrediting professional associations. The network is important, and often vital, because of the variety of oversight responsibilities exercised across it (Lane 2007), but also because the network can facilitate diffusion of best practices and infusion of values to individual units in higher education.

Participants in, and observers of, higher education are familiar with oversight responsibilities and diffusion of best practices roles of external stakeholders, but there has been less attention to understanding value infusions from external stakeholders to a more ethical academy. This chapter focuses on value infusions to higher education from the network of external stakeholders and how to better realize the potential of this network in promoting the ethical academy while ignoring the impact of external stakeholders on the shaping of unethical conduct (as seen prominently in chapters 7 and 8). I argue that inattention to the prospect and promise of value infusions from external stakeholders will limit the possibilities for shaping a more ethical academy. The argument proceeds from defining what is meant by value infusions, explaining why it is so difficult, to probing how to understand and utilize the rhythms of value infusions to shape a more ethical academy.

Value Infusion: Definition, Skill Sets, and Architecture

Values can come in various shapes and sizes, and external stakeholders often have perspectives on values that differ from those of internal stakeholders. Values of transparency and accountability, for example, are essential to a monitoring and oversight process by external stakeholders, but internal stakeholders frequently resist or delay efforts by accreditation agencies or government to get reliable statistical reports from the campus (public safety being a very recent example). Values of student access to higher education or internationalization of the curriculum, on the other hand, are chosen as a result of public pressure—in the case of access—or—in the case of internationalization—as a result of the calculation of how higher education can advance economic development in a globalizing world; after some initial resistance, these kind of values are often embraced. Other values emerge from broader societal shifts in norms, such as attitudes toward women or members of the lesbian, gay, bisexual, and transgender (LGBT) community, and may indeed be led by internal stakeholders themselves.

I define values as goals responsive to legitimate public purposes essential to maintenance, adaptability, and thriving of social groups and institutions and which individuals are expected to operationalize and affirm in their behavior. Infusion is the process of transmitting those values into a social group or institution that retains substantial autonomy and thus can resist or slow that transmission. Some might deny that external stakeholders can transmit values in any robust manner but rather are ordinarily only catalysts—speeding or slowing the process of change without being intimately involved in it. Although this may have superficial advantages in displaying deference to the autonomy of a given institution of higher learning, it seriously understates the roles and participation of external stakeholders in the processes of change.

The key skills for value infusion needed by external stakeholders are twofold, then: (1) overcoming resistance; and (2) monitoring the implementation of the values. Overcoming resistance requires diagnostic leadership and diplomatic skills (Zartman & Berman 1982), whereas monitoring relies on skills such as benchmark design and statistical acumen. Diagnostic leadership is the ability to comprehend and articulate the special structures and configurations of institutional resistance. Diplomatic skills are those that set the stage for negotiating with a given institution of higher learning and formulating a strategy that stipulates more than modest objectives. Whereas monitoring may seem mundane, it is crucial because it must be patient and persistent. It also is not a strictly mechanical process, but one that displays qualitative judgments that, like arms control, demand conclusions about whether progress can be verified; that is, are there elements of acceptance of a value that are deeply held and virtually irreversible? These judgments are essential to sustaining a radius of trust between internal and external stakeholders and lay the basis for future co-operation and conflict resolution between them.

Success at value infusion, I will argue, requires "thinking institutionally" (Heclo 2008) by both internal and external stakeholders but with external stakeholders taking a primary role in helping internal stakeholders to think institutionally. Heclo (2008) speaks to those within institutions being "committed to the ends for which organization occurs rather than to an organization as such" (Heclo 2008: 90). For Heclo (2008: 66), thinking institutionally has a "moral quality" and is more than professionalism. Heclo (2008: 15) is particularly useful in helping us develop a perspective toward the ethical academy that is more attentive to the moral demand of "excellence" and a more limited, although important, demand of preventing abuse or ethical failure. Value infusions can reflect a panoply of legitimate public purposes even if Heclo's model synthesizes them into a value which he calls "thinking institutionally." This chapter explores both the infusion of a panoply of values and the power of the Heclo synthesis.

Values in a panoply can conflict, of course. Environmental sustainability is often in conflict with the value of economic development, for example. Or meritocratic values can be perceived as antagonistic to access values. External stakeholders can find ways to assist the academy in adapting in ethical ways even when values are in conflict by (1) balancing values; (2) privileging one value over others in a given time period; and (3) supporting the addition of organizational layers to represent and create interests associated with a value. Government may encourage and provide funding for the establishment of ethical centers on college campuses, for example, or foundations can establish awards for colleges and universities that excel with campus organizational initiatives that help to further the ethical academy. The STARS system, to rate and reward environmental stewardship by higher education organizations, created by the Association for the Advancement of Sustainability in Higher Education (AASHE), is one example of the possible success of such external stakeholder involvement.[1]

Although it can be argued that some values enter the academy through osmosis (i.e., are picked up because of social changes such as in women's rights), most values are explicitly reinforced by external stakeholders or even mandated (such as affirmative action). External stakeholders also help define the patterns in the distribution of values. For example, the value of shared governance was developed by the American Association of University Professors (AAUP). The AAUP not only proselytizes it, but also monitors the process to see that it is consistently implemented and sanctions campuses when it is not. External stakeholders also monitor the *pacing* of implementation; even though a given university may show interest in a value, it may take a protracted period of time to begin to inculcate the new value. Accreditation agencies are often more crucial than government in ascertaining the pacing process; goading and scolding are often used by accreditation agencies—the examples of articulating learning objectives and recruitment of under-represented students, faculty, and staff are among the most recent.

External stakeholders can also play roles in confronting collapsing values or corruption (Bruhn, Zajac, Al-Kazemi, & Prescott 2002). The National Collegiate Athletic Association (NCAA), for example, reformed its own processes in order to offset the decline of academic standards for student athletes on many campuses or even penalized higher education institutions that flaunted NCAA rules or failed to enforce them. Because much of the oversight process is peer review, the possibilities of "going native" are great. External stakeholders must retain a proper social distance between themselves and internal stakeholders. This is difficult in a peer review process and is dependent on the development and retention of autonomy by the external stakeholder itself. Foundations and government have a greater social distance from given institutions of higher education and are therefore of utility in maintaining perspective. However, they do not have the task-specific capacity and resources that peer review processes tend to possess in greater abundance. The United States has such a decentralized governmental system that oversight is exceptionally uneven. Centralized education ministries can often apply common, uniform standards but that may not solve corruption issues or set sufficiently high ethical standards (Hallak & Poisson 2007). Competition and complexity may have advantages in promoting the ethical academy over centralized approaches.

Foundations, on the other hand, have less generalized agendas than government but fewer "sticks." Their ability to target and leverage resources to promote specific goals and values is often greater than that of government and may indeed stimulate government involvement in value infusions or revitalize a value that government has moved beyond. Foundation activity before Sputnik, for example, made it easier for government to rapidly increase scientific research and foreign language acquisition values after Sputnik. As another example, foundations were often crucial in helping individual colleges and universities pursue affirmative action goals after the federal government shifted its attention to technology, the internet, and computer literacy in the 1990s.

Although osmosis and explicit transmission of values from external stakeholders can be a noisy and tumultuous process (especially in the United States), there is a basic architecture of values that establishes the general parameters, if not specific configuration, of those values. That architecture in America is surprisingly consensual and robust and is defined in a triad: (1) teaching-learning; (2) research; and (3) service. External stakeholders transmit values into this triad typically by encouraging refinements, adjustments, and connectedness among the three legs. Research, teaching, and service to society are reinvigorated by external stakeholders in the United States in ways that are not possible in most countries where the goals/functions are separated organizationally. The research and teaching values often tug one another in the United States, but even at research universities faculty report more career satisfaction from teaching than from research (Boyer 1990). Service to society is of particular concern to external stakeholders in the United States and has been the motif and motive of government and foundations, in particular. Government has linked support for research and service frequently, from the development of the land-grant university in the nineteenth century to the National Defense Education Act in the 1960s that sponsored graduate education for a generation of future college and university teachers. Foundations often link teaching with service in grants to schools of education to train teachers for urban and minority education, for example, or in encouraging educators to participate in foreign assistance endeavors and projects.

Despite the consensual and robust character of the triad, there is a nagging sense by many that it is insufficient in addressing the ethical challenges either in the academy or without. Public concern with research fraud, student cheating scandals, and financial mismanagement is frequently expressed, as seen throughout this book. Even well-regarded colleges and universities have been tainted. Layered on top of this have been the culture wars and battles over political correctness in the academy over the last two decades. Public cynicism has increased, and fears about value and cultural relativism abound. Yet more disconcerting is a sense among educators themselves that professionalism in the academy is weak and weakening and that tweaking the triad is insufficient for creating a more ethical academy. I will return to this issue more directly in my conclusions, but first we need to establish why value infusion is so difficult and analyze the rhythms and possibilities for successful value infusions by external stakeholders.

Difficulties of Value Infusion

Change is difficult. We all know this whether in making personal New Year's resolutions or implementing new technology in the workplace. The literature on organizational change is extensive, and we know much about it. But organizations and institutions can adapt; they can also be receptive to new goals and purposes expressed as values. It is hard to achieve change alone, whether as an individual or an organization, thus the importance of external stakeholders and developing a receptivity to them. General Motors (GM) apparently learned this hard lesson in 2009 when it went through bankruptcy. David Brooks (2009) of *The New York Times* quotes a GM executive as saying, "we have vastly underestimated how deeply ingrained are the organizational and cultural rigidities that hamper our ability to execute." It took an external stakeholder, the federal government, to help GM survive. Whether or not it can thrive again is yet to be seen.

The cultural and organizational rigidities of higher education may or may not be as great as those of General Motors, but it would be imprudent to underestimate them in any case. Corporations fail or merge in much higher proportions than institutions of higher education. The fear of failure rarely grips the college or university even during the darkest days of reaccreditation or funding shortages. Colleges and universities are supposed to be learning organizations, but their virtual immunity to failure and dissolution may actually contribute to their cultural and organizational rigidities.

Three specific attributes of that rigidity are parts of the conventional wisdom on academic structures: (1) faculty power; (2) preoccupation with process; and (3) bureaucratization. The last two developed historically to deal with aspects and flaws of the first. Although this is an oversimplification of the morphology of higher education, it is a useful way to probe the nature of academic rigidities and highlight how and why external stakeholders have developed the roles they have.

Faculty power in higher education may itself be an exaggeration. Academic freedom is frequently defined by faculty in absolute rather than relative terms, but there are numerous constraints on it in any event. Deference to the faculty member in a classroom setting is still large despite the movement to learning assessment. But individual faculty, while setting pedagogical strategies or designing research programs, do have to defer to collegial curricular norms and a peer review process for research publication. And higher education administrators often had and have great power, even in the alleged "golden years" of the liberal arts college. The rush to unionize faculty in the last half of the twentieth century was led by faculty resentful of administrator power and fearful that the external stakeholder of government would also challenge faculty prerogatives and power.

The perception and realities of faculty power also led to attentiveness to process. The jurisdictional sensitivities of faculty had to be spelled out and clarified to protect junior faculty from arbitrary rank and tenure decision making and other faculty, such as women and minorities, from discrimination. Students required some mechanisms for grade grievances and protection from sexual harassment. And faculty researchers needed blind reviews in an effort to insulate themselves from insider games. Although all this, and other procedural preoccupations, prevented a range of abuses, it hardly was a call to excellence in the pursuit of the goals of the triad. Preventing abuse, by itself, does not create the ethical academy—but it is where we have historically begun. This is why, as Kezar and Sam noted in their chapter, ethical codes of conduct are the most common of any possible organizational levers for creating the ethical academy.

In order to rationalize procedures and deal with the huge expansion of American higher education, a wave of bureaucratization occurred in higher education that more frequently diminished rather than augmented the faculty role. Administrators proliferated in student affairs, budget, information technology, and even public safety along with the very distinctive American academic–athletic complex. This administrative explosion led to a proliferation of regional and national professional associations in each area, which took on many attributes of an external stakeholder. The complexity of higher education represented by the rise of the managerial class may have contributed to adaptability by internal organizational development responsive to new values, social forces, and pressures from external stakeholders; but higher education also may have lost flexibility in the inexorable stasis that accompanies bureaucratization. From another perspective, the proliferation of national and international professional associations connected with these new internal stakeholders created new paths for value infusion and diffusion of best practices, and not all for the good of the ethical academy as we saw in earlier chapters.

Value infusions are difficult not only because of the rigidity of higher education institutions, but also because external stakeholders are frequently unskilled, non-persistent, or miss obvious opportunities for value infusion. Value infusions from government frequently have unintended but foreseeable consequences. Early government efforts to protect human subjects in research projects, for example, were not only awkwardly and too rapidly developed but led to immense confusion and delayed research on many campuses. Sexual harassment legislation, on the other hand, is so general that it took most colleges and universities decades to implement it in a uniform fashion and was immersed in litigiousness that slowed the process of implementation.

The skills most needed by external stakeholders, as indicated earlier, are to diagnose well the shape of the resistance to change on a given campus and possess strategic patience to pursue implementation of a value. The anomalies prove the rule. The value of technological modernization was promoted well for research and basic administrative logistics; but distance education, combining technology and access values, has been more problematic because of threats to the traditional campus (Drucker 1999). Reforms in teacher education and quality, while urgently pressed over the years, had been mired in a stasis intimately shared by internal and external stakeholders. And the value of a liberal arts education, although articulated well and with strong evidence, has been incredibly difficult to implement because of the proliferation of professional programs, fragmentation of disciplines in the academy, and societal pressure for students to have "marketable" skills.

Although there has been less attention to missed opportunities for value infusions from external stakeholders, it is not insignificant in describing difficulties these stakeholders may have. Perhaps the most glaring of the missed opportunities has been the virtual failure to infuse the value of student academic integrity and honesty into the academy even as student cheating scandals received publicity and even as more scholarly research has been published over the last twenty years on the topic. "Integrity" is frequently mentioned in accreditation standards, but there has been little attention to value infusion on the matter of academic integrity and student academic honesty except from professional associations such as the International Center for Academic Integrity (ICAI).[2]

What explains the lack of traction or value infusion on academic integrity? One could ask the question more precisely by wondering why more powerful external stakeholders, such as accreditation agencies and government, did not include academic integrity high on their agendas. In the absence of survey data of accreditation staffers and relevant opinion leaders on key legislative education committees, it is difficult to come up with compelling answers. However, the experience of the ICAI is suggestive. It developed, with support from the William and Flora Hewlett Foundation and the Kenan Institute for Ethics, a comprehensive examination of statements on student academic integrity from U.S. colleges and universities that identified a cluster of five values supporting student academic honesty held in common throughout postsecondary education.

The ICAI document, published in 1999 as *The Fundamental Values of Academic Integrity*, was circulated widely, and the precise language on academic integrity from the ICAI was frequently recycled to postsecondary mission statements as these were being redone in the decade following the publication.

Given a fairly responsive attitude toward the value infusion suggested by the ICAI, at American and even foreign educational institutions, what constrained the effectiveness of implementing the value infusion? Scholars, including this author, have hypothesized at least four explanations:

1. The issue is still young and has not been picked up yet by accreditation agencies.
2. Student academic dishonesty is considered an intractable matter, with only honor code schools showing much progress on constraining student cheating, and the creation of student-run honor codes is exceptionally difficult.
3. The issue may complicate work on student learning outcomes assessment by both "crowding out" that agenda item and undermining it by calling into question the legitimacy of testing and measurement projects in assessment.
4. Other initiatives, such as regaining academic control of student athletic programs or pursuing diversity and access, also "crowded out" the value infusion of student academic honesty (Davis, Drinan, & Bertram Gallant 2009: 1–30).

There are not many glaring opportunities that have been missed for value infusion, but academic integrity/student academic honesty must be on any list. Academic integrity is so central to the value structures of higher education in both teaching and research that failure to make progress on value infusion in this area will taint not only the reputation and status of individual colleges and universities but also those of external stakeholders themselves. Of the external stakeholders, accreditation agencies have the most to lose in this missed opportunity given their frequent verbalizations on integrity and institutions.

The Power and the Promise of External Stakeholders

Although we have been attentive to the four primary external stakeholders of government, accreditation agencies, foundations, and professional associations, there are two others, one potential—the public—and one real—religious bodies, that have been excluded in this analysis, and a rationale for not including them should be briefly noted. Although the general public is often given status as an external stakeholder by some (Kells 1992), it is being excluded in this chapter under two assumptions: (1) the four designated external stakeholders are a prism through which public opinion and concerns are expressed; and (2) the general public tends to have value roles that are more inchoate, such as socialization of young people before they enter the academy or attitudes of support or non-support toward faculty and administrators as they evaluate student work or engage in discipline.

The role of religious bodies as an external stakeholder is a relatively small slice of higher education today. A century ago, religious bodies had a significant role in infusing values into the private colleges they sponsored. Most of these private colleges no longer have religious control, and secularization is the rule. Roman Catholic and Baptist/Evangelical colleges still have close relations with sponsoring religious societies, but these are excluded from my analysis given the relatively small number and/or size of these institutions and the fuller treatment of the issue by other scholars (Pelikan 1992).

The structure and network of the primary external stakeholders hold great promise for value infusion for three primary reasons:

1. the linkage of value infusion to the roles of oversight and diffusion of best practices;
2. external stakeholders' perspectives and decision making on the "ripeness" of a value or issue; and
3. the power and reach of external stakeholders in the governance of higher education.

Oversight, diffusion of best practices, and value infusion exist on a spectrum and are not compartmentalized. Oversight, for example, can lead to reforms that are diffused in best practices (as in financial aid). Diffusion of best practices is often originally driven by attention to values (as, for example, how research expectations have been ratcheted up even at non-research, "teaching" institutions). Value infusions are distinctive because values are substantive and often contentious whereas oversight and best practices tend to be more process oriented.

Oversight and a given best practice do involve values of transparency, accountability, and professionalism along with the negatively expressed value of avoidance of ethical failure. But the attention to moral quality and excellence *as an institution* is a much higher expectation. An example of a minimal expectation could be asking whether or not a college has a general education requirement and whether it is regularly reviewed. Attention to excellence, on the other hand, would mean the deep pride that faculty take in the connectedness of disciplines and creating space for interdisciplinary programs that define the uniqueness of a given institution of higher learning.

External stakeholders hold a particularly potent position in deciding the "ripeness" of a given value or best practice as an issue to be transmitted to a given institution or set of institutions. Assessment is an example of the network of external stakeholders (but accreditation agencies in particular) recognizing and affirming the value of teaching-learning and "forcing" colleges and universities to define and measure learning outcomes.

A very recent example of "ripeness" is NAFSA: Association of International

Educators's strategic effort to include peace and justice as a value to be integrated into study abroad/international education. It resulted from leadership within NAFSA committed to increasing the moral quality of international education around the notion of "global citizenship" (Lewin 2009). The transmission of this value into higher education was designed to provide a common discourse for international educational professionals as they connect with faculty. Although this effort is just underway, it is clear evidence that professional associations can identify and participate in value infusions when they sense "ripeness" even if the professional association's primary purpose is diffusion of best practices.

Despite these prominent examples of value infusion, external stakeholders often underestimate or do not see their power and reach that can be used for such purposes. This may happen if they are overly deferential to the institutional autonomy of colleges and universities or if they are preoccupied with oversight or diffusion of best practices. Social scientists often define power in terms of social capital, that is, the ability to both range over a network that extends beyond the family unit and have influence in the network (Fukuyama 1999). Reach, then, is a feature of power and is frequently defined in positive terms as a "radius of trust" (Fukuyama 1995). This radius of trust means a recognition of common and complementary missions among social actors and a sense that there must be some reliance on one another.

To see better the power and reach of external stakeholders, two visualizations are proposed that capture the structure and potential of social interactions between colleges and universities and their external stakeholders. Visualization I (the pendulum metaphor) is derived from the work of Adam Watson and is used to describe the swing of international society from isolated states on one extreme to world government or world empire on the other (Watson 1992: 13–18). An adaptation of the metaphor to higher education is shown in Figure 12.1. The two extremes do not describe the U.S. higher education system. The pull of the pendulum is away from the extremes. The movement of the pendulum suggests a device for explaining infusions of value as the pendulum swings. In the United States, the pendulum, or radius of trust, moves mostly in the center

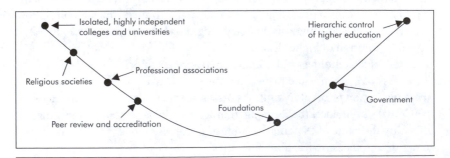

Figure 12.1 Visualization I: The Pendulum Metaphor.

from professional associations to government oversight (but not control). Each of these points gathers energy as the pendulum swings so that infusions of value can occur and be connected, if not orchestrated. The two extremes represent a lack of trust either in the anarchic world of isolated units or in the bureaucratic world of an education ministry. Successful infusions of values in this metaphor come from the *weight* of the pendulum and its *direction*; for the United States it also means that creating the ethical academy involves, then, avoiding extremes. It also means that the agendas of professional associations, accreditation bodies, foundations, and the government must overlap and not be coterminous. In the absence of overlap, the pendulum does not swing; the fact that agendas do not completely overlap simply describes the different identities of the various stakeholders.

The utility of Visualization I is primarily to see external stakeholders as part of a *society* and not just a *system*. "Society" implies norms, reciprocity, and a common language of discourse for mutual influence beyond that of a more formal conceptualization of a "system" of higher education. The existence of a higher education society implies greater social capital than a more formal system and begins to depreciate the notion that given higher education institutions are so autonomous that they can be isolated. The "swing" of the pendulum thus privileges the center of the spectrum occupied by external stakeholders.

Visualization II (institutional thinking and the radius of trust) helps external (and even internal) stakeholders analyze the possibilities and opportunities for effective value infusions and is derived from Hugh Heclo's 2008 work, *On Thinking Institutionally* (Figure 12.2). In this schema, "weak institutional thinking" represents more instrumental and bureaucratic approaches whereas "strong institutional thinking" pays "respect in depth" (Heclo 2008: 66) to the moral quality of the institution. "High trust" refers to solid relationships between internal and external stakeholders whereas "low trust" refers to very modest relationships of responsiveness and effectiveness between internal and external stakeholders.

Quadrant I would be characterized by mundane and regularized relationships between internal and external stakeholders. Quadrant II would be the ideal of robust and legitimate relationships that could characterize responsive and effective value infusions into the ethical academy. Quadrant III is the opposite, inviting poor relationships between internal and external stakeholders and/or a retreat toward isolation by the institution. Quadrant IV is surprising in that strong institutional thinking by both internal and external stakeholders can work directly on trust and therefore open new opportunities for infusion of values.

Value infusions, using the Heclo approach, shape the ethical academy by placing the moral quality of higher education ahead of instrumental, bureaucratic thinking. Although Heclo is not optimistic about institutional thinking increasing its general profile, higher education is used to the language of institutions. The distance of external stakeholders from a given campus ironically may give

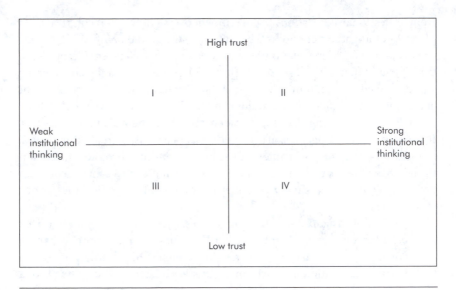

High trust

I

II

Weak
institutional
thinking

Strong
institutional
thinking

III

IV

Low trust

Figure 12.2 Visualization II: Institutional Thinking and the Radius of Trust.

them the space and perspective to encourage institutionally minded behavior
on our campuses.

External stakeholders should not think value infusion is easy to accomplish
(as if they would!). If internal stakeholders are badly divided on a given campus,
lack organizational and leadership skills, or are generally deficient in coherence,
value infusions will be aborted, be poorly done, or simply fail. No amount of
external stakeholder skill or persistence can compensate for lack of coherence at
the level of the organization or institution. Huntington (1968: 22) states:

> An effective organization requires, at a minimum, substantial consensus
> on the functional boundaries and on the procedures for resolving disputes
> which come up within those boundaries. The consensus must extend to
> those active in the system. Non-participants, or those only sporadically
> and marginally participant in the system, do not share it to the same extent
> as the participants.

Value infusions are, then, regulated by internal stakeholders, and they are
primarily responsible for the shape of any value infusion originated by external
stakeholders.

The key to institutional adaptability is not the *speed* of adaptability but the
balance of adaptability and coherence at a given college or university. Adaptability
refers more to the dimension of external challenges, including from external
stakeholders, that are dealt with by a college or university. Coherence, on the

other hand, is attention to the values to be infused, which redirect institutional mission without uprooting it.

Conclusion: The Heclo Synthesis and Visualizing the Ethical Academy

Heclo (2008) has been a leader in the effort to connect, first, discussions of "moral quality" with "infusion of value" and, second, "thinking institutionally" with an expansion of trust. The advantage of the Heclo synthesis is not its abstraction but its *concreteness*. It is concrete in at least two ways: (1) a recognition of the centrality of practicality; and (2) the attention to the individual. According to Heclo (2008: 193), "to acquire a way of thinking, institutional or otherwise, is probably the most practical thing a person ever does." Heclo (2008: 193) goes on to link being "institutionally minded" to the effort "to be trustworthy" and "to enhance a culture of institutional values." After all, Heclo might argue, values are about not only maintenance and adaptability of social groups and institutions but also their thriving.

Heclo's passion for thinking institutionally explains his hostility to bureaucratic thinking. He argues that the latter is about doing "a particular job" in an organization not "the deeper commitments that express one's enduring loyalty to the purpose or purposes that lie behind doing the job in the first place" (Heclo 2008: 101). For Heclo (2008: 101), then, *individuals*, whether internal or external to the organization, are crucial. He states that we should "never lose sight of the individual and his or her responsibilities to institutions." External stakeholders interested in value infusions and the ethical academy must find, nurture, and connect with champions of thinking among internal stakeholders, and not just in the formal hierarchies of our colleges and universities. Sustained efforts by external stakeholders in nurturing institutional thinking among both other external stakeholders and internal stakeholders may be the next frontier in constructing the ethical academy.

How might one take this lofty and yet practical way of thinking and integrate it more specifically into the values architecture of higher education and a more ethical academy? One answer is to amend the triadic structure of values (teaching-learning, research, and service) of American higher education and vividly include institutional thinking as a foundation for the triad or even as a fourth leg. The language of institutions is already endemic to the academy and thus could easily be recognized more explicitly as foundational to the ethical academy. Even institutional thinking as a fourth leg to the values architecture may not be as farfetched as it may sound; many rank and tenure documents have a "fourth criterion" that expects a sense of responsibility and also support of institutional mission from faculty. This is often difficult for faculty to conceptualize with their disciplinary loyalties. It may be less difficult for the growing class of non-faculty academic professionals to articulate. There may be a large opportunity to open a conversation between faculty and these professionals about what institutional thinking may mean on their individual campuses. Faculty loyalty to discipline could be transcended and non-faculty professionals likewise could have their already developed organizational sensibilities upgraded.

Faculty and non-faculty professionals also can provide a key nexus in partnering with external stakeholders. The International Center for Academic Integrity, for example, has already attempted this by providing for conversations between student affairs professionals and faculty and by soliciting foundation support for infusion of the value of student academic honesty into institutions of higher education. I have alluded to the array of non-faculty professionals who are organizing professional societies beyond individual campuses and thus are nurturing authentic, and quite new, partnerships that are primarily about diffusion of best practices. NAFSA efforts in this regard were highlighted earlier in the chapter, particularly by displaying the dynamic relationship of diffusion of best practices to value infusion.

Visualizing the potential for value infusion is a crucial tactic in its acceleration and can augment strategies that are overly dependent on connecting with formal academic hierarchies. If a wider array of both internal and external stakeholders begins to see the potential for the pendulum to swing, they may realize how even small nudges can produce weighty outcomes and a more ethical academy.

Notes

1. For more information, visit the AASHE website at http://www.aashe.org (accessed 9 June 2010)
2. Formerly known as the Center for Academic Integrity (CAI).

References

Boyer, E.L. (1990) *Scholarship Reconsidered: Priorities of the Professoriate*, New York: Carnegie Foundation for the Advancement of Higher Education.

Brooks, D. (2009). 'The quagmire ahead', *The New York Times*, 2 June, A23.

Bruhn, J.G., Zajac, G., Al-Kazemi, A.A., and Prescott, L.D. Jr. (2002) 'Moral positions and academic conduct: Parameters of tolerance for ethics failure', *Journal of Higher Education*, 73: 461–93.

Center for Academic Integrity. (1999) *The Fundamental Values of Academic Integrity*, Durham, NC: Center for Academic Integrity. Available at http://www.academicintegrity.org/fundamental_values_project/pdf/FVProject.pdf (accessed 5 July 2008).

Davis, S.F., Drinan, P.F., and Bertram Gallant, T. (2009) *Cheating in School: What We Know and What We Can Do*, Malden, MA: Wiley-Blackwell.

Drucker, P.F. (1999) *Management Changes for the Twenty-First Century*, New York: Harper Collins.

Fukuyama, F. (1995) *Trust: The Social Virtues and the Creation of Prosperity*, New York: Free Press.

—— (1999) 'Social capital and civil society'. Paper presented at the IMF Conference on Second Generation Reforms, Washington, DC, November 1999.

Hallak, J. and Poisson, M. (2007) *Corrupt Schools, Corrupt Universities: What Can Be Done?*, Paris: International Institute for Educational Planning.

Heclo, H. (2008) *On Thinking Institutionally*, Boulder: Paradigm Publishers.

Huntington, S.P. (1968) *Political Order in Changing Societies*, New Haven: Yale University Press.

Kells, H.R. (1992) *Self-Regulation in Higher Education*, London: Jessica Kingsley Publishers.

Lane, J.E. (2007) 'The spider web of oversight: An analysis of external oversight of higher education', *Journal of Higher Education*, 78: 615–44.

Lewin, R. (2009) *The Handbook of Practice and Research in Study Abroad: Higher Education and the Quest for Global Citizenship*, New York: Routledge.

Pelikan, J. (1992) *The Idea of the University: A Reexamination*, New Haven: Yale University Press.
Watson, A. (1992) *The Evolution of International Society*, New York: Routledge.
Zartman, I.W. and Berman, M.R. (1982) *The Practical Negotiator*, New Haven: Yale University Press.

13
Toward Global Academic Ethics through Accountability Systems

BRIAN L. HEUSER AND TIMOTHY A. DRAKE

In his renowned work, *After Virtue*, the noted twentieth-century Scottish ethicist, Alasdair MacIntyre, offered the analogy of a child learning to play chess as a way of reflecting on the nature of virtuous behavior and the potential goods it produces. In so doing, MacIntyre focused his attention on the learning process and on the role of incentives for determining the character of success. Significantly, the hypothetical scenario he developed does not distinguish cognitive from ethical development. Rather, both are embedded in the overall exchange. Motives for participation in the game emerge, but remain mostly grounded in narrow self-interest.

> Consider the example of a highly intelligent seven-year-old child whom I wish to teach to play chess, although the child has no particular desire to learn the game. The child does, however, have a very strong desire for candy and little chance of obtaining it. I therefore tell the child that if the child will play chess with me once a week I will give the child 50 cents worth of candy; moreover I tell the child that I will always play in such a way that it will be difficult, but not impossible, for the child to win and that if the child wins, the child will receive an extra 50 cents worth of candy. Thus motivated the child plays and plays to win. Notice however that, so long as it is the candy alone which provides the child with a good reason for playing chess, the child has no reason not to cheat and every reason to cheat, provided he or she can do so successfully. But, so we may hope, there will come a time when the child will find in those goods specific to chess, in the achievement of a certain highly particular kind of analytical skill, strategic imagination, and competitive intensity, a new set of reasons,

reasons now not just for winning on a particular occasion, but for trying to excel in whatever way the game of chess demands. Now if the child cheats, he or she will be defeating not me, but himself or herself.

(MacIntyre 2007: 188)

Over time, the student is taught how to distinguish simple transactions from those of greater purpose and value. In so doing, personal integrity becomes linked with self-actualization. However, where MacIntyre offers merely an anticipation that these understandings become imbued over time, realistically, the ideal dynamic requires intentionally embedding the learning process with the necessary elements that will enable the student to internalize them. In this way the relationship between student and teacher becomes a significant part of the process—methodology becomes the catalyst for transformation—and the game of chess itself serves as both the object to be mastered in and of itself and a way of thinking about how to master it. At this point in the development process, it is "ethically sufficient" if the student progresses to desiring the "higher goods" associated with strategic mastery of the game. Of course, if the student could generalize the found value to some virtue beyond the self, even better. Here, then, emerges the role of colleges and universities in creating and sustaining ethical environments.

MacIntyre's analogy, like much of the literature on corruption in education, is clearly focused on the task of shaping individual decision making. And although it is not our goal to examine dimensions of individual ethical behavior, his analogy provides us with a rich construct around which to organize a system-level ethic for higher education—*the creation of contexts that encourage the pursuit of the goods intrinsic to the processes of higher education*. Although colleges' and universities' core activities involve systematic research, teaching, and learning, they also foster extensive social functions in every country of origin. So although the primary activities of students and faculty are pedagogical in nature, these activities are accompanied by complex social processes through which norms, values, attitudes, and ethics are transmitted from the societal to the individual level. These processes involve a constant dialogue—a communication of understandings and expectations regarding ways of being in the organization—between faculty, students, administrators, government officials, international organizations, and numerous other groups. Accordingly, the achievement of the goods associated with academic work product is informed by ethical codes that have been established by various institutional stakeholders and, of course, market forces.

From MacIntyre, we begin to understand that the causes of corruption may have much to do with the transactional nature of individuals' relationship with higher education institutions, as implicated by Heyneman in chapter 2 of this volume. When driven primarily by external rewards or benefits (especially monetary) rather than by enhanced capabilities that may also carry those rewards, there may be little incentive for individuals—students, but also faculty, administrators, and even policy makers—to engage with institutions in virtuous ways. Although increasing personal earnings (and thus well-being) through the attainment of a college degree is certainly a fine motivation, serious problems arise when it is merely the degree itself and not the intellectual capabilities associated with that degree that drive the whole exchange.

What most studies have failed to do convincingly is to equate the monetary reward structure with empirically validated cognitive traits or measures of real productivity. This missing information (and the discrepancies it implies) represents a real challenge to our standard ways of calculating the benefits of higher education. Importantly, if earnings are based mostly on degree attainment and degree attainment is based on something other than developing human capital, then earnings represent an artificial (and flawed) indicator of aggregated higher education's contribution to societal productivity. Moreover, if earnings that are based primarily on either degree attainment or social status attainment (or both) disproportionately incentivize the certification process over the learning process, then the work of colleges and universities is placed in jeopardy when they bend to the demands of prevailing market forces.

Additionally, if the educational process dissolves to the point where coursework and learning activities (such as writing papers, taking exams, class discussion, lab exercises, field research) become primarily equated to earning numerical scores, then the desired learning outcomes will likely be supplanted by an external economic exchange. Students cease to find value in academic work when earning an "A" (think MacIntye's 'candy') becomes the primary motivation for success. In these cases, the goods internal to academic work (cognition, strategy, application of formulae, theory adaptation) become secondary by-products of the process.

Similarly, if the incentive (pay and promotion) structure for faculty and/or administrators is based on narrow criteria that prioritize monetarily lucrative endeavors (likely as a result of parallel institutional priorities), then it is, quite rationally, in those activities that they will invest their time and effort. In relation to MacIntyre's ethical construct, when the goods that are produced by the academic profession serve individual faculty and institutions more than students, communities, or even the fields of knowledge in which they are located, then there is reason to doubt whether higher education any longer serves society's common good. Neglecting educational processes and the human capabilities they can develop places the social contract between faculty, tertiary institutions, and the public in jeopardy.

What is instructive to higher education about this construct of virtue is that, if academic "rules of law" are to be adopted by students and faculty, the value of the underlying purposes of those rules must be embedded throughout multiple institutional policy mechanisms. Academic virtue must be not only defended in terms of individual levels of compliance with codes of conduct, but rather communicated as a comprehensive aspect of institutional activities and priorities.

Although it is true that aversion to retribution for malfeasance creates some level of individual compliance, it cannot motivate faculty, students, and administrators to actualize the benefits associated with the virtuous acquisition of academic goods. On the other hand, when the pursuit of the internal goods of education is strategically embedded in educational processes, it is far more likely that academies will succeed in building environments of integrity—namely because the individuals therein will seek value in the inherent productivity of their work. Although national, cultural, and organizational differences certainly influence how different systems of higher education relate to institutional corruption, there seems to be broad agreement that safeguarding the primary educational goods associated with tertiary education is fundamentally important to the future development of stable and productive societies.

Early Global Responses to Education Corruption

Transparency International, whose global mission is to create change toward a world free of corruption, was chartered and established in Berlin in 1993.[1] Transparency was the first civil society organization of its kind—a global organization dedicated entirely to exposing widespread national and systemic issues of corruption. Fundamental to Transparency's organizational philosophy is the recognition that unethical behavior must be not only evaluated ex post, but also systematically dealt with ex ante. Among other strategic goals, Transparency seeks to increase knowledge production through high-quality research, promote anti-corruption norms and principles, enhance global communication and knowledge sharing, reach a broader base of citizens, and monitor global trends.[2]

One of Transparency's greatest contributions to the fight against corruption is the development of the Corruption Perceptions Index (CPI), a composite index using surveys of business professionals and assessments of country analysts. The strength of this instrument comes from two core characteristics. First, Transparency administered comparable surveys across locations, enabling perception to become a valuable barometer for cross-country comparisons. Second, by leveraging a diversity of data sources into a single index, each individual component becomes more reliable.

In addition to the CPI, Transparency also developed the Global Corruption Barometer (GCB)—a survey that assesses the general public's attitude toward and experience with corruption—and the Bribe Payers Index (BPI)—a tool to measure the likelihood that firms within industrialized nations will "bribe abroad." Although the validity of these metrics is currently under debate (even more than the CPI), Transparency is one of the first organizations to operationalize international corruption. In effect, by creating a way to numerically compare each nation's perceived level of corruption, Transparency International made corruption more transparent. Society could no longer case corruption within vague terms or rhetorical statements. Rather, the publication of quantitative levels of world corruption resulted in international pressure to develop specific strategies toward lowering and eliminating these figures.

If Transparency International helped draw attention to the seemingly ubiquitous spread of systemic corruption, the World Bank's efforts mobilized the fight against it. In 1996 President James Wolfensohn of the World Bank Group gave his now famous address "The Cancer of Corruption" at the World Bank/International Monetary Fund (IMF) annual meeting. Up until this point, Wolfensohn (2002) described how the issue of corruption was taboo.

> You may be amused to know, when I arrived, that the general counsel was giving me guidance on what it is that I could and couldn't do within the context of this, then rather more bureaucratic, organization than it is now. He said very quietly to me: "Of course, we are not allowed to engage in politics, and you cannot mention the 'C' word"; and I said: "What is the 'C' word?" And he more or less took me behind some shadowy place and whispered in my ear: "That's corruption." And I said: "Why can't I mention corruption?" And he said that corruption is essentially political and it gets into the concerns of our Board members and we are a non-political organization.
>
> (Wolfensohn 2002: 2)

For Wolfensohn, labeling corruption as a political issue was myopic, neglecting to account for the moral, social, and economic elements inextricably linked with the concept. Further, he felt that to ignore its presence out of political sensitivity would be disastrous to the future of the institution of the World Bank and to its various stakeholders (Wolfensohn 2002).

Accordingly, Wolfensohn implemented institutional reforms to allow for a more liberal environment of open communication, including an anonymous whistleblower hotline and ethics programs to facilitate discussions about important World Bank policy and practice. From these two interventions alone Wolfensohn discovered that "corruption was one of the greatest inhibiting forces to equitable development and to the combating of poverty" (Wolfensohn 2002: 3). Additionally, in 1999 Wolfensohn created the Department of Institutional Integrity (INT), which was charged with the dual mission of investigating allegations of corruptible practice in World Bank-financed projects (external) and among World Bank staff (internal). Although the INT's duties were primarily investigative, its reports went to groups with the power to levy sanctions, including letters of reprimand, restitution, and temporary or permanent debarment. Furthermore, the Bank publishes it sanctions of companies and individuals on the World Wide Web (Integrity Vice Presidency 2009).

At the turn of the century, many other regional and international players had implemented similar systematic institutional reforms to address the issue of corruption. In Latin America, the Network of Institutions for Combating Corruption and Rescuing Public Ethics (RICOREP) with twenty-one institutional members was formed in 1998 to conduct forums, exchange ideas, share information, provide consultation, and disseminate publications on the issue of Latin American corruption. The Council of Europe (CoE) established the Group of States against Corruption (GRECO) in 1999 to monitor each member state's compliance with CoE anti-corruption standards through the process of mutual evaluation and peer pressure.

In 2000, the Asian Development Bank (ADB) released its first Governance Action Plan recommending that a consensus on regional benchmarks, codes of conduct, and best practices across both public and private sectors be developed.[3] Around that same time, the United Nations called for a Convention against Corruption (UNCAC), which "introduced a set of standards, measures, and rules that all countries can apply in order to strengthen their legal and regulatory regimes to fight corruption" (Annan 2004: iii). And in 2003, the European Commission issued a communiqué arguing, among other things, that "Member States and EU institutions and bodies should redouble their efforts to combat corruption" and "develop and improve investigative tools and allocate more specialised staff to the fight against corruption."[4] That same year, the Organisation for Economic Co-operation and Development's (OECD) Development Assistance Committee published the Principles for Donor Action in Anti-Corruption, which recommended that aid donors (1) collectively foster, follow, and fit into the local vision; (2) acknowledge and respond to the supply side of corruption; and (3) marshal knowledge and lessons systematically and measure progress.[5]

All of these movements taken together signaled a profound shift toward addressing international corruption on a global scale. Although national systems still bore the central burden of eradicating unethical practice from within their own borders, these historical developments highlighted the future role that international organizations would play in combating global corruption. As Pasi Sahlberg notes, "Domestic political strength and will of countries that suffer from corruption are normally not enough to make any significant progress in governance and transparency that are often related to alleviating corruption. Therefore international organizations have an important role to play in combating wide-spread corruption" (Sahlberg 2009: 135).

Toward a Global Higher Ed Market of Openness and Accountability

The open boundaries between colleges and society foster interaction among internal organizational and external influences and allow for transformation of one type of influence to others especially as it moves from society to campus . . . the boundary is permeable as colleges accept and adapt to external influences and begin to see them as organizational and internal imperatives.

(Stark & Lattuca 1997: 337–8)

In the past decade, cross-border student mobility has increased by nearly one million students per year (Altbach, Reisberg, & Rumbley 2009). Participation rates of the roughly three million college students (undergraduates and graduates) who study outside their country of nationality are still trending upward despite the global economic crises of the past year (Altbach, et al. 2009; Council of Graduate Schools 2009). Perhaps most significantly related to issues of educational corruption and integrity are the emerging priorities of internationalization in higher education. In their preliminary report for 2009, the International Association of Universities found that 30 percent of the 745 institutions surveyed named "student preparedness" as their number one priority. Additionally, nearly 17 percent responded that their primary internationalization agenda was related to enhancing institutional and curricular quality, and just over 15 percent said they were most concerned with their "profile and reputation." "Research and knowledge production" maintained the fourth spot in the rankings with just over 14 percent of institutions listing it as their top priority. And in the 115 countries in which these surveys were administered, heightened exchange of students, research, curriculum, and faculty and staff were cited as the activities most sought after by colleges and universities (International Association of Universities 2009: 3). In sum, tertiary institutions in all parts of the world have never been more open to collaboration around their core functions or concerned with their image.

These increasing trends toward collaborative openness and increasing prestige have been accompanied by very intentional economic motivations on behalf of countries' governments, international organizations, higher education institutions and the global marketplace. By the start of the twenty-first century, the trend toward 'mass' higher education was already well established, and scholars and policy makers were united in their understanding as to the individual and public financial benefit.

In an influential policy paper entitled *Responding to New Demand in Tertiary Education*, the OECD surmised that obtaining some level of postsecondary education had become "both an expectation and perceived necessity" for a significant and increasing number of individuals and societies looking to broadly participate in the new world order (OECD 1997: 20). Similarly, some scholars were advancing even more urgent reports regarding the macro-level effects of higher education, arguing for its advance as the "principal economic engine [of] today's world economy . . . that determines a society's evolutionary potential" (Alexander 2000: 412). Combining such economic arguments with their civic counterparts, whereby "the construction of knowledge economies and democratic societies" was cast as the joint product of higher education, was another common theme echoed in both the literature and debates regarding the emergence of what had become know as the new 'knowledge-based society' (World Bank 2002: xxi). Common to all of these perspectives was also a strong emphasis on higher education's role in laying the educational foundations for the inevitably changing economic and human capital demands of a globalized society.

The international community was now moving in lockstep around the goals of expanding the range and quality of human capital though higher education, understanding it (quite rightly) as a central force driving the changing world economy and simultaneously being shaped by its increased potentiality. In response to this 'new demand' (and the accompanying economic expectations), countries, colleges, organizations, development banks, and citizens all coalesced around scaling up the provision of tertiary opportunities (OECD 1997). While governments wrestled (as they continue to do so) with issues of demand, access, quality, and equity, many tertiary institutions (public and private) quickly reacted to the technological demands of the burgeoning knowledge- and service-based societies by dramatically expanding their programs of study. The prevalence of private colleges and for-profit institutions increased, as did the emphasis on private tutoring as a means of accessing tertiary education. Common to the many approaches of higher education expansion was the universal recognition by governments, organizations, and the market that higher education institutions could serve the varied needs of both individuals and institutions that desired participation in the emerging knowledge economy.

For economies that traditionally relied heavily on human capital as a physical means of production, promoting higher education represented a new promise for social mobility and access. For countries that were already considered 'knowledge-based economies' with 'massified' systems of higher education, investment in tertiary education continued to be seen as essential to the maintenance of a high standard of living and as the primary driver of future innovation. For both developing and developed economies, prioritizing institutional collaboration became a significant means of expanding broad capacities; and building a robust system of higher education was normatively understood as an imperative economic strategy (Knight 2003).

Also during the first part of this decade, the expanding market for higher education and increasing openness of tertiary systems—particularly those parts associated with cross-border mobility of students, faculty, and resources—prompted serious concerns about institutional quality assurance. Policy makers, faculty, and administrators began to fear that the proliferation and diversification of educational exchange was outpacing the accrediting capacities of state and regional agencies. Adding fuel to these concerns was skepticism over the rise of for-profit providers of higher education services and a general uncertainty associated with the trade provisions for higher education included in the General Agreement on Tariffs and Services (GATS). Overlaying all of these issues were also basic questions related to the relationship between national regulatory frameworks for quality assurance and international agreements. It was during this same period of time (2000–4) that the United Nations Educational, Scientific and Cultural Organization (UNESCO) began to seriously focus its attention on the links between the global expansion of higher education and the corruption of higher education.

With corruption now at the front of the international agenda due largely to the work of multilateral international organizations, UNESCO's International Institute for Educational Planning (IIEP) launched a campaign to define and address the issue of corruption in education. In 2000–1, IIEP conceptualized and launched a new research project dedicated to "Ethics and Corruption in Education." This project's main objective was "to improve decision-making and the management of education systems by integrating governance and corruption concerns in educational planning and administration methodologies" (Hallak & Poisson 2002: 15). After encountering numerous issues of educational corruption in the course of conducting several audits of the educational sector, the organization very intentionally shifted focus, noting that, "the issue of corruption [in education] has never been specifically addressed, and requires new approaches and even new partners" (Hallak & Poisson 2002: 15).

Accordingly, the IIEP organized and sponsored an Expert Workshop in November of 2001, designed "with the aim of generating fruitful debate on the optimal design, methodologies, and execution of this new research project" (Hallak & Poisson 2002: 15). The education policy experts who were brought to Paris to inform the deliberations included representatives from the OECD, World Bank, and Transparency International, along with

> experts in methodologies of diagnosis and audits, used either in the field of education (ADEA), or in the specific sphere of corruption (the Asian Development Bank), and people having an intimate knowledge of the main features characterizing corruption in the domain of education, in the case of particular countries.
>
> (Hallak & Poisson 2002: 11).

Although there were many positive outcomes of this unprecedented gathering, the most significant was likely that the evidence presented challenged each of these organizations and agencies to confront corruption in education systems in relation to corruption within adjoining systems. Jacques Hallack and Muriel Poisson of IIEP encouraged the international community to move beyond compartmentalized organizational approaches of conceptualizing and addressing corruption and focus instead on the complex linkages of systemic corruption. The meetings and deliberations of this workshop brought these organizations together in an intentional effort to synergize their work and leverage each other's technical expertise, skills, and methodologies. It established a precedent of collaborative practice that has come to characterize the current effort to combat educational corruption.

Though relatively limited in scope, issues of corruption specifically within higher education were nonetheless an important topic of conversation at this workshop. One of the participants even suggested that the project should be led at the tertiary (rather than secondary) level. As supporting evidence, two major issues were highlighted as areas of concern—*the proliferation of academic fraud through the creation of diploma mills* and *the influence of private enterprise on the results of scientific research.* Furthermore, this same working group acknowledged that higher education considerations had too often been neglected and that increased attention needed to be paid to the significant issues of corruption that tertiary institutions were facing (Hallak & Poisson 2002: 11).

As a result, the IIEP began focusing their efforts more deliberately on the relationship between internationalism in education and the global rise of issues of corruption. In 2003, they published Max Eckstein's (2003) *Combating Academic Fraud: Towards a Culture of Integrity*, a report that dealt heavily with the forms of academic corruption that bridge secondary to higher education. Hallak and Poisson (2005) found that, with a deepening financial crisis facing higher education in many countries, especially those countries with state-backed financing, institutions were enrolling an increasing number of foreign students who were charged significantly higher fees. Furthermore, because of the profitability of this practice, many fraudulent institutions offered bogus courses, degrees, and programs. In a particularly notorious case, fifteen Malaysian students of an Australian-run university in Kuala Lumpur who had initially been failed for plagiarism were granted passing grades because of the university's fears of losing revenue from offshore students (Hallak & Poisson 2005).

In addition, the rapid development of electronic technology facilitated a new market for diploma and accreditation mills. In response, the OECD and UNESCO formulated non-binding international guidelines for cross-border higher education, more particularly with regards to student recruitment and support.[6] To specifically address the issue of accreditation fraud, UNESCO developed the Portal on Higher Education Institutions—a searchable database that lists all legally accredited higher educational institutes and programs in twenty-seven participating countries. The IIEP also launched student-led campaigns in the Republic of Moldova and Serbia by supporting reforms within their respective tertiary systems.

Other organizations began to address corruption within the global academy as well. In the former Soviet republic of Georgia—where bribery, nepotism, and extensive private tutoring undermine equitable access to higher education—a World Bank initiative led to the passing of a state law requiring all students to take a unified university entrance exam.[7] Similarly, in Ukraine, a partnership of the Open Society Institute, the International Renaissance Foundation, the American Councils for International Education, the American Institutes for Research, and a few international experts provided technical support to the government to implement a fair and transparent entrance examination to higher education.

Finally, significant integrity concerns have been emerging related to the exponential rise of sponsored and collaborative research by many tertiary institutions and higher education systems. In their last full survey report, *Internationalization in Higher Education: Practices and Policies*, the International Association of Universities (IAU) reported that "strengthening international research collaboration" was one of only two "primary priorities" for the institutions surveyed (Knight 2003). From IAU's data, frequent policy initiatives emerging from numerous countries, and universities' consistent international outreach efforts, it is evident that tertiary institutions worldwide have recognized the potentiality of collaborative research to generate both operating capital and higher levels of human capital. Unfortunately, the rules, norms, and accountability mechanisms that govern research conducted by mature tertiary research institutions are not as easily acquired as the partnerships and/or funds necessary to conduct research. As these international research relationships continue to emerge and become more a part of institutions' priorities, enhancing and co-ordinating existing regulatory frameworks is absolutely necessary to safeguard higher education's research functions from additional corruption.

Encouragingly, in 2008, the Government–University–Industry Research Roundtable (GUIRR) created a formal Working Group on International Research Collaborations (I-Group) to examine growing concerns about the nature and functioning of cross-national research arrangements in higher education (Carfora, Casey, & Killoren 2008/2009). Though they have yet to produce either a final report or recommendations (at the time of writing of this chapter), the I-Group *has* identified nine general categories of primary concern, four of which are directly related to our present examination: "Differences in Ethical Standards, Responsible Conduct of Research, Intellectual Property, and Research Integrity" (Carfora, et al. 2008/2009: 10). Institutionalizing any of these domains is obviously replete with significant cultural, definitional, and technical challenges; and whether I-Group's final recommendations will be (1) robust enough to adequately safeguard research processes from corruption; (2) amenable enough to be broadly adopted at the policy level; or (3) enforceable enough to create substantive accountability will not be known for some time.

These examples demonstrate the feasibility that global organizational partnerships that are well managed can positively affect ethical behavior within higher education. Furthermore, the current trend toward international co-ordination and co-operation suggests that international demand is rising for a more concerted effort to end corruption in the academy. There are many reasons to be encouraged that steady and significant progress is being made at the institutional level that is taking hold throughout systems of higher education; but there is also much more work to be done to enhance the integrity of the global higher educational enterprise.

Toward a Unified Global Approach to Building Ethical Academies through Quality Assurance[8]

> Norms are intentionally established, indeed as means of reducing externalities, and their benefits are ordinarily captured by those who are responsible for establishing them. But the capability of establishing and maintaining effective

> norms depends on properties of the social structure . . . over which one actor
> does not have control yet are affected by one actor's action. These are properties
> that affect the structure's capacity to sustain effective norms, yet properties that
> ordinarily do not enter into an individual's decision that affects them.
>
> (Coleman 1988: S117)

In a survey conducted for this chapter, we asked international education policy experts to comment on whether they thought the work of international organizations has helped to increase general public awareness of the problems associated with educational corruption, particularly for higher education. They were in strong, unanimous agreement that it has, especially in those countries and regions where these organizations have been most active and when their efforts have been joined by smaller grassroots organizations and afforded the support of governments. However, each of these experts also expressed significant reservations as to whether building awareness of these issues among the public will translate into any kind of positive behavioral change without the adoption of institutional mechanisms of accountability. In fact, none of our respondents thought that any substantive change could occur without broad, systemic approaches that involve multiple stakeholders—colleges and universities, government agencies, international organizations, accrediting agencies, employers, and the media. In sum, a systems approach is deemed necessary for establishing norms of academic and professional integrity in higher education and ensuring that they are upheld.

As the nature of social and political systems varies among country and region, new institutional arrangements may be necessary to unite various systems of quality and integrity assurance. The hard work of creating effective norms has already begun as part of the broader movement toward quality assurance (QA). Although QA mechanisms within higher education have always been (and will continue to be) a fundamental part of institutional identity and procedure, nationally structured QA processes are increasingly becoming priority themes for governmental ministries and agencies around the world (Materu 2007). Currently there are more than 130 national QA agencies in about 100 countries, all established in the last decade or so (Gnanam 2008). These national QA agencies center around two strategic priorities. First, as higher education systems continue to expand through increased private investment, QA agencies are forced to regulate the development of the sector. Second, these agencies work to enhance accountability and quality assurance measures in both public and private institutions through assessment, academic audit, and/or accreditation (Gnanam 2008; Materu 2007).

Intrinsic to the process of creating a national QA strategy is the establishment of national qualification frameworks. As Gnanam (2008: 4) explains,

> Whatever may be the unit or process of assessment used by the national
> Quality Assurance bodies . . . the outcome of such assessment should

ultimately reflect on the Qualifications offered by them. In a sense the qualifications offered are the academic 'currency' for the transaction among the nations to promote academic mobility . . . . The development of National Qualifications Frameworks (NQF) and suitably retooled National Quality Assurance (NQA) mechanisms are therefore considered essential to enhance the acceptability of any qualification at the global level.

Nevertheless, although the development of NQF and NQA mechanisms provides the impetus for a more transparent administration of tertiary education, these processes do not inherently create a system more conducive to international quality assurance. In fact, this movement is relatively new and is predominately nation-centric, with no guarantee that national quality assurance ensures international quality (Gnanam 2008).

However, parallel to the development of NQA and NQF systems has been the formation of networks of regional and international QA bodies. One of the earliest of these, the International Network for Quality Assurance Agencies in Higher Education (INQAAHE, established in 1991), was formed to collect and disseminate "information on current and developing theory and practice in the assessment, improvement and maintenance of quality in higher education."[9] In addition to its more than 200 institutional members located in eighty countries, the INQAAHE has signed a Memorandum of Cooperation with various regional QA networks, including the Arab Network for Quality Assurance in Higher Education (ANQAHE, established 2007), the Asia-Pacific Quality Network (APQN, established 2003), the Eurasian Quality Assurance Network (EAQAN, established 2004), the European Association for Quality Assurance in Higher Education (ENQA, established 2004), the Central and Eastern European Network of Quality Assurance Agencies in Higher Education (CEEN, established 2000), and the European Consortium for Accreditation (ECA, established 2003). In essence, these memoranda pledge mutual support by leveraging each organization's resources, information, and professional expertise.

Additionally, the INQAAHE has formed partnerships with the Caribbean Area Network for Quality Assurance in Tertiary Education (CANQATE, established 2003), the Ibero-American Network for Quality Assurance in Higher Education (RIACES, established 1999), and the Quality Assurance Network for African Higher Education (AfriQAN, established 2007). All of these regional networks share the common objectives of (1) information sharing; (2) liaison; (3) collaboration; (4) good practice; (5) quality improvement; and (6) capacity building (Woodhouse, n.d.).

Within the context of these partnerships the World Bank and UNESCO teamed up in 2008 to launch a Global Initiative for Quality Assurance Capacity (GIQAC). According to their website, the GIQAC was established to "assist emerging quality assurance systems in building capacity by sharing information on good practices world-wide, facilitating communication among the diverse set of agencies and professionals, and supporting the production of analyses and guidelines."[10] In addition, the World Bank and UNESCO have provided significant financial support to the INQAAHE and other regional QA networks through the GIQAC.

Likewise, NQFs have adapted to the internationalization of higher education by forming transnational agreements. Most notable within this movement is the European Qualifications Framework (EQF). The EQF, initially conceived in 2004 when EU member states demanded increased transparency and portability of qualifications, relates each member's NQF around a common reference of eight levels, ranging from basic (Level 1) to advanced (Level 8) skills, knowledge, and competence (Commission of the European Communities 2006). The recommendation by the European Commission set a target date of 2010 for each country to relate its national qualification systems to the EQF, and 2012 for individual countries to ensure their individual qualification certificates contain a reference to the appropriate EQF level. The EQF has also served as a model in proposals for other regional qualification frameworks, including in Asia-Pacific and South Africa. In addition to these larger networks, individual nations have signed bilateral agreements, as in the case of the Chinese government, who by 2006 had signed agreements with Britain, France, Germany, New Zealand, Australia, and Ireland for mutual recognition of higher educational qualifications.[11]

Taken together, quality assurance mechanisms and qualification frameworks are two of the most potent weapons in the fight against higher education corruption (Bergan 2009). As government agencies, regional bodies, and international organizations continue to strengthen collaborative relationships, systemic forces will have to continue to coalesce around an internationally recognized set of ethical norms. The primary work moving forward will involve leveraging institutions' political and economic interests to develop and synchronize quality–integrity policies and programs through binding agreements, the provision of which must be subject to rigorous accountability and monitoring.

U.S. accrediting agencies have long been ahead of the world community in their requirements for rigorous assessments of the activities of higher education. Even so, as has been thoroughly discussed, international institutions are catching up quickly and may even be gaining advantage where collaborative quality assurance systems are quickly being instituted. The primary policy challenges ahead for the American system will involve (1) refocusing strongly on producing (and justifying) the *outcomes* of higher education while (2) respecting the complexity and autonomy of U.S. colleges and universities, and (3) ensuring that the accountability mechanisms are incorporated at the systemic level, which insures comprehensive institutional integrity that broadly complies with our international counterparts.

Notes

1. For more information, see the Transparency International website at http://www.transparency.org (accessed 1 February 2010).
2. See the *Transparency International Strategic Framework 2008–2010*, available at http://www.transparency.org/about_us/strategy_2010 (accessed 1 February 2010).
3. They have now released their second plan. See http://www.adb.org/Governance/gacap.asp (accessed 1 February 2010) for more information.
4. For a summary of this document, visit http://europa.eu/legislation_summaries/fight_against_fraud/fight_against_corruption/l33301_en.htm (accessed 1 February 2010).
5. Available at http://www.u4.no/themes/coordination/dacprinciplesabout.cfm (accessed 1 February 2010).
6. See http://www.unesco.org/education/hed/guidelines (accessed 1 February 2010).
7. See http://web.worldbank.org/WBSITE/EXTERNAL/COUNTRIES/ECAEXT/GEORGIAEXTN/O,,contentMDK:20872345~menuPK:3949564~pagePK:1497618~piPK:217854~theSitePK:301746,00.html (accessed 1 February 2010).
8. The authors wish to acknowledge the valuable input of Muriel Possion and Jacques Hallak of IIEP UNESCO.
9. For more information, see the INQAAHE website at http://www.inqaahe.org (accessed 1 February 2010).
10. For more information, see the GICAQ website at http://www.inqaahe.org/giqac (accessed 1 February 2010).
11. Available online at http://www.nfq.ie/nfq/en/about_NFQ/recognition_international_qualifications.html (accessed 1 February 2010).

References

Alexander, F.K. (2000) 'The changing face of accountability: Monitoring and assessing institutional performance in higher education, *Journal of Higher Education*, 71: 411–31.

Altbach, P., Reisberg, L., and Rumbley, L. (2009) 'Trends in global higher education: Tracking an academic revolution'. Report Prepared for the UNESCO 2009 World Conference on Higher Education, Paris.

Annan, K. (2004) 'Foreword', in *United Nations Convention Against Corruption*, New York: United Nations. Available at http://www.unodc.org/documents/treaties/UNCAC/Publications/Convention/08–50026_E.pdf (accessed 20 November 2009).

Bergan, S. (2009) 'The European higher education area as an instrument of transparency?', in S.P. Heyneman (ed.) *Buying Your Way into Heaven: Education and Corruption in International Perspective*, Rotterdam: Sense Publishers.

Carfora, J., Casey, J., and Killoren, B. (2008/2009) 'GUIRR gives green light to examine international research collaborations', *NCURA Magazine*, December/January: 10–11.

Coleman, J.S. (1988) 'Social capital and the creation of human capital', *American Journal of Sociology*, 94: S94–120.

Commission of the European Communities. (2006) *Implementing the Community Lisbon Programme: Proposal for a Recommendation of the European Parliament and of the Council on the Establishment of the European Qualifications Framework for Lifelong Learning*, Brussels: Commission of the European Communities. Available at http://ec.europa.eu/education/policies/educ/eqf/com_2006_0479_en.pdf (accessed 1 February 2010).

Council of Graduate Schools. (2009) *Findings from the 2009 GSC International Graduate Admissions Survey. Phase 1: Applications*, Washington, DC: Author.

Eckstein, M.A. (2003) *Combating Academic Fraud: Towards a Culture of Integrity*, Paris: UNESCO International Institute for Educational Planning (IIEP).

Gnanam, A. (2008) *Globalization and its Impact on Quality Assurance, Accreditation, and Recognition of Qualifications*. Available at http://www.unesco.org/education/studyingabroad/highlights/global_forum/presentations/gnanam.doc (accessed 20 November 2009).

Hallak, J. and Poisson, M. (2002) *Ethics and Corruption in Education: Results from the Expert Workshop held at IIEP, Paris 28–29 November 2001*, Paris: UNESCO International Institute for Educational Planning (IIEP).

Hallak, J. and Poisson, M. (2005) 'Ethics and corruption in education: An overview', *Journal of Education for International Development*, 1: 1–16.

Integrity Vice Presidency. (September 28, 2009) Available at http://web.worldbank.org/WBSITE/EXTERNAL/EXTABOUTUS/ORGANIZATION/ORGUNITS/EXTDOII/0,,contentMDK:21182440~menuPK:2452528~pagePK:64168445~piPK:64168309~theSitePK:588921,00.html (accessed 20 November 2009).

International Association of Universities. (2009) *Initial Results: 2009 IAU Global Survey on Internationalization of Higher Education*. Available at http://www.iau-aiu.net/internationaliza-tion/pdf/Key_results_2009.pdf.

Knight, J. (2003) *Internationalization of Higher Education: Practices and Priorities: 2003 IAU Survey Report*, Paris: International Association of Universities.

MacIntyre, A. (1981; 3rd edn 2007) *After Virtue*, Notre Dame, IN: University of Notre Dame Press.

Materu, P. (2007) *Higher Education Quality Assurance in Sub-Saharan Africa: Status, Challenges, Opportunities, and Promising Practices*, World Bank Working Paper No. 124, Washington, DC: World Bank.

Organisation for Economic Co-operation and Development (OECD). (1997) *Responding to New Demand in Tertiary Education*, Paris: OECD.

Sahlberg, P. (2009) 'The role of international organizations in fighting education corruption', in S.P. Heyneman (ed.) *Buying Your Way into Heaven: Education and Corruption in International Perspective*, Rotterdam, Netherlands: Sense Publishers.

Stark, J.S. and Lattuca, L.R. (1997) *Shaping the College Curriculum: Academic Plans in Action*, Needham Heights, MA: Allyn & Bacon.

Wolfensohn, J.D. (2002) 'Opening address to Third Conference of International Investigators of United Nations Organizations and Multilateral Financial Institutions', Washington, DC. Available at http://web.worldbank.org/WBSITE/EXTERNAL/NEWS/0,,contentMDK:20040023~menuPK:34472~pagePK:34370~piPK:34424~theSitePK:4607,00.html (accessed 26 October 2009).

Woodhouse, D. (n.d.). 'Internationalization of quality assurance: the role of networks of quality agencies', Available at http://www.inqaahe.org/admin/files/assets/subsites/1/documenten/1258452442_obhe-paper-internationalisation-of-qa.pdf (accessed 20 November 2009).

World Bank (2002) *Constructing Knowledge Societies: New Challenges for Tertiary Education*, Washington, DC: Author.

14

The Future of the Ethical Academy

Preliminary Thoughts and Suggestions

TRICIA BERTRAM GALLANT AND PATRICK DRINAN

In his book, *Collapse*, Jared Diamond (2005: 438) supplies what he calls a "road map" to the collapse of societies: "failure to anticipate a problem, failure to perceive it once it has arisen, failure to attempt to solve it after it has been perceived, and failure in attempts to solve it." Although it is doubtful that higher education will collapse, except as the direct consequence of the collapse of global society itself, the academy—its purpose, its ideals, its manifestations—as we know it, might. We have already seen the autonomy, respect, and credibility of traditional higher education questioned and challenged through the rise of for-profit education and diploma mills and the disintegration of tenure, as well as increasing accountability pressures from external stakeholders. Although some of these changes may be considered by some to be natural evolutionary responses, they could also be interpreted as a sign that the academy is having difficulty anticipating, perceiving, and resolving serious issues at its ethical center—which is, after all, the infrastructure and base for the pursuit and transmission of knowledge. If the ethical center cannot be defended, the prospects for collapse—or at least severe loss of faith in our educational institutions—will dramatically increase.

Some may be skeptical of a "sky is falling" prognosis. If a reader is in this camp, it would still be hard for him or her to deny that a failure to thrive is a realistic possibility even if societies invest more and more resources into education, research, and training. Indeed, those very investments increase the likelihood that society will monitor education more closely. And, the more vigorous the monitoring, the greater the chance that anomalies of performance, ethical or otherwise, will be discovered (in chapter 6 we saw that this scenario is already true for federally funded research activities).

Education at its best is a call to excellence. Educators create high expectations for themselves and their students (or at least they should), and societies expect much from educators given their investments. However, the higher the expectations, the greater the disappointments if high standards are not met—let alone if misconduct eats away at morale. We may not know exactly where the "tipping point" will be in societal support for education, but it is likely to manifest itself in two ways: (1) resource withdrawal and (2) loss of confidence within educational elites. The first of these two may be at hand, at least in the United States. The second can display itself if educators are inattentive to their ethical center, and the educators responsible for the direction of higher education begin to lose confidence in an ethical academy. The combination of the two is a real danger, if not *the* tipping point.

Throughout this volume, the contributing authors have been attentive to the possibilities for reaching this tipping point, whether collapse or failure to thrive, on all four dimensions suggested by Diamond. Heyneman's chapter and those in Part II may help some campuses anticipate ethical problems not yet experienced while helping others perceive problems already occurring. Of course, we were unable in this volume to cover all of the ethical challenges facing the academy. Some emerging challenges not discussed include student cheating in online education (which may or may not differ from cheating in face-to-face classes),[1] financial aid fraud committed by students, non-students, and parents,[2] and financial/accounting fraud committed by administrators.[3] These challenges, among many others, do require extensive consideration and analysis, and we encourage readers to use the systems framework from chapter 3 to do so. We hope that the common misconduct challenges presented in this volume help to illustrate the complexity of academic ethics and generate an awareness regarding the seriousness of the issue.

We also did not cover in this volume the common ethical dilemmas facing colleges and universities every day. Questions such as "How do we enhance diversity without bending our academic standards?," "How do we honor free speech and academic freedom while condemning hate speech?," or "How do we decide which academic programs to cut when facing budget crises?" are all important to ask. Of course, the ethical decision-making frameworks provided by Goodchild (chapter 9) could be used by readers to work toward the resolution of such ethical dilemmas. We chose not to include such ethical dilemmas because the purpose of this volume was to call attention to ethical misconduct—those behaviors that violate professional standards and expectations and undermine the integrity of the education system.

Although we wanted this volume to call attention to the ethical problems occurring in the academy, the central preoccupation of this book was to convince readers to attempt to resolve the problems once they are perceived. This book will fail—as might the academy itself as a thriving institution—if ethical challenges continue to be ignored or downplayed as issues of individual dysfunctionality. Chapter 3 provided readers with a framework for understanding misconduct as a systems issue, and Part III offered ideas for addressing misconduct within each systems level. Together, these ideas help to forward the creation of the ethical academy, one in which misconduct and corruption will not be able to thrive. Although we cannot dictate what each individual campus needs to do specifically, we will repeat a point worthy of repetition—colleges and universities can no longer afford to do nothing. For far too long, ethics has not been an intentional strategic priority for higher education and we are seeing the consequences of that.

Ignoring the problems will not make them go away or minimize their negative impact.

The systemic forces that have shaped the ethical problems of the past will certainly not be dissipating in the future. Technology, a powerful force in the shaping of misconduct, will only become more integrated into the daily lives and operations of students, faculty, staff, and administrators as it becomes more sophisticated and omnipresent. We saw throughout this book that technology not only makes misconduct easier to execute by more people (Bertram Gallant 2008 has previously referred to the impact of technology as the "democratization of cheating"), but it also makes misconduct easier to deter and fraud easier to detect. However, without strategic and intentional attention to the creation of the ethical academy, campuses will over-rely on technology and an ineffective "arms race" between people and institutions will ensue (Davis, Drinan, & Bertram Gallant 2009). The wide use of plagiarism detection software by faculty has not been effective at stemming student plagiarism, so we should not think that any other technologies will be the "magic bullet" solution either. Instead, campuses need to work toward understanding the impact that technology has on misconduct, including the changing nature of information and knowledge (Bertram Gallant 2008), and how it might function as merely one tool within a systematic ethical academy strategy.

The globalization of education will also not reverse or cease. Rather, the consequences of globalization (such as a concentrated focus on standardized testing, expanded campus diversity, and increased intra- and intercampus competition) will necessitate greater attention to ethical standards and expectations (Bertram Gallant 2008). A concentrated focus on standardized testing will continue to mean less (or no) attention paid to ethics education including decision-making, critical thinking, and reasoning skills. Expanded campus diversity means that shared assumptions and understandings of ethical or legitimate academic conduct cannot be assumed; without proper socialization and education, misconduct may increase as people unintentionally violate ethical standards of which they are unaware. And increased competition encourages people and institutions to do "whatever it takes" to get ahead. We saw this in Part II—students and parents are cheating to secure limited college spots; researchers are cheating to earn tenure and promotion points; and universities are cheating to enhance prestige within the competitive system. The globalization of education also expands the impact felt by misconduct—when Professor Chiranjeevi in India submitted fraudulent manuscripts for publication in science journals, the impact was felt not just by his colleagues but by researchers and users of research around the world (see chapter 6). So when one campus refuses to address the ethical misconduct being perpetrated by its students, faculty, staff, and administrators, it is failing to address the ethical damages to the education system as a whole.

Of course, misconduct and corruption are not the only factors precipitating the failure of the academy to thrive, but they certainly have not helped to thwart the failure. And considering that both those professionals who are unethical outside the academy and those who are unethical within the academy are "products" of our colleges and universities, we should be inspired to pause and reflect on what we might do better. We certainly cannot be expected to control the ethicality of every person who studies in, works within, or graduates from our campuses. However, we must be able to at least demonstrate to society that we are able to anticipate the problem, perceive it once it occurs, and work to resolve or reduce it. If we do not do this, we will continue to see the erosion of public trust, individual ethical responsibility, and institutional integrity, all of which will likely precipitate the collapse of our autonomy and authority to be the architects of the worldwide education system. It is not necessary to allow this to happen.

This volume provides a way forward—we encourage readers to use it to craft new research agendas, to begin conversations on individual campuses, and to facilitate movement toward the creation of an ethical academy.

Notes

1. See http://www.westga.edu/~distance/ojdla/fall123/stuber123.html (accessed 2 June 2010) for one study that found students are less likely to cheat online than in traditional classes.
2. See an article in *The Chronicle of Higher Education* for just one example of the kinds of financial aid fraud that can occur; this one just happens to be connected to online education: http://chronicle.com/article/Online-Scheme-Triggers-New/63532/ (accessed 2 June 2010).
3. The *Los Angeles Times* posted one such story in 2003: http://articles.latimes.com/2003/jun/13/local/me-rcc13 (accessed 2 June 2010).

References

Bertram Gallant, T. (2008) *Academic Integrity in the Twenty-First Century: A Teaching and Learning Imperative*, San Francisco: Jossey-Bass.
Davis, S.F., Drinan, P.F., and Bertram Gallant, T. (2009) *Cheating in School: What We Know and What We Can Do*, Malden, MA: Wiley-Blackwell.
Diamond, J. (2005) *Collapse: How Societies Choose to Fail or Succeed*, New York: Viking.

List of Contributors

Melissa S. Anderson is a higher education professor in the College of Education and Human Development and director of the Postsecondary Education Research Institute at the University of Minnesota. Her scholarship focuses on research integrity, research misconduct and related ethical issues, graduate education, and academy–industry relations.

Michael N. Bastedo is an associate professor in the Center for the Study of Higher and Postsecondary Education at the University of Michigan. His scholarly interests are in the governance, politics, and organization of public higher education in the United States and abroad.

Tricia Bertram Gallant (editor) runs the Academic Integrity Office for the University of California, San Diego and chairs the International Center for Academic Integrity Advisory Council. Tricia has authored two books as well as multiple journal articles and book chapters on academic integrity.

John M. Braxton is a professor of education in the Higher Education Leadership and Policy Program in the Peabody College of Education and Human Development at Vanderbilt University. One of his major programs of research centers on the study of the academic profession with particular emphasis on the social control of faculty teaching and research misconduct.

Timothy A. Drake is a graduate student in the International Education Policy and Management (IEPM) Program at Peabody College of Education and Human Development at Vanderbilt University. His research interests are related to quality assurance and accountability in higher education.

Patrick Drinan is a professor in the Political Science Department at the University of San Diego and former dean of the College of Arts and Sciences. He has written several journal articles and book chapters on academic integrity.

Lester F. Goodchild is the director of the Higher Education Program and professor of education at Santa Clara University. He is also a scholar at its Markkula

Center for Applied Ethics. He has taught an academic ethics course for thirteen years there and at the University of Denver.

Nathan F. Harris is a doctoral student in the Center for the Study of Higher and Postsecondary Education at the University of Michigan. His scholarly interests include colleges and universities as organizations.

Brian L. Heuser is an assistant professor of the practice of international education policy at Peabody College of Education and Human Development at Vanderbilt University. His research interests include internationalization and ethics in higher education, specifically related to quality assurance and accountability.

Stephen P. Heyneman is a professor of international education policy with the Peabody College of Education and Human Development at Vanderbilt University. Stephen researches the effect of higher education on social cohesion, the international trade in education services, and the economic and social cost to higher education corruption.

Michael Kalichman is the director of the Research Ethics Program at the University of California, San Diego and adjunct professor of pathology. Mike leads national and local ethics and education groups and publishes in the area of research ethics.

Mark Kavanaugh is the policy analyst for the Texas Senate Higher Education Committee. Mark's primary academic interests include conflicts of interest, research integrity, and the higher education law.

Peter A. Keller is a professor of psychology and provost for Mansfield University of Pennsylvania. The author or editor of a dozen professional books, Peter recently completed sabbatical work with the Institute for Global Ethics to explore strategies for promoting ethical cultures in academic communities.

Adrianna J. Kezar is an associate professor in the Rossier School of Education at the University of Southern California. Her numerous books, book chapters, and journal articles have focused on higher education change and innovation, leadership, diversity issues, governance, and organizational theory.

Cecile Sam is a research associate at the University of Southern California Center for Higher Education and Policy Analysis. Her research focuses on ethics, leadership, and organizational studies of higher education.

J. Douglas Toma is an associate professor at the Institute of Higher Education at the University of Georgia with an appointment in the School of Law. Doug writes primarily about strategy and management in higher education, and is currently interested in how institutions position themselves for greater prestige.

Index

abuse: of authority 14; preventing 185, 188

academic: ethics *see* ethics, academic; integrity *see* integrity, academic; misconduct *see* misconduct, academic; records 53; selection 48, 52, 54, 56–9; *see also* misconduct, academic selection

accountability 94, 115, 118, 126, 183, 191, 204, 209, 212; measures 49, 210; mechanisms 209, 210; movement 34; pressures 215; public funds 4; standards 163

accreditation 14–16, 21, 210; agencies 183–5, 189; bodies 193; European Consortium for 211; institutional 41; mills 208; standards 189–91

Adidas 101

administration 4, 15, 153, 159, 162, 164, 207, 211

admissions: athletes 101; competition in 40, 56; consultants 52–3, 54, 56, 57; fraud 52–3, 56, 58; process 5, 48–50, 52–4, 58–9; process, formal 119–20; process, shadow 119–25

Advanced Placement (AP) Exams 48, 49, 54–5

American Association of University Professors (AAUP) 185

American Council on Education (ACE) 115–16; 126

anomie theory 66

Asia 15, 17; Central 15; Pacific 212; –

Pacific Quality Network Region, 211; South 16

assessment 4, 34, 64, 191, 210–11; learning 188; outcomes 175, 190

Association of American Colleges & Universities (AAC&U) 175

Association of Fundraising Professionals (AFP) 99

Association of Governing Boards (AGB) 115–16, 126

athletics 6–7, 97–9, 106, 108–10, 161; administrator 28, 102, 107; associations 100, 102; boosters 100; budget 108; conference, mid-American 108; conference, Western 109; giving 103; intercollegiate 97, 101, 106; Mountain West Conference 109; programs 100–2, 107–8; reform 108–9; revenue 107, 108, 109; scholarships 100; Southeastern Conference 109; spending on 107

audit *see* ethical, audit

Australia 54, 212

authority: abuse of, 13–14, 117, 121; figure 54; formal 117, 156–8; limits of 163

authorship 31, 84

boards of governors/trustees 23, 115, 127

brand equity 104, 106

bribe 13, 14, 52; Payers Index 202

bribery 15, 19, 20, 50, 208

bullying 71

bureaucratization 187–8

221

learning: about ethics 177, 180; centered
cultures 180; environment 75–6, 77;
organizations 187; process 63–4, 199–
200, 201; social–emotional 172–4;
student 49, 77, 190
legal 7, 31, 94, 118, 130, 147, 148, 204
Liberal Education and America's Promise
(LEAP) 175

mandates: federal 31; *see also* regulations
Markkula Center for Applied Ethics
145–6
Medical College Admissions Test
(MCAT) 49, 51
meritocracy 18, 57, 58, 94, 185
Michigan State University 108
Middle East 15
misbehavior: professional 13, 15; research
84–6, 88–95; scientific 83, 91; *see also*
misconduct
misconduct: academic 7, 66; academic
selection 54–7; admissions 53; ethical
4, 13, 23, 27, 36, 116–19, 216, 218;
faculty 69, 73; individual 4, 7–9,
13, 36; institutionalization of 123;
organizational 117, 122, 216–18;
professional 13, 16; research 14, 33,
36, 84–91, 93–4; scientific 91; teacher
50, 69; testing 15, 56
moral: action 172, 177; beliefs 30;
character 155, 172; choice 39, 137;
conduct 55; crisis 3; development
86, 155, 157–8, 172–3, 175, 180;
dilemmas 86, *see also* ethical,
dilemmas; duties 137; education
169–74; exemplar 156–8; identity 117,
157–9; imperative 42; judgment 143,
177; motivation 177, 179; obligations
29, 33, 35; principle 17, 21, 138, 140;
quality 191–3, 195; reasoning 7, 38,
156–7, 174–5; responsibility 123;
sensitivity 177, 180; standards 16,
179; theories 136–41; thinking 179;
turpitude 70–1
morality 135–6, 139, 155

National Collegiate Athletic Association
(NCAA) 99, 102, 107, 110, 185
Network of Institutions for Combating
Corruption and Rescuing Public
Ethics (RICOREP) 203
Nike 101
No Child Left Behind Act 40
norms 23, 35, 39, 66, 70–4, 77–8, 98,
117, 122, 137, 148, 153–4, 156–7, 161,

164, 176, 184, 188, 193, 200, 209–10;
admonitory 70–3, 75, 78; anti-
corruption 202; faculty research 137;
faculty teaching 69; ethical 118, 158,
212; inviolable 69–73, 75; moral 136;
peer 66; professional 84, 94; social
156; societal 97, 105; teaching 72–4,
78; undergraduate college teaching 63;
violations of 63, 70–8
North Africa 15
North America 15, 17

obligations: moral *see* moral, obligations;
to society 30–5, 105; *see also* ethical,
obligations
Office of Research Integrity (ORI) 90
Ohio State University 100, 108, 109
Oklahoma State University (OSU) 100,
109
Open University 47
Organisation for Economic Co-operation
and Development (OECD) 16, 204
organization: level (of the framework)
39–40, 55–6, 66–8, 72–3, 87–9
organizational: levers 159–64
organizations, international 23, 200, 204,
205, 206, 210, 212
originality 31, 89

peer influence 158
peer review (as a method of
accountability) 84, 88, 93, 94, 161,
185–6, 188
Penn State 101
Pepsi (or PepsiCo) 100–1
plagiarism 7, 14–15, 17, 23, 31–2, 39,
41–2, 64, 84, 87–9, 137, 208, 217
policies *see* policy
policy: challenges 212; conflict of interest
130; education 207, 210; fraud 55;
initiatives 209; institutional 68, 74,
77–8, 136–7, 201; instructor 70;
makers 128, 201, 205–6; research
misconduct 84; Studies, Carnegie
Council on 5; Office on Science and
Technology 84; World Bank 203
power: authoritative 156–7; distributed
39, 158; external stakeholder 192–3;
faculty 187–8; monopolistic 57
prestige 20, 40, 90, 99, 101, 103
(institutional), 104, 105, 109, 205, 217
prevention, of corruption *see* corruption,
prevention
private: enterprise 17, 207; sector 20
privatization 17